D1116183

YALE HISTORICAL PUBLICATIONS

DAVID HORNE, EDITOR

Miscellany 82

Published under the Direction of the Department of History

SCIENTISM IN CHINESE THOUGHT 1900–1950

D. W. Y. KWOK

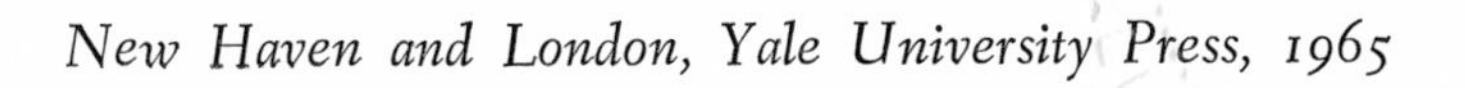

New Haven and London, Yale University Press, 1965

Designed by Arthur G. Beckenstein,
set in Fairfield type,
and printed in the United States of America by
The Colonial Press Inc., Clinton, Mass.
Distributed in Canada by McGill University Press.

Library of Congress catalog card number: 65–22330
Published with assistance from the foundation
established in memory of Philip Hamilton McMillan
of the Class of 1894, Yale College.

To N. C. K.

PREFACE

This book is intended for those interested in the modern transformation and transvaluation in Chinese thought. I have written it primarily to illustrate China's response to one of the major intellectual forces in modern civilization, science. I approached the subject as a student of the history of thought, not as a philosopher, scientist, or an historian of science.

It has been necessary to use a high degree of selectivity in the choice of thinkers to demonstrate the depth, intensity, as well as pervasiveness, of scientism as an autonomous intellectual phenomenon. Not every thinker could satisfy all three of these goals. Ch'en Tu-hsiu, for example, might have provided the intensity but failed in giving the reader a sense of the pervasiveness of the intellectual phenomenon of which he was an inextricable part. This intensity, furthermore, seems short-lived, as Ch'en's writings revealing scientism covered only a short span of time. Despite these and other difficulties that invariably accompany such selectivity, I have chosen the thinkers for a qualitative portrayal of scientism in Chinese thought. I realize that other thinkers could have been included if the quantity of this phenomenon were the major concern.

Generally, I have tried to let the men of thought speak for themselves on their understanding of science, their scientific critique of past culture, and their new scientific world-views. For this reason, I have relied mainly on Chinese sources and have produced numerous and sometimes lengthy translations.

The range of thought of each thinker is large, and the unwary reader should be cautioned against assuming that science was all they were concerned with. The fact that the majority of the thinkers in this book were not scientists, but commented significantly on science, should serve as good authority for China's response to the idea of science.

I am indebted to many scholars of modern China for providing the intellectual milieu in which a treatment of this kind is possible. In its earliest form, this book benefited much from the interest and comments of the late Ralph E. Turner, Harry R. Rudin, David N. Rowe, and Chitoshi Yanaga. Mary C. Wright kindly read through this work during its various stages and gave valued suggestions which have been incorporated into the present book. T. Y. Li and Mikiso Hane have always given me valuable advice and encouragement. John McDonald and James J. Y. Liu freely gave hours of discussion and criticism. Eugene Wu, formerly Curator of the East Asian Collections at the Hoover Library and presently of the Harvard-Yenching Library, lent me valuable assistance. The librarians of Yale, Harvard, and the Library of Congress extended me courtesies for which I am very grateful. I wish also to thank Knox College and the University of Hawaii for providing grants for study during the summers and reducing my teaching hours. David Horne of Yale University Press has always given encouragement. Finally, my admiration and respect go to Jane Isay for her suggestions and meticulous editing of the manuscript. I am, of course, responsible for any shortcoming and misjudgment.

D. W. Y. K.

Honolulu
1965

CONTENTS

ABBREVIATIONS

ESSC *Erh-shih shih-chi* 二十世紀 (*Twentieth Century*)

FEQ *Far Eastern Quarterly* (now *Journal of Asian Studies*)

HCH *Hsin Chung-hua* 新中華 (*New China*)

HCN *Hsin ch'ing-nien* 新青年 (*New Youth*)

HSC *Hsin shih-chi* 新世紀 (*New Century*)

HSWT *Hu Shih wen-ts'un* 胡適文存 (Collected Essays of Hu Shih) 1st coll., 1921; 2nd coll., 1924; 3rd coll., 1930; Shanghai, Ya-tung. 4th coll., 1953; Taipei, Yuan-tung—rearranged from 1935 collection (see below)

HSLHCC *Hu Shih lun-hsüeh chin-chu* 胡適論學近著 (*Recent Academic Writings of Hu Shih*), Shanghai, Commercial Press, 1935

KHYJSK *K'e-hsüeh yü jen-sheng-kuan* 科學與人生觀 (*Science and the Philosophy of Life*), 2 vols. Shanghai, Yatung, 1923

KT *Kai-tsao* 改造 (*La Reconstruo*)

KWCP *Kuo-wen chou-pao* 國聞週報 (*National News Weekly*)

MTTHC *Mao Tse-tung hsüan-chi* 毛澤東選集 (*Selected Works of Mao Tse-tung*), 4 vols. Peking, Jen-min, 1951, 1952, 1953, 1960

TFTC *Tung-fang tsa-chih* 東方雜誌 (*Far Eastern Miscellany*)

THWT	*Tu-hsiu wen-ts'un* 獨秀文存 (*Collected Essays of Ch'en Tu-hsiu*) 2 vols. 9th ed. Shanghai, Ya-tung, 1922, 1933
TLPL	*Tu-li p'ing-lun* 獨立評論 (*Independent Critic*)
TSTC	*Tu-shu tsa-chih* 讀書雜誌 (*Reader's Miscellany*)
TYWT	*T'ang Yüeh wen-ts'un* 唐鉞文存 (*Collected Essays of T'ang Yüeh*) 2 colls. Shanghai, Commercial Press, 1925, 1929
WCC	*Wu Chih-hui ch'üan-chi* 吳稚暉全集 (*Complete Works of Wu Chih-hui*), 10 books. Shanghai, Ch'ün-chung, 1927
WWT	*Wu Chih-hui hsien-sheng wen-ts'un* 吳稚暉先生文存 (*Collected Essays of Wu Chih-hui*), 2 vols. Shanghai, I-hsüeh, 1925

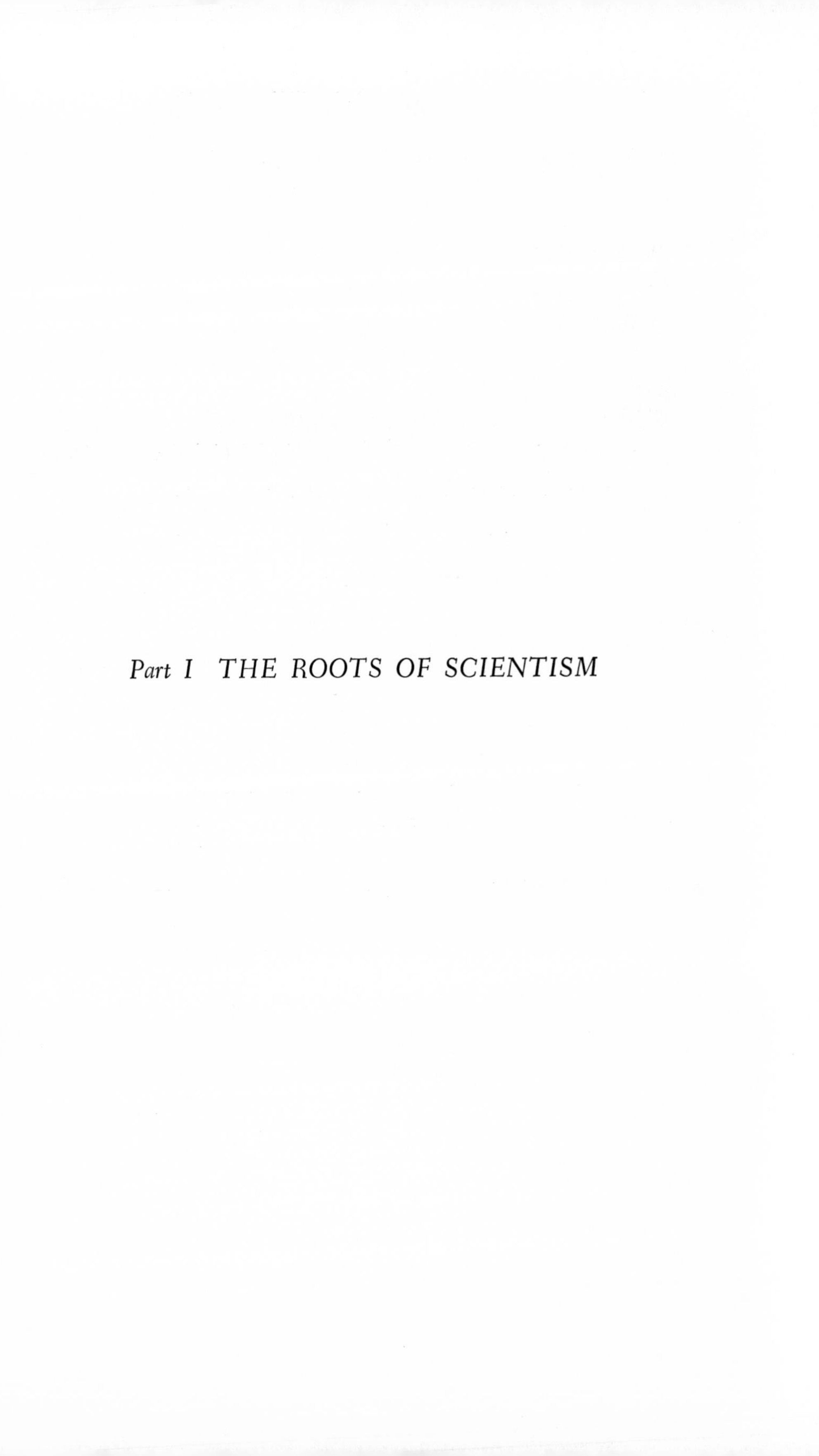

Part I THE ROOTS OF SCIENTISM

Chapter 1 THE DOCTRINAL IMPACT OF MODERN SCIENCE ON CHINESE THOUGHT

Conditions during the first half of the twentieth century in China discouraged the wholesale application of science but encouraged an intellectual appreciation of it, which we may call "scientism." Scientism, in general, assumes that all aspects of the universe are knowable through the methods of science. Proponents of the scientific outlook in China were not always scientists or even philosophers of science. They were intellectuals interested in using science, and the values and assumptions to which it had given rise, to discredit and eventually to replace the traditional body of values. Scientism can thus be considered as the tendency to use the respectability of science in areas having little bearing on science itself. In China, the desire for national growth was accentuated by the weakness in technology, and it is thus not surprising to find among her Western-educated intellectuals great enthusiasm for science.

The initial impact of the West had been made on China at the time of the Opium War of 1839–42. It was not until the 1860s that China began to adopt Western ways. Goaded by motives of national survival, China began to look toward the West for guidance in technology, the force behind Western strength. It would be a mistake to assume that the Chinese at this time had been completely won over to the spirit and substance of modern scientific civilization. Their faith in the adequacy and vitality of the Confucian doctrinal framework hardly wavered. By far the best expression of this sentiment was provided by Chang Chih-tung who, in his collection of essays entitled "An Exhortation to Learning" (*Ch'üan-hsüeh p'ien*),[1] gave a consummate summary of the reformist tendencies throughout the last forty years of the nineteenth century. Chang stressed the need to retain the Chinese classics as the basis of inculcating spiritual values, while at the same time he pleaded for the introduction of Western studies (*hsi-hsüeh*). This was a new attitude, compared with China's first response to Western science in the seventeenth century, when the findings of Jesuit astronomers—the prediction of eclipses and reformation of the calendar, for example—suited and supported the traditional interests and did not conflict with Confucian doctrine. In contrast to the superficial grasp of seventeenth-century science, modern China accepted the technological trappings of the West in order to strengthen military defenses of the country. Chang's essays also called for more industrial and economic effort and advocated the study of science as a means to bring the country material wealth. His efforts and the general response to the impact of Western knowledge were epitomized in one of his own phrases—"Chinese learning as the substance and Western learning for application."

China's contact with Western science dates back to the seventeenth century,[2] when science was introduced by the Jesuits. The Jesuits' superior knowledge of the science of the heavens helped them penetrate China's self-imposed isolation. Astronomy and the prediction of celestial phenomena such as eclipses were important functions of the officials at the imperial court. The Jesuits established their reputation in China through the aid of a small group of Chinese scholar-officials

1. Published in 1898, this collection received imperial endorsement, and a million copies were said to have been distributed throughout the empire. Noted by Cyrus H. Peake, "Some Aspects of the Introduction of Modern Science into China," *Isis,* 22 (1934), 190.

2. For the early introduction of science into China see excellent article by Henri Bernard, "Notes on the Introduction of the Natural Sciences into the Chinese Empire," *Yenching Journal of Social Studies,* 3 (1941), 220–41. Bernard suggests the incompatibility of the mind of ancient China with the spirit of these sciences. No composite work on the history of the introduction of modern science into China has been attempted. Joseph Needham's *Science and Civilization in China* (Cambridge, 1954) stops at the Ming just before the introduction of modern science. Good articles on the subject are: Cyrus Peake, "Some Aspects of the Introduction of Modern Science into China," *Isis,* 22 (1934), 173–219, and C. H. Liu, "Introduction of Modern Science into China," *China Journal,* 34:3 (1941), 120–25; 34:5 (1941), 210–19.

who felt the inadequacy of their own traditional knowledge of science.[3] The first contact with Western science was successful, not because the Chinese basically understood the nature of the Western findings, but because these particular views suited and supported the traditional interest and did not conflict with Confucian doctrine. There was no cause for the gentry-scholar to fear a weakening of traditional doctrines as the result of the scientific spirit. The last two thirds of the eighteenth century found China again in isolation, and the introduction of modern science was put off until the nineteenth century when the main purveyors of new beliefs were Protestant missionaries.

One might say that the feverish activities of this period, when the attempt was made to match the Western pattern in its outward trappings, provided good exercise for the mind but little stirring of the soul. In order to facilitate the learning of Western methods of manufacturing guns and building ships, the Kiangnan Arsenal was established in 1865, and the Foochow Shipyard in 1866, as well as many vocational schools for the training of technicians. A school of foreign languages was founded in Peking in 1862, the Naval Academy in Fukien in 1867, and the Telegraphy School in Tientsin in 1879. An indication of the laborious attempts to introduce the technological aspects of modern science was the fact that the translation work[4] begun by the Kiangnan Arsenal in 1871[5] lasted until 1905. During this time, 178 works were published, including 66 on the natural sciences, 38 on military science, 35 on engineering and manufacturing, 11 on medicine, 7 on agriculture, and 21 on history and institutions.[6] The inadequacy of a partial adoption of science, however, as contrasted with Japan's wholehearted institutionalization and idealization of science in the 1870s and 1880s, became apparent in the Sino-Japanese War of 1894–95. Japan's mechanized power, outmatching Chinese numerical superiority, awakened many Chinese to the neces-

3. Most well-known of these men is Hsü Kuang-ch'i, for whom the famous observatory at Sze-ka-wei near Shanghai was later named.

4. For the general impact of translation on China, see Tsien Tsuen-hsuin, "Western Impact on China Through Translation," *FEQ*, 13 (1954), 305–27.

5. For an interesting history of this institution, see Wei Yün-kung, *Chiang-nan chih-tsao-chü chi* (*A Record of the Kiangnan Arsenal*) (Shanghai, 1905).

6. Noted by Tsien Tsuen-hsuin, "Western Impact on China Through Translation," *FEQ*, 13 (1954), p. 317.

sity for fundamental changes in thought. For the first time, the Chinese framework of spiritual reference seemed to many intellectuals to be inadequate and incongruous with the modern temper. The weakening of confidence in the intellectual authority of the past was accompanied by the desire to capture the Western spirit of science, which had made possible the advances in the West's material strength.

Most instrumental in introducing modern Western concepts of science, philosophy, and political thought was Yen Fu, who translated into Chinese Huxley's *Evolution and Ethics,* Spencer's *Synthetic Philosophy,* Montesquieu's *L'Esprit des lois,* Smith's *Wealth of Nations,* and Jevon's *Elementary Lessons of Logic.* Writing as early as the mid-1890s in a Tientsin newspaper, Yen Fu tried to determine the essential difference between the two civilizations. For him the main contrast between China and the West was that Western culture "in intellectual matters detests falsehood and respects truth [the term closest to scientific impartiality at that time] and in political matters subjects the private and personal to the majority [then the term closest to democracy]." [7] The designation of *chen,* impartial or scientific truth, and *kung,* democratic egalitarianism, as the essence of Western civilization was put into more concrete and emotional terms twenty years later by Ch'en Tu-hsiu, the impresario of the New Thought. Yen Fu set the stage for the thinkers of the new century to accept modern science as a value system. Because of his later retreat from his forward-looking position of the 1890s and because of the archaic language he used for the new concepts, Yen cannot be thought of strictly as a progenitor of the new thought in China.[8] However, the doctrinal acceptance of modern science by China began, for all practical and symbolic purposes, with the twentieth century.

The Reform of 1898 had been the earliest sign of a fundamental tendency to question the adequacy of the traditional framework to cope with the modern world. For a short while the reform seemed to be succeeding, but it was squelched by the ever jealous and interfering Empress Dowager after only one hundred days. The spirit of

7. Yen Fu, "Lun shih-pien chih chi" (On the Extremes of World Change), *Yen Fu shih-wen hsüan* (Selected Poems and Essays of Yen Fu), ed. Chou Chen-fu (Peking, 1959), p. 5.

8. Nevertheless his translations did serve as important reading matter for the New Thought generation and were treated by this generation as signs of the arrival of new thought.

fundamental change, however, was not dampened. Students began to go in large numbers to Japan, Europe, and the United States for education. The hold of the Confucian order began to weaken, and the new education abroad was destined to bear fruit in the twentieth century. Moreover, the tottering Manchu house was now faced with the threat of revolution by Chinese led by Sun Yat-sen and others.

The intellectual fervor of the first fifty years of the twentieth century rose amid major political disunity and factional strife, economic infancy imperiled by foreign interference, basic social upheavals, and invasions and wars. For China this was a period of search, trial, and transvaluation. The antireformist forces which had thwarted the Reform of 1898 now supported the fanatical Boxer Rebellion of 1900. Because of this outburst of unenlightened antiforeignism (as opposed to articulate nationalism), resulting in injuries to persons, goods, and "dignity" of the foreign nations, Manchu China was humbled by the Boxer Protocol and indemnity of 1901. The Empress Dowager assumed full responsibility for this primitive uprising and began to institute reforms. These efforts were too late in coming and only piecemeal in nature. In 1905 the imperial examinations were abolished, thus doing away, at least symbolically, with the institution of the scholar-gentry, long the stabilizing force in the traditional society. Confucian China, by this act, lost one of its two main props. (The other, monarchy under an exemplary sage-king, collapsed with the Revolution of 1911.) New measures were introduced: the adoption of a constitution in 1909, the establishment of a new educational system, the offering of scientific subjects in the schools, and many others. However, this series of changes only paved the way for the revolutionaries who were now intent solely on the elimination of the Manchus and dynastic politics. The fading of the old order brought into open confusion social and political forces which the busy revolutionaries had not had time to consider. The elimination of the scholar-gentry left the rural areas without their main stabilizing element, creating a power vacuum and inviting ambition. The slakening of power of the central government, plus a slate of flux caused by the series of revolutions, allowed regional forces, in ferment for a good part of the nineteenth century, to become strong.

No sooner was the Republic established than it fell prey to the ambitions of Yüan Shih-kai, a man much accustomed to regional politics. Yüan maintained a sham parliamentary government until 1915, when he tried to reestablish a monarchy. After his death in 1916, China entered her darkest period of warlord rule, which lasted until the Nationalist unification in 1927–28. None of the warlords was strong enough to unify the country alone, and the effect of their aggregate presence was disunity, havoc, and widespread confusion about national goals.

The humiliations of the Japanese victory of 1895 and the Boxer Protocol of 1901 had sent men abroad for new knowledge. The subsequent failure of the parliamentary government after 1911 and the Twenty-one Demands Japan presented in 1915, in the hopes of establishing a protectorate over China, strengthened the awareness that Chinese society must somehow be fundamentally reorganized. In this atmosphere of urgent nationalistic concern, Chinese intellectuals, who carried on the tradition, if not the institution, of the scholar-gentry as an intellectual elite, began to speak out strongly for a new culture. The propagators of new ideas were seldom the military and political leaders of China. They were a group of thinkers who did not (some did not want to) participate in warlord and regional politics, which they preferred to criticize.

One of the foremost attacks on the old order was the call for a vernacular language and literature. Hu Shih, while still a student in America, advocated the adoption of *pai-hua* (vernacular Chinese) in all written expressions. His proposal found an enthusiastic reception in China, where Ch'en Tu-hsiu helped to popularize this proposal in the influential journal *New Youth* (*Hsin Ch'ing-nien*). For all the enthusiasm for science shown by the new intellectuals, the language and literary reform was not primarily technological—to enable the Chinese language to absorb modern scientific terminology. It was based on social considerations—to achieve a unity of the spoken and the written languages for mass application. The reform had a leveling effect as the new ideas conveyed through the *pai-hua* reached an ever-growing reading public. Journals led by the example of the *New Youth* began to flood the bookstalls. Contributors to this popular medium discussed the application of Western ideas to China's age-old culture.

Hu Shih's advocacy of a general application of the critical attitude, Ch'en Tu-hsiu's call for a modern civilization built on science and democracy, and Wu Chih-hui's forthright demand for a scientific industrial society favorably impressed the thinkers of the new century. This New Thought Tide was centered at the National University of Peking after Ts'ai Yüan-p'ei assumed its chancellorship in 1917. The University (commonly abbreviated Peita) became the symbol of liberal tendencies in China. Ts'ai's enlightened demand for freedom of expression earned for Peita a new prestige, attracting to its faculty such leading thinkers as Hu Shih, Ch'en Tu-hsiu, Li Ta-chao, and other newly returned students. More significantly, a new generation of students found in Peita an identity for their aspirations. Without these students, the intellectual movement could not have achieved the significance that it did.

For almost twenty years after 1911, China witnessed centrifugal political tendencies. If Japan's successful modernization is explained chiefly by the presence of centralized effort, China's lack of success in these years is understandable because she sorely lacked this requisite. Though heavy industries and highly technical processes lagged, China did experience a growth in light industry after the founding of the Republic. The relative absence of foreign attention, now given to the First World War, meant a breathing spell during which the Chinese developed their own industries in textiles, flour milling, match and cigarette production, and other commodities. Towns and cities, with wage-earning opportunities, began to multiply and to attract people from the countryside. The old Chinese family system cracked slowly under the industrial pressure. The growth of cities gave a new importance to China's merchants, who had formerly thrived as compradors in the treaty ports. Now they were becoming "Chinese" merchants. Influenced by Western ideas, they were eager to send their children abroad to learn. Through contact with modern ideas, the merchants developed a keen sense of patriotism and began to think of national independence and unity. This awakening sense of national identity was revealed when the merchants adopted frequent use of the boycott against foreign goods. Their resentment of the Twenty-one Demands led them to conduct a nationwide boycott of Japanese goods in 1915.

World War I instilled in Chinese students a dedicated sense of common destiny. The Wilsonian Fourteen Points were received by thinkers and students as the message of liberation for peoples everywhere. The Versailles Treaty was disappointing, as the Powers decided to yield to Japan's demand for the former German rights and concessions in Shantung. On May 4, 1919, the students of Peking, led by those of Peita, demonstrated in protest against this decision. By extension the May Fourth Movement has come to signify the trend of thought and action in China immediately before and after 1919. As a political movement, the student demonstration accomplished little except to prevent the government from signing the Versailles Treaty. As a cultural movement, it achieved great significance in that the students became the "appliers" of the ideas articulated by the major thinkers.

After 1919 the students began to organize into federations on the municipal and national levels. In their spare time, they went in teams to the countryside to propagate the New Thought to the masses. Just as the scholar-gentry had in the past served to bring Confucian morality and thought to the lower strata of society, the students wasted no time in disseminating their new awareness. The role of the students is all the more remarkable when one realizes that they were propagating ideas not identified with the existing governmental and political philosophies. Their popularity is shown by the patriotic support given them by the merchants in the large-scale boycotts against Japanese goods.

The Versailles Treaty, interpreted in China as a failure of the democracies, turned many Chinese to the message of "liberation" proclaimed by the Bolshevik Revolution. A Marxist study group had formed at Peita in 1918. Three years later, the Chinese Communist Party was formed under the leadership of Ch'en Tu-hsiu and Li Ta-chao. The '20s saw struggles between communism and nationalism for leadership of the "National Revolution" to create a new China. This political issue was temporarily settled in 1928 when the Kuomintang (Nationalist Party) restored unity to the country. During the '20s much concern for the national destiny was evident. On May 30, 1925, another nationwide movement took place in which the object of protest was the lingering structure of the "unequal treaties" and extraterritoriality. The merchants, again led by the students, conducted huge boycotts against all foreign goods. Never before had there been such a show of unity of purpose and aspiration.

The thirty years after 1900 contain numerous clues to the subsequent development of China. The first decade saw the rapid crumbling of the old order, the next saw critical discussion of new ideas as applied to China, and the third witnessed mass application of the new culture. The events of the '30s were an intensified continuation of the trends of the '20s. During these decades, while China was supposed to be unified, many projects were only partly carried out because of the internal threat of communism and the external menace of a militant Japan. Probably the basic cause of the slowness of true national unification was the fact that the aspiring government could not rid itself totally of regionalism and traditionally tinged political habits which survived unification. Also, toward the end of the '30s, World War II had practically come to China with the Sino-Japanese Incident (called "incident" in deference to the Kellogg-Briand Pact of 1928 which denounced war as an instrument of national policy) in 1937. After the war the Communist struggle for power in China enlivened and embittered the second half of the '40s.

As the ability of Confucianism to provide a frame of intellectual and cultural reference declined, many trends of thought were introduced, causing spirited debates and polemics on history, language, philosophy, and sociology. The world of thought in China faced the complex components of modern civilization with the same intensity and desire for comprehensiveness with which it had approached the Confucian world of values and attitudes, including the Buddhist and Taoist aspects of Chinese life. To all the proposals and counterproposals, the New Thought Movement, the student movements, and various other movements, a basic note was attached—the all-sufficiency of science. The scientific spirit was replacing the Confucian spirit, and science was thought to supply a new philosophy of life.

THE POPULARITY OF SCIENCE

The intellectual summons to adopt the scientific world-view and to discard the traditional philosophy of life was begun in the first twenty years of the new century. Hu Shih characterized the position of esteem which science began to hold.

> During the last thirty years or so there is a name which has acquired an incomparable position of respect in China; no one, whether informed or ignorant, conservative or progressive, dares openly slight or jeer at it. The name is Science. The worth of

> this almost nationwide worship is another question. But we can at least say that ever since the beginning of reformist tendencies [1890s] in China, there is not a single person who calls himself a modern man and yet dares openly to belittle Science.[9]

Chang Chun noted the increasing importance of science to the intellectuals.

> In the days since the Boxer Incident when modern schools were on the rise, scientific subjects were listed in the curricula and were compulsory for students at all levels of education. In addition, the young intellectuals studying abroad who noted the extremely close relationship between science and the profundity of modern civilization rose up to disseminate it. For several years now, the widespread nature of such a tendency [to disseminate science] has actually become an independent movement.[10]

Science was an ideological entity, imported to replace the old cultural values. These men could not have been commenting on any high degree or development of scientific research which, even in the '20s, was still weak in quantity, if not in quality.[11]

In July 1907, before the establishment of the Republic, the *New Century* (*Hsin Shih-chi*), a weekly initiated by veteran revolutionaries Wu Chih-hui and Li Shih-tseng, appeared in Paris. Produced abroad, it was widely read by exiled Chinese as well as by overseas students who were to return with the 1911 Revolution. The first issue contained a credo indicative of the temper of subsequent decades:

> The discovery of scientific laws and the expansion of waves of revolution are truly the characteristics of mankind during the nineteenth century. These two mutually complement and affect each other, so that society may merge into the laws of nature . . . What has in the past been called a revolution is merely a surface change . . . On the other hand, the revolution of the New

9. Hu Shih, "K'e-hsüeh yü jen-sheng-kuan hsü" (Preface to Science and Philosophy of Life), *KHYJSK*, 1 (Shanghai, 1923), pp. 2–3 of 2nd preface.

10. Chang Chun, "Wu-shih-nien-lai Chung-kuo chih k'e-hsüeh" (Chinese Science of the Past Fifty Years), *Tsui-chin chih wu-shih-nien* (The Past Fifty Years), anniversary issue of *Shen Pao* (Shanghai, 1923), 2, p. 1 of 4th art.

11. Jen Hung-chün, mathematician and cofounder of the Scientific Society of China, noted this in "Science: Its Introduction and Development in China," *Symposium on Chinese Culture,* ed. Sophia H. Zen (Shanghai, 1923), pp. 170–71.

> Century considers that all that does not conform to the laws of nature is undesirable and must be changed. Not only that, but this revolution will persist, forever nearing the right and the truth. Therefore, this is a relentless and progressive revolution, a revolution that has as its object the happiness of mankind.[12]

Much of modern China's effort to develop a new literature and a new world-view must be seen in the context of this loose interpretation of the word revolution. The quotation also demonstrates the easy equation, reminiscent of the West during the late seventeenth and eighteenth centuries, between the laws of nature that governed the natural sciences and the natural law that was thought to describe an ordered and analyzable human society. Revolutionary efforts in China began in earnest from about 1914–15 on; its supporters were armed with a flexible notion of revolution, and with "scientific exactness" to give their cause stature. These efforts have had a number of names: New Culture Movement, the Chinese Renaissance (Hu Shih's term), and New Thought Wave. They generally have been studied under these designations, and the "popular" nature of the movements has received documentation by numerous able students of modern China.[13] Although the institution of the scholar-gentry disappeared with the downfall of the monarchy, the tradition of an intellectual elite remained. When they spoke, the country listened. "Popular" refers to the new generation of students who propagated the fresh ideas which came from abroad. The scientific spirit pervaded all these movements.

When Hu Shih and Ch'en Tu-hsiu called for a literary and language revolution in *New Youth,*[14] that magazine became the vehicle of intellectual change in China. When Ch'en Tu-hsiu designated sci-

12. *HSC,* 1 (1907), 1.

13. Most of these works are by Kiang Wen-han and Chow Tse-tsung. Kiang's *Chinese Student Movement* (New York, 1948) stresses the more important currents of thought. Chow's *The May Fourth Movement: Intellectual Revolution in China 1915–1924* (Cambridge, 1960) is the leading comprehensive treatment of the period. Notable Chinese works are: Kuo Chan-po, *Chin wu-shih-nien Chung-kuo ssu-hsiang shih* (Chinese Intellectual History of the Past Fifty Years) (Peiping, 1935), and Wu Ch'i-yüan, *Chung-kuo hsin-wen-hua yün-tung kai-kuan* (China's New Culture Movement) (Shanghai, 1934).

14. C. T. Hsia in *A History of Modern Chinese Fiction* (New Haven, 1961) draws an interesting and valid line between Hu the empirical and cautious reformer and Ch'en the firebrand revolutionary in this sphere. It was the decisive and emotional language of Ch'en, however, which seemed to have carried the day.

ence and democracy as the bases of modern civilization in *New Youth,* the popular demand at once was for cultural reform through adoption of the scientific world-view and political reform through adoption of democratic practices. This journal set the tone for subsequent publications. *Hsüeh-i* (with its Western title, *Wissen und Wissenschaft*) first appeared in 1917, advertising itself in the front of the journal as a vehicle for the "promotion of learning and for criticism based on truth." It became an influential vehicle for scientism.[15] *The New Tide* (*Hsin-ch'ao*) was a publication organized in the winter of 1919 by a group of students at the University of Peking, headed by Fu Ssu-nien, Ku Chieh-kang, and Hsü Yen-chih. Hu Shih was their inspiring leader. The journal carried in its preface a credo—"The adoption of a critical spirit, scientific thinking, and a reformed rhetoric." *Young China* (*Shao-nien Chung-kuo*), established by the Young China Association, began publication in 1919. It followed the same practice; the frontispiece of the journal carried the dedication to "social services under the guidance of the scientific spirit in order to realize our ideal of creating a Young China." This journal represented such scientistic tendencies that for a while the Association refused membership to anyone belonging to a religious organization. *New China* (*Hsin Chung-kuo*) first appeared in 1919. It was devoted to almost every variety of modern thought but with a strong undercurrent of faith in science.[16]

These publications were numerous. One estimate stands at four hundred titles then available in the bookstalls.[17] Most indicative of the rising sentiment of scientism was the effort of the members of the Science Society in China to popularize the scientific spirit. An organization of Chinese men of science, the Society was originally formed in 1914 by a group of students at Cornell University and moved to China in 1918. As a research organization, its slogan, stated in numerous advertisements, was "the diffusion of the scientific spirit and knowledge for scientific growth and industrial prosperity." The journal of this Society was supposedly devoted to serious professional ar-

15. See especially *Hsüeh-i,* 2 (1920).

16. See particularly the contributions of Kao I-han and Liu Shu-ya, two men whose support for science as a popular doctrine was unreserved.

17. Estimated by Ch'en Ping-k'un, *Tsui-chin san-shih-nien Chung-kuo wen-hsüeh shih* (A History of Chinese Literature of the Past Thirty Years) (Shanghai, 1930), p. 214.

ticles on science proper. But in every issue of the *Science Journal* (*K'e-hsüeh*) until the late '20s, the first article argued for the adoption of the scientific world-view. These lead articles were later grouped into a popular book on science, *Essays on Science* (*K'e-hsüeh t'ung-lun*), published by the same society in 1919. The titles are symptomatic: "Scientific Spirit," "Scientific Method," "Science and Education," "Science and Morality," "Scientific Philosophy of Life," and so the list continues, bringing science into the varied provinces of life.

Printed matter of this description, then, was the vehicle for publicizing the idea of science as a value orientation. The audience was the generation of youths in schools and universities who felt particularly compelled to learn these ideas and then to propagate them.[18] The mere introduction of the scientific world-view was not enough for them. Scientism, as we have said, is necessarily a critique of improper ideas and beliefs. This the Chinese intellectuals adopted from their earlier Western counterparts. Just as the problem of the confrontation of the theistic world-view and the mechanistic world-view provided spirited discussion in the West, the problem of religion now came under Chinese scrutiny also. In borrowing science and democracy, the question of whether the religious component of the borrowed culture was also worth adopting had to be answered, and answered responsibly. What started merely as a critical discussion, lasting from about 1917 to 1921, became a vicious year-long attack on religion in 1922.[19] Behind the antireligious movement was the growing vogue of positivism and its inevitable exclusion of pluralistic philosophies. Behind it also, of course, was the hold which the respectability of the physical and natural sciences had upon several influential thinkers who found identification with an old system exceedingly untimely.

18. The special role of cultural messianism felt by the students is described well by T. C. Wang in *The Youth Movement in China* (New York, 1927). See also Kiang Wen-han, *Chinese Student Movement* and Chow Tse-tsung, *The May Fourth Movement.*

19. For a complete presentation of the antireligious movement in China, see Neander C. S. Chang, ed., *Kuo-nei chin shih-nien-lai chih tsung-chiao ssu-ch'ao* (Religious Thought Movements in China 1917-1927) (Peking, 1927). See also Chow Tse-tsung, "The Anti-Confucian Movement in Early Republican China," in *The Confucian Persuasion,* ed. A. F. Wright (Stanford, 1960), pp. 288–312. For anti-Christian sentiments of the 1920s, illustrating the growing positivism, see T. and S. Yamamoto, "The Anti-Christian Movement in China, 1922–27," *FEQ,* 12 (1953), 133–48.

As the attack on religion was being waged, another issue emerged as a result of World War I, which many Chinese viewed as the triumph of mechanism over spiritual values. Science was held responsible for producing a valueless mechanistic outlook and was blamed for the destruction and bloodshed of the war. Traditionalists thought they had found the means to challenge the omnipotence claimed for science by their modern compatriots. Immediately the cry arose that the spiritual civilization of the East was superior to the materialistic civilization of the West. The traditionalists were not alone in expressing this sentiment. Bertrand Russell, on a lecture tour in China during 1920–21, commented glowingly on the spiritual civilization of China, and belittled in no uncertain terms the mechanistic outlook of the West.[20] Foremost in proclaiming the bankruptcy of science and the return, at least partially, to traditional Chinese values was Liang Ch'i-ch'ao, who was considered the most prolific journalist of the time.

Finally, under relentless pressure for a new scientific culture, the problem of Chinese cultural and intellectual continuity broke into an open debate. The participants called it a battle, and in many ways it was a battle between the traditional and the scientific world-views. The Debate of 1923, treated fully in Chapter 6, can be said to have been won by the proponents of scientism before it even started. The illustrious names on the side of the antagonists of science show the seriousness of the challenge posed by scientism; these inroads into the intellectual continuity of China had to be contested. The Debate dwelled on several issues, the most obvious of which was the problem of knowledge. The antagonists led by Chang Chün-mai (Carsun Chang), contested the epistemology based on the concepts of substance and causality in the scientific method, while V. K. Ting, leading the protagonists of scientism, argued from his position as a phenomenalist. The major cause of (and also an issue in) the debate was the claim of the antagonists that Eastern civilization was superior to the materialistic civilization of the West. A third issue, which prob-

20. See his *The Problem of China* (New York, 1922), pp. 78–79. It should be noted that, while helping traditionalists sing the praises of Chinese spiritual civilization, Russell helped the proponents of science by his critique of religion. His more serious lectures did center on the use of the logical method, just as John Dewey's did in China the year before. Russell's visit was so popular that the *Russell Monthly* (*Lo Su yüeh-k'an*) was published to carry his lectures by the Lecture Society of the National University of Peking.

ably showed most clearly the penetration of modern science into the Chinese mind, was the adequacy of science in providing a philosophy of life.

In the years of the New Culture, with traditional orientation threatened, the question of value-orientation became tremendously important. The Chinese expression for the philosophy of life, *jen-sheng-kuan,* is literally "outlook on man's life." Ordinarily a philosophy of life is a personal matter; but during this time of change, when threats to traditional cultural references were real, the philosophical and academic meaning was shed in favor of a more emotional and ideological expression. Both antagonists and protagonists of the scientific worldview thought philosophy of life an unavoidable issue. The difference was that the antagonists tried to salvage a philosophy of life that would not be submerged under a scientific monism, while the protagonists thought a new life-outlook could be built on scientific principles, method, and spirit. In the 1923 Debate on science and the philosophy of life (sometimes called the debate on science and metaphysics), most of the notable Chinese scientists countered with a philosophy of science in defense of their position. They were supported by nonscientists led by Wu Chih-hui, Ch'en Tu-hsiu, and Hu Shih. The nonscientist support in this polemic gives convincing substance to the rise of scientism in Chinese thought.

The reverberations of the Debate continued into the '30s and '40s. But science no longer had to fight its own battles; the intellectual activities of the late '20s, '30s, and '40s covered other subjects: debates on history, society, and the mode of Westernization, were all waged in primarily scientific terms. The Debate of 1923 actually helped publicize science to such a degree that the term, scientism, became generally applicable to the basic current of positivist thought from then on. Bookstores in the '20s were flooded with "philosophies of life," most attempting a synthesis of the conception of life and science. Such collections numbered anywhere from fifty to two hundred and fifty.[21] Under the pressure of the "new" vision of natural and physical life, these works undertook to examine, or rather reexamine, such questions as the nature and origins of life, man's relationship to the universe,

21. O. J. Brière, *Fifty Years of Chinese Philosophy 1898–1950,* Eng. trans. L. G. Thompson (London, 1956), p. 90. See also a work of the '30s that counted 274 philosophies of life: Huang Ching-wan and Hsü Wan-ch'eng, *Ko-chung jen-sheng-kuan* (Varieties of Philosophies of Life) (Shanghai, n.d.).

his natural, physical, social, and intellectual nature, his morality, and his religion. Many leaders of Chinese thought came to a position of scientific monism.[22] This trend of the '20s led to an even more rigid insistence in the '30s and '40s on the power of science and the compatibility of scientific laws with "laws" of human development. Two periodicals, in particular, propagandized the spirit of science: *Scientific China (K'e-hsüeh ti Chung-kuo)*, first published in 1932 by the Nanking Association for the Movement of the Dissemination of Science in China; and *Collections of Writings on Science (K'e-hsüeh lun-ts'ung)*, a vehicle for the Marxist sociological version of science and the scientific method. Both publications showed a lack of any real understanding of science, on the one hand, and an excessive enthusiasm for it, on the other.

While journals were disseminating scientism, several debates proved further that the Chinese imagination was gripped by the spirit of science. In the 1928 Controversy of the History of Chinese Society,[23] enacted along strictly Marxist lines, each participant tried to project himself as the "scientist" solving societal problems according to the immutable laws of material forces. While differing in modes of presentation, the participants all followed Marx's assumption that social existence determines man's behavior. Where Marx contributed this hypothesis as merely a tool with which to analyze society, his followers (Chinese included) turned it into the inexorable law of historical determinism. Thus the two contending camps, led by T'ao Hsi-sheng in the periodical *New Life (Hsin sheng-ming)*, and by Kuo Mo-jo in *New Thought Tide (Hsin ssu-ch'ao)*, raged a furious battle over the mode of Marxian periodization of Chinese history.[24] Arguments dwelled on the nature of Chinese society. The controversy lasted well into the '30s, when materialistic positivism was carried on uninterrupted by a group of Marxist theoreticians including Li Ta, Liu Shao-ch'i, Ai Ssu-ch'i, and Mao Tse-tung. Mao, for instance, clearly stated in 1940 the Communist understanding of the role of science:

22. Brière, *Chinese Philosophy*, pp. 88–89.

23. Chung-kuo she-hui-shih lun-chan. See Chinese collection by the same title in *TSTC,* ed. Wang Li-hsi (4 vols. Shanghai, 1932). All subsequent references are to *TSTC.*

24. Much of the conflict was carried on by *TSTC,* a journal of materialistic and deterministic expression.

> The culture of this New Democracy is scientific. It opposes all feudal and superstitious thought; it advocates practical realism, objective truth, and the union of theory and practice. From this point of view, the scientific thought of the Chinese proletariat, along with the comparatively progressive material monists and natural scientists of the capitalist class, must unite to oppose imperialism, feudalism, and superstition; [they] must not ally themselves with any reactionary idealism.[25]

The Nationalists, whose theoretical spokesman leaned toward what is generally called "vitalism," felt compelled to minimize the philosophical and popularistic position of the material positivists by also appropriating the name of science for their emphasis on a combination of Bergsonian and Euckenian vitalism with the intuitionism of Wang Yang-ming. Sun Yat-sen himself had voiced this sentiment as early as 1918 in *On Psychological Reconstruction* (*Hsin-li chien-she lun*), a work which was clearly echoed during the '30s in the writings of Chiang Kai-shek and Ch'en Li-fu.[26] Both writers felt a need to use science as a cloak for the return to Confucian virtues. The serious effect these writers had on a large segment of the population was seen in the New Life movement begun in 1934 and in the efforts and thought of a number of provincial leaders.[27] The Nationalist enchantment with science was a sign of its immense popularity and of the strength of scientism. When a school of thought founded on the notion of the union of theory and action (not an exclusive property of the Communists), and harking back to ancient morals and intuitive thought, called itself scientific, there is interesting evidence of scientistic misapplication of labels.

Somewhere between the Communist and Nationalist positions stood another form of scientism in the '30s. Caught between the growing vogue of scientific and material monism and science-cloaked vitalism, the empiricist form of scientism eventually disintegrated. Largely because the power struggle between the main contenders was un-

25. See "Hsin min-chu chu-i lun," *MTTHC* (Peking, 1952), 2, 700. This essay was written in Jan. 1940.

26. See Chiang's *Chung-kuo chih ming-yün* (China's Destiny) (Chungking, 1943), a work which embodies much of the thinking behind his writings of the '30s. See fuller treatment in Chapter 7.

27. Brière, *Chinese Philosophy*, p. 60.

settled, the empiricists enjoyed a phase of popularity during the '20s and '30s. This creed tended to favor not just the modern but Western civilization as well. With the publication of an article by Hu Shih in the 1929 *China Christian Year Book* entitled "The Conflict of Cultures in Modern China," in which Hu advocated wholesale Westernization for China,[28] heated arguments arose. Throughout the '30s Chinese intellectuals debated wholesale Westernization versus China-centered Westernization. Arguments for and against an Anglo-American type of society were made. This was a controversy involving upholders of the empiricists' creed, defenders of traditional civilization, and the selectivists.

World War II tended to eclipse and disperse the squabbles of the late '30s and '40s. The empiricist tendency, in the political and military metaphor of the times, was neutralized and lost its campaign in China. The pseudo-scientific vitalism of the Nationalists collapsed with the Communist take-over in 1949. The trend to monistic, positivistic scientism, long dominant since the early crusade by Ch'en Tu-hsiu, followed the political tide to triumph. Scientism's vision of an inexorable scientific law for human development seemed fulfilled.

THE NATURE AND VARIETIES OF SCIENTISM

R. G. Owen, in his *Scientism, Man, and Religion,* attacks scientism as a form of idolatry, which he terms "scientolatry." "As a result of the exalted status of science," he writes, "it has, in some quarters, come to be worshipped as omniscient, omnipotent and the bearer of man's salvation."[29] This "scientolatry," according to him, claims that it can solve all problems scientifically and even examine questions of spirit, values, and freedom. A more sophisticated definition of scientism is provided by John Wellmuth, who states, "The word 'scientism' . . . is to be understood as meaning the belief that science, in the modern sense of that term, and the scientific method as described by modern scientists, afford the only reliable means of acquiring such knowledge as may be available about whatever is real."[30]

These characterizations complement one another. The former con-

28. Hu later relented and changed his appelation to "wholehearted modernization." See *HSLHCC* (Shanghai, 1935), pp. 558–59.

29. R. G. Owen, *Scientism, Man, and Religion* (Philadelphia, 1952), p. 20.

30. John Wellmuth, *The Nature and Origins of Scientism* (Milwaukee, 1944), pp. 1–2.

ceives of scientism as a cultural phenomenon with the emotional attribute of a substitute religion. The latter sees in it a conscious and identifiable philosophy, hence an intellectual phenomenon.[31] For our study we will attempt another definition. Scientism, in general, is a form of belief arising from a tradition or heritage in which the limiting principles of science itself have found general application and have become the cultural assumptions and axioms of that culture. More strictly, scientism ("scientistic" is the adjective) should be defined as that view which places all reality within a natural order and deems all aspects of this order, be they biological, social, physical, or psychological, to be knowable only by the methods of science.

Indeed, modern science would not be what it is today without the scientific method. John U. Nef points out, "What distinguishes modern science from all science of the past is not the observation of nature but a peculiar purpose and method in the examination of nature. What distinguishes modern science is, first, the persistent use of the experiment or of controlled observation as the final arbiter in reaching any result and, second, the employment of quantitative methods as the major means of achieving the results which are subject to the control of positive evidence." [32]

The scientific method operates on four fundamental principles. First, the need for observation, hypothesis, experimentation, and the return to observation: the empirical principle. Second, to achieve exactitude in measurement such a method must employ quantitative means: the quantitative principle. Third, the scientific method deals with causal relations and often uses abstractions to represent them. For this end, it must locate meaningful recurrences of behavior and then formulate general laws or equations which describe and explain such behavior: the mechanical principle of science. Fourth is a general assumption of all scientists which may be called an attitude of mind, a principle inherent in the concept of research: the principle of progress through science. This idea is clearly stated by Edgar Zilsel:

> Science, both in the theoretical and the utilitarian interpretation (by theoretical is meant a scientist doing a piece of work sheerly

31. Although Owen sometimes becomes emotional about scientism, he gives a capable analysis of its phases.

32. John U. Nef, "The Genesis of Industrialism and of Modern Science," *Essays in Honor of Conyers Read,* ed. Norton Downs (Chicago, 1953), p. 218.

> for that end; by utilitarian is meant a scientist doing a piece of work who links progress of science with progress of civilization, and has in mind the benefit to mankind by the practical application of theory), is regarded as the product of cooperation for nonpersonal ends, a cooperation in which all scientists of the past, present and the future have a part. Today this idea or ideal seems almost self-evident. Yet no Brahmanic, Buddhistic, Moslem, or Catholic Scholastic, no Confucian scholar or Renaissance humanist, no philosopher or rhetor of classical antiquity ever achieved it. It is a specific characteristic of the scientific spirit and of modern Western civilization.[33]

Gradually, with the success and improvement of science, these principles, supported by laboratory methods of controlled experimentation, became the assumptions of that culture which had itself benefited from both the theoretical and the applied aspects of science. Here R. G. Owen's analysis of how these principles together form "the scientific heritage of the modern West" is helpful. According to him, the general limiting principles of science can be illicitly generalized and transformed. Hence, the empirical principle becomes the empiricist axioms: no beliefs are respectable if they are not scientifically verifiable; the scientific method is the only method for arriving at truth. The quantitative principle is translated into materialistic axioms: the only reality is physical reality; the scientific method is the only valid method capable of measuring it. The mechanical principle becomes the mechanistic presupposition: knowledge is real only if it is knowledge of mechanical behavior. The progressive principle develops into the optimistic assumption that all work of men advances in linear fashion, and that in the future science itself will bring perfection.[34] Owen continues that these cultural presuppositions which form the scientific heritage can be easily turned into dogmas of scientism. Empiricism becomes the dogma that science is all-truth; the materialistic assumption becomes the dogma which denies the reality of spirit and the objectivity of values; the mechanical presupposition becomes the dogma of determinism, denying the reality of freedom; finally the progressive principle puts on the cloak of utopianism, envisaging the

33. Edgar Zilsel, "The Genesis of the Concept of Scientific Progress," *Journal of the History of Ideas,* 6 (1945), 325.

34. Owen, *Scientism, Man, and Religion,* pp. 18–20.

future society guaranteed by science and evolution in its perfection.[35]

Historically, such transitions from original principles to assumptions and then to their dogmatic conclusions found their best expression in the nineteenth century. This faith in the applications and implications of science is characterized by Sir William C. Dampier, who called the nineteenth century the Scientific Age not only because of the rapid growth of knowledge of the natural world, but also because in that century,

> the whole conception of the natural Universe has been changed by the recognition that man, subject to the same physical laws and processes as the world around him, cannot be considered separately from the world, and that scientific methods of observation, induction, deduction, and experiment are applicable, not only to the original subject-matter of pure science, but to nearly all the many and varied fields of human thought and activity.[36]

The materialistic determinism of the second half of the eighteenth century contributed a good measure of stimulus to the nineteenth-century temper. It is most representatively summed up in de la Mettrie's *L'Homme Machine* and Holbach's *Système de la Nature.* The latter work has often been called the Bible of Materialism.

The fact that scientism arises from cultural assumptions derived from scientific principles makes it an autonomous intellectual phenomenon, often unconsciously propagated by admirers of modern civilization. As such, it generally has two manifestations. Both are products of the scientific age; both possess immense implications for the biological, psychological, physical, and social aspects of the natural order; they are not necessarily exclusive of each other.[37] First, materialistic scientism, with its deterministic tendencies and explanations of the human situation, assumes that man is in no way different from the rest of nature, the nature of the physical sciences. Second, the variety of scientism called the empiricist creed, though not as dogmatic

35. Ibid., p. 23.

36. Sir William C. Dampier, *A History of Science* (4th ed., rev. New York, 1949), p. 200.

37. On the varieties of scientism, I have adopted in essential outline, but with varying emphasis, Owen's analysis of the materialistic and empiricist modes of scientism.

in its conclusions as the materialistic variety, is equally summary in its assumptions. The unquestioned acceptance of science as the ultimate good and of the scientific method as the only method to find truth and knowledge is basic.

Materialistic Scientism

Defined strictly, materialism is the belief that matter constitutes the only and ultimate reality of the universe. Thought and consciousness are its by-products, and there is nothing real beneath or beyond matter. Upon this hypothesis is built a whole materialistic metaphysic, best characterized by the line of thought from Hobbes to Haeckel, with important development of its social implications by Comte and Marx. Hobbes attempted a system of reality based on physics, while Comte and Marx—at all times maintaining the materialist premise—saw materialism as a science of society. Actually, Hobbes, considering all reality physical in essence and mechanical in behavior, arrives logically at the type of society he advocated, the Leviathan state. His view could only encourage his successors. Hobbes' view of human nature—with man's consciousness explained away as matter in motion; his behavior governed by the same laws of motion which exercise their influence through pleasure and desire, fear and pain; and his values reduced to powerfully motivated desires—joined with the ascending Newtonian physics to give a materialistic picture of man and the universe. The Darwinian theory gave it further explanation and sanction.

With the impetus given by Hobbes, the school of philosophical materialism received its best late eighteenth-century expression in the works of de la Mettrie and Holbach. De la Mettrie denied the existence of any mind, and the phenomenon called "mental being" was for him nothing more than the functioning of the brain. But, comparing man to a machine, detailed and regular in its parts and workings, de la Mettrie was never able to answer how this machine could wind itself. This naïve concept of materialistic and mechanistic determinism found a relatively more systematic expression in Holbach, who contended: "There are no unknown forces, but only attraction and repulsion, to which all process is referable, of which the causal relationship forms a closed and boundless system." [38] The mechanism derived from

38. W. P. D. Wightman, *Science and Monism* (London, 1934), p. 162, quotes R. Eisler, *Die Geschichte des Monismus* (Leipzig, 1910).

Newton's explanation of the movements of heaven and earth is taken to the extreme in this deterministic philosophy.

This essentially naïve and dogmatic eighteenth-century attitude evolved into the full-blown scientific monism of Ernst Haeckel in the nineteenth century. Materialistic monism, based on science and emboldened by the Darwinian hypothesis, reached its culmination with Haeckel, the first philosopher to erect a speculative monism based on the unitary concept of the natural sciences. He believed it false to think man a special creature simply because he is supposed to be endowed with a "soul," and false to think that other animals differing from our bodies only in a diminishing complexity and adaptation should have "souls" differing from ours accordingly. W. P. D. Wightman summarizes Haeckel's scientific monism:

> The universe [for Haeckel] is bounded neither in space nor time; its substance (with its two attributes matter and energy) fills the whole of space, and is in constant motion, resulting in the periodic development and decay; countless worlds move through all-pervading ether; of these, one is our sun, and of its planets, one is our earth; on the earth during the course of ages have arisen successively simple organisms, vertebrates, primates, and man.[39]

The social dimension given by Comte to materialism is another sign of the growing popularity of science. By applying the scientific method to the study of human society, another sphere of nature could be brought under control. Comte attempted to construct a scientific society based on his conception of the intellectual development of man. This development, as Comte saw it, was divided into three phases: the religious state, in which knowledge was mainly derived from revelation and superstition; the philosophical stage, in which knowledge was mainly speculative and metaphysical, and which indulged in such terms as "essences" and "forms"; and the positive stage, or the scientific age, in which only the understanding of scientific laws leads to true knowledge. Comte's greatest influence on the admirers of modern civilization we will consider was his linking the greatest intellectual respectability to the age of scientific industrialism. His original contribution in introducing the scientific study of society is often ignored, in favor of his more emotional vision of the employment of scientific

39. Wightman, *Science and Monism*, pp. 244–45.

tools in the creation of the scientific industrial society. Finally, as a natural sequel to this vision of a future society, Comte revealed a new object of worship, humanity. In this new orientation were the implications for a science of society and the inherent materialistic utopianism which gave Marx the premise for his creed, though Marx stated it in a more sophisticated and biased form. His dialectical materialism, explaining all stages of human development in terms of vying and changing modes of production, purports to deal "directly" with society. It may be thought of as the basis of social scientism.

In short, then, science proper used this view of the material world to develop (at least during the eighteenth and nineteenth centuries), but this view was seized by the worshippers of science and made into a general philosophy. Materialistic scientism assumes that all aspects of life belong to a natural order and are controllable and knowable by methods of science, for they are simply matters of nature and move according to definite scientific laws. This view of the world was received with great enthusiasm by many Chinese intellectuals in the first half of the twentieth century, even though the age of modern physics was dawning and would someday dispel the narrow determinism of nineteenth-century science.

In China the two best representatives of philosophical materialism are Wu Chih-hui and Ch'en Tu-hsiu. The former manifested a crude blending of late eighteenth-century mechanistic materialism and nineteenth-century evolutionary thought. In the proper fashion of the materialistic determinist, Wu read into the Darwinian *hypothesis* of natural selection the *law* of organic evolution. Indeed, all Chinese thinkers who admired Western civilization held this view of Darwin. To them, evolution theory was proof positive that man is only matter, functioning in obedience to the laws of motion. Ch'en Tu-hsiu shared many philosophical premises with Wu, although he was primarily the uncritical and propagandistic popularizer of science. In Ch'en we find the basic premises of philosophical materialism taken to their dogmatic extremes.

Empirical Scientism

The second variety of scientism is much less dogmatic in its conclusions than materialistic scientism. But the two share common assumptions (taken from the scientific method and the "scientific tradition") and common ancestry. This second variety finds its best expression in empiricism, long a major mode of thought of Western society.

Empiricism, as an attitude of mind, has always existed. As philosophy and epistemology, however, it has its modern beginnings in the philosophy of Francis Bacon. Responding to the findings in the natural sciences, Bacon believed that the method which led to discoveries in science could be applied to philosophy. His most notable contribution, of course, lies in his advocacy of the induction, as opposed to deduction, which philosophers since Aristotle had favored. The deductive method could not be useful in the discovery of new knowledge, because, in any deductive reasoning, the conclusion is already contained in the premise. Bacon did not fully explain or understand the scientific method, for both the deductive and inductive methods do play mutually important roles, but his proposal of induction is a clear example of empirical philosophy's debt to scientific method. Empiricism rests upon observation of experience, analysis of data observed, and formulation of hypotheses which, in turn, are tested by further observation and experiment. Bacon insists that the only real knowledge is that gained by the method of the natural sciences. This insistence constitutes the beginning of the "scientistic" assumptions of the school of empirical philosophy. Bacon's wholehearted acceptance of inductive method in areas concerning human understanding was to receive further refinement from Locke and Hume.

The problem of reliability of the senses in observation, unsolved by Bacon, was faced by John Locke. Locke explained the element of unreliability by introducing his concept of primary and secondary qualities. Primary qualities, number, dimension, figure, and motion, represent qualities inherent in things; secondary qualities, color, taste, smell, and sound, are products of our sensual perception. Primary qualities compose precisely the picture of reality as understood by seventeenth-century science. Locke never admitted that there was material substance existing by itself in which these primary qualities inhere and to which they pertain. He was thus found saying that knowledge of the material substance beneath the primary qualities comes from an act of faith or conviction. This inferential knowledge cannot fulfill the empirical demand for verifiability.

David Hume pushed Locke's position even further and found himself in the position of utter skepticism. If knowledge of matter were merely inferential, there could be no real knowledge to speak of. Locke had turned substantive matter, the main object of scientific investigation, into a thing of the mind; Hume injected the idea of causality into his scheme of sense impressions and found that even the idea of causality lacked objective validity. The belief in causality was, for Hume, a habit of mind, resulting from constant association of two events so that when one comes to mind the other is also recalled. Constant conjunction merely creates a subjective correlation of two events and does not necessarily amount to an impression of an actual and objective connection. Thus, the second main prop of inductive science, namely causality, also eludes empirical verification. Although Hume remained in his logical skepticism, he never manifested a fundamental distrust of substance and causality, just for want of objective proof. He considered them useful assumptions in the scientific study of things.

Hume's crippling skepticism seemed altogether to have weakened and discredited the empirical claim of scientific sanction and verifiability. Yet again, the power of science proper and its enormous practical success came to the rescue. Darwin revived faith in the empirical method. His contribution lay in the formulation of an hypothesis of the evolution of man. This hypothesis need not be repeated here. Most important is the fact that it lowered the exalted level of the human intellect and moral faculties, formerly thought to be marks of man's ineffable spirituality. Man was now different from beast only in degree and not in kind, his so-called intellectuality considered an evolution of primitive animal intelligence and his moral sense thought to be a higher degree of sophistication of the instinctual faculties of the animal. Empirical scientism, thanks to Darwin, now flourished once more. Science became glorified for those who were persuaded that the scientific method led to truth and knowledge.

The world-view of the last half of the nineteenth century was largely composed of the Newtonian universe and the Darwinian world of man. Likened to a machine, the world consisted of the reality of matter in motion, according to the laws of mass and gravity. Man, like the particle, was a product of natural forces; his origin, development, and character were accounted for in these terms. Such knowledge of the universe and man could have been achieved only by the scientific method. This faith in science and its method had produced much of modern civilization in the West. Many Chinese intellectuals of the twentieth century adopted it with enthusiasm.

Most representative of the empiricist tendency was Hu Shih. While accepting this creed throughout his life, Hu, by philosophical preference, was influenced by William James, John Dewey, and Charles Peirce. Pragmatism, a further development of the empirical style of philosophy, is a break in the empiricist tradition of Locke and Hume. It defies precise definition, partly because it is not a systematic doctrine that evolved from a single principle and partly because its different exponents had different points to make. It does solve, however, the empiricist problem which led Hume into a logical skepticism. The older empiricists tried to define true knowledge as that which corresponds with external reality. James, for example, maintains that there is a functional value to truth and knowledge; an idea is true if it leads to a kind of experience in which that function is served. Pragmatism, therefore, emphasizes the practical side of the scientific tradition, with the principle of utility as its criterion of truth.

Although tentative and cautious in its conclusions, empirical scientism is, after all, based on the assumptions of the scientific tradition, and the objects of worship are still within the province of scientific method. Hu Shih, a student of empirical philosophy in general and of pragmatism in particular, expounded this belief in China's period of New Thought.

Both varieties of scientism share an indispensable feature: the critical sense. Scientism stands essentially against anything that cannot be verified; it opposes all forms of deductive and speculative reasoning which inhibit empirical investigation. Bacon called unfounded ideas "idols." Because of its basic acceptance of matter as the only reality and its denial of the separate existence of spirit or soul, scientism is a critique of religion and popular beliefs. Comte, with the help of the eighteenth-century rationalists, had replaced religious worship with the new faith in humanity. Marx struck a contemptuous note by calling religious beliefs and ethical ideas "superstructures" grafted on the material forces of society, which in turn would change them anyway. Huxley's agnostic demand for proof of the existence of God and Dewey's ruling that religious beliefs are incongruous with the scientific habit of mind are components of the essentially antireligious temper of scientism.

This antireligious view was shared by the Chinese thinkers whose scientistic beliefs this study explores. They attacked not only religion but also the traditional world-view. Thus their critique partakes both of a Baconian critique of idealism and a positivistic attack on religion. Even though the Chinese tradition was not religious in the Western sense, the intensity with which the "old" (beliefs, religions, and institutions) was attacked can cause us to see in the worship of science in modern China a substitute religion or religious substitute. Scientism exhibits first, a particular understanding of the power of science, second, a critique of tradition, and, third, a form of substitute religion.

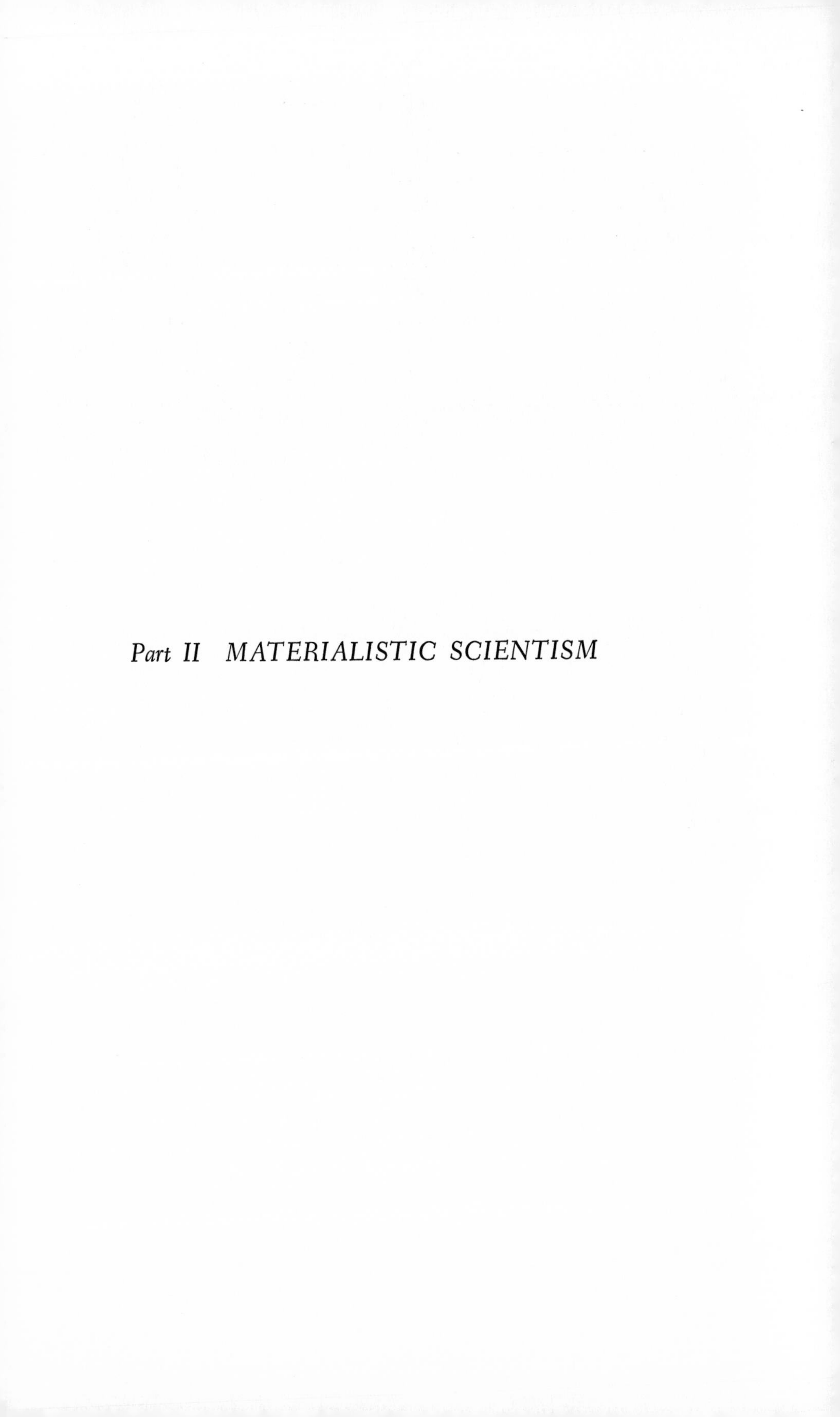

Part II MATERIALISTIC SCIENTISM

Chapter 2 THE PHILOSOPHICAL MATERIALIST: WU CHIH-HUI (1865–1953)

Born in 1865,[1] Wu Chih-hui, the philosophical materialist, was remarkably consistent in his beliefs throughout most of his long life. Alfred Forke once named him the representative thinker of modern China,[2] a significant tribute to Wu, who was already in his fiftieth year when *New Youth* first appeared. Though primarily known for his use of the vernacular (his native Wu-hsi, at that), Wu was first educated in the classics. In 1891 he went up for the degree of *chü-jen* (second highest imperial degree through examination). During this examination, an incident occurred which indicates Wu's satirical and humorous nature and his contempt for the trappings of "old China." The candidate for the examinations had to show proficiency in composing poetry, a literary pursuit which, by self-admission, Wu feared. He solved the problem by rendering in *chuan* script, the ancient seal style of calligraphy, a poem which, as a second precaution, he had copied onto the fan he had brought into the examination hall.[3] The episode and the *chuan* script became famous, possibly because Wu Chih-hui did receive his degree. Wu's habit of mocking

1. No adequate biography of Wu exists as yet. Good brief sketches are by Hu Shih, "Chi-ke fan-li-hsüeh ti ssu-hsiang-chia," *HSWT,* 3rd coll., bk. 2 (1930), 151–85; and by Liou Ho, "Notice biographique sur C. H. Wood," *Annales Franco-Chinoises de Lyon,* 1er Trimestre (1931), 2–4. See also an interesting treatment by Chang Wen-po, *Chih-lao hsien-hua* (Random Notes on Wu Chih-hui) (Taipei, 1952).

2. Alfred Forke, *Geschichte der neuren Chinesischen Philosophie* (Hamburg, 1938), p. 646.

3. Chang Wen-po, *Random Notes,* p. 9.

the unpopular appears often in his later scientistic critique of traditional civilization. His writings are noted for their fresh, yet serious, content, satirical intent, humorous style, and biting condemnation of all forms of thought standing in the way of progress.

During the humiliating years from 1894 to 1903, which saw him teaching in various schools in Peking, Tientsin, and Shanghai, Wu Chih-hui was aroused by the technological supremacy of the Japanese and the inadequacy of the Manchus, and began the life of a revolutionary. With Ts'ai Yüan-p'ei, he founded the famous Society of Patriotic Scholars (*Ai-kuo Hsüeh-shih She*) and the *Kiangsu Journal* (*Su Pao*). The journal propagated Wu's early revolutionary ideas, and its inflammatory articles so angered the Manchu ruling house that Wu, its editor-in-chief, had to flee to Japan in 1902 to avoid arrest. In 1903, after a struggle with the Japanese police, he left for England. The trip proved advantageous, for in England Wu became acquainted with the theories of evolution and paleontology. He began writing on these new theories in Chinese and did translations. The major ones were Dennis Hird's *A Picture Book of Evolution* and Joseph McCabe's *La Paléontologie*. The ideas of modern civilization gave a new dimension to Wu's revolutionary fervor. They freed him from the narrow political concern of a revolution to overthrow the Manchus. His knowledge of the natural sciences and theory of evolution led him to doubt the so-called spiritual base of Chinese civilization and to begin advocating a fundamental reorientation of values. While in England in 1905, Wu met Sun Yat-sen and was won over to his cause, joining Sun's *T'ung-meng Hui* at the end of that year.

What he discovered in England was to be coupled with new ideas Wu learned in Paris. The Paris sojourn saw him collaborating with Li Shih-tseng and Chang Ching-chiang[4] on the *New Century* (*Hsin shih-chi*) and *The Illustrated World* (*Shih-chieh hua-pao*).[5] By the

4. Li Shih-tseng, the anarchist, was the Chinese translator of Kropotkin's works. Chang Ching-chiang, though one of the richest men of the time, was extremely sympathetic to the revolutionary cause and with the help of Li and Wu established the first bean curd factories in Paris to raise funds for Sun Yat-sen's revolution.

5. The *New Century*, a weekly, was published first on June 22, 1907, and went through 121 issues until it was suspended on May 21, 1910. Many writers used one-word pseudonyms. The paper reflected much of the anarchistic beliefs of this group of Chinese intellectuals. *The Illustrated World*, not as well-known, was considered a sister publication. Both periodicals were published by the Shih-chieh She.

time the first issue of the *New Century* appeared in June 1907, Wu seemed to have achieved systematic expression of his intellectual convictions. No longer was he troubled by the confrontation of the old and the new, of the Chinese and the foreign. He started to formulate his new beliefs in terms of a new cosmology, a new world-view, in which he considered such questions as religion, morality, knowledge, and the correct society for humanity. In the end, Wu was completely captivated by the values of the modern scientific society.

At the creation of the Republic, Wu Chih-hui, a distinguished philologist, was made President of the Committee for the Unification of the Pronunciation of Characters for All China (*Ch'üan-kuo Tu-yin T'ung-i Hui*), which owes to him the invention of a phonetic alphabet. In his attempts on behalf of a new Chinese culture, Wu was one of the most active promoters of an overseas education for young Chinese. He had devised a program for training professors and creating Chinese universities abroad to improve higher education at home. The Université Franco-Chinoise at Lyons was founded in 1920. In 1921, Wu personally escorted the first contingent of students and became the institute's first director. From the time he returned in 1922 until his party assumed control of the government, Wu Chih-hui, a veteran member of the Kuomingtang, did not participate in the government. Instead, he busied himself with public affairs, educational and philanthropic endeavors, both at home and abroad.[6]

An ardent admirer of materialistic civilization by philosophical conviction, and at the same time very much an idealist by temperament, he did not agree completely with the Marxists and Communists; the latter he early considered brutal and despotic. He was captivated by the doctrines of Proudhon and Kropotkin and believed in the continuous evolution of the world toward perfection. This could be achieved eventually, Wu believed, in a hundred years or even a thousand years, with the absence of government by sages and with universal adoption of industrial and vocational education. He was devoted to Sun Yat-sen, for in Sun's plan of reconstruction he saw not only the material organization necessary to China but also progress toward the happiness of mankind. Wu's wisdom and worth aside,

6. In 1924, for instance, he was named member of the Commission of Intellectual Cooperation of the League of Nations, a project suggested by S. E. Briand, the French Minister of Foreign Affairs.

his tenacious faith in Sun was remarkable, and it lasted until his own death.

Wu Chih-hui was a prolific writer. His major work, written in the style of a novel-travelogue but containing much information on mankind's evolution, is entitled *Sayings about the World and Times of Old and New* (*Shang-hsia ku-chin t'an*).[7] His most important philosophical writing is a long essay entitled "A New Belief's Conception of the Universe and the Philosophy of Life" ("I-ke hsin hsin-yang ti yü-chou-kuan chi jen-sheng-kuan").[8] Other writings include numerous articles commenting elaborately on education, politics, religion, morality, traditional Chinese values, scientific industrialism, and the art of nongovernment.[9]

In this study, emphasis is laid on Wu's conception of science, his critique of traditional values, and his new philosophy of life based on the acceptance of the omnipotence of science.

CONCEPTION OF SCIENCE

Science was closely woven into Wu Chih-hui's conception of the new society. The new society of anarchy could be realized by a new morality which was to be nurtured by scientific education. Wu had arrived at these convictions at the time of the appearance of the *New Century* in Paris (1907). In fact, most of his writings on morality, religion, education, and anarchism were produced in 1907 and 1908. In an article, "On the Carefree Realm of Anarchy," he states:

> The name "anarchy" is the most auspicious in the world . . . [with anarchy] each country would remove national boundaries . . . each would renounce different languages and adopt a common tongue; the state without government uses seventy or eighty percent of its total effort to educate people in scientific knowledge, and twenty or thirty percent to teach the ethics of nongovernment. Anarchy, the result, is inevitable and will have ethics but not laws. One will have "from each according to his ability," but cannot call that "duty"; one will have "to each according to

7. First published in 1911, now reprinted by Chung-yang wen-wu kung-yin she (2 vols. Taipei, 1955).

8. This article (hereafter cited as "A New Belief") was written in 1923 for the Debate. It appears in many collections, but my reference is to *WWT*, 168–308.

9. All of his writings until 1927 are collected in *WCC* (10 bks. Shanghai, 1927).

> his need," but cannot call that "right." When everyone voluntarily places himself in the realm of truth and equity, and when the state of the ruler and the ruled exists no longer, then we will have true anarchy.[10]

This statement illustrates Wu's faith in the modern scientific society and his humanitarian concern for the general progress of mankind. Although he often said that education and revolution were the sole means to promote man's progress, he meant a specific scientific education and a revolution, not necessarily political in nature, which overthrows old habits of mind and reactionary ideas of social organization. His view of a correct education is found in a letter dated September 28, 1908: "The only education that deserves the name is in the physical, chemical, and mechanical sciences and industries, for these pursuits can constantly press for new theories and inventions, creating the happiness of mankind and bringing about the progress of the world." [11] There can be no doubt about Wu's preference for an industrial education; he wanted the whole of China to forget the so-called spirituality of her culture (and, for that matter, the spirituality of any culture) and concentrate on achieving a "dry and tasteless materialistic civilization" by perfecting the knowledge of scientific industrialism.[12]

Concern with the inhibitory effects of China's traditional culture on scientific and industrial development proved to be an obsession with Wu. He believed that even the introduction of science would be difficult if the nation were not taught the notion of manual, mechanical arts and crafts. In a celebrated letter to Ts'ai Yüan-p'ei,[13] he praised Ts'ai for sending his son to Belgium to learn technology. Wu, while stressing China's pitiful technological lag and her meager contribution to mankind's progress, nevertheless considered science proper more important than mere technology. Given the disharmony between

10. "T'an wu-cheng-fu chih hsien-t'ien" (The Carefree Realm of Anarchy), *WCC,* bk. 8, 49–51.

11. "Ta jen shu—chiao-yü . . . ke-ming" (An Answer to a Letter—Education . . . Revolution), *Wu Chih-hui hsüeh-shu lun-chu* (Selections of Wu Chih-hui's Academic Writings) (Shanghai, 1925), p. 237.

12. Wu's August 24, 1924 editorial of "K'e-hsüeh chou-pao" (Science Weekly), *WCC,* bk. 1, 123.

13. "Fu Ts'ai Chieh-min shu" (A Return Letter to Ts'ai Yüan-p'ei), *WWT,* 1, 146–51.

the old humanistic ideal and the idea of technology, however, Wu was acutely aware of the danger of just promoting science (as theory and discipline) while the people still held old habits of meditative speculation, for this might draw the scientists into metaphysical polemics.

Wu's conception of science as the helpmate of progress and the coming industrial society is stated in clear terms in three articles which appeared in the *New Youth* in 1916 and in 1918. In "Youth and Tools" and in "Again on Tools," he clarifies his concept of material civilization. "I absolutely do not worship material civilization as such, but, if 'material civilization' means that which is directed by a concern with spiritual enlightenment, then I absolutely believe in it."

What he meant, of course, was that material civilization should be directly proportional to mankind's happiness and that many materialist values are inherent in the notion of happiness. What is material civilization?

> It is none other than [the world of] man-made things. What then are man-made things? They are none other than handmade things. Hence, hands are the mother of all man-made things. Animals use horns, mouths, and feet as tools of creation . . . Man's ancestor first stood on his two hind legs in order to support his whole body, freeing the front two legs to become arms and hands. Hands are the best tools of the animal world. Why? Because, in being tools themselves, the hands can create other tools.[14]

As the process of toolmaking progresses from the simple to the complex, it not only multiplies power but also achieves a new degree of precision. Wu saw in this process the maturation of the human being and the development of his mentality from crude simplicity to refined and precise mechanism. Wu was more interested in the state of mind that could comprehend the multiplicity and precision attainable through the use of tools than in the tools themselves. He wanted to combat the traditional Chinese disdain for people who use their hands and are mechanically clever. In the same article, he urges

14. "Ch'ing-nien yü kung-chü" (Youth and Tools), *HCN*, 2:2 (1916), p. 2 of 2nd art.; see also his "Tsai lun kung-chü (Again on Tools), ibid., 2:3 (1916), 9th art.

China's youth not to be satisfied with mere finished products, but to "play" with the machines which created them—needles, scissors, openers, and screwdrivers (themselves tools). To him, no one has the right just to enjoy the fruits of industrialized labor; everyone should contribute to the process of creating goods for all mankind.

From this discussion of the virtues of tools, Wu moves to the assertion that "great harmony" could be achieved by machines. He expresses this sentiment in his "Treatise on the Promotion of the Universal Harmony by Machines,"[15] in which he especially condemns the people (such as Lao-tzu and Tolstoi) who taught that tools could not help mankind, that the world could be improved by reverting to a form of moral nihilism. There are two kinds of dreams of the great harmony: one is a primitive naturalism which pictures a hut on a mountain where man can breathe fresh winds, contemplate the bright moon, and enjoy a selfsustaining agricultural life; the superficiality of such a vision is readily seen if one considers what a few months of strong winds and torrential rains can do to the hut, the well, and the fields. The second is the more realistic vision, for it puts faith in the social implications of a mechanistic and materialistic civilization:

> [W]hen the world of great harmony is reached, all forms of labor shall have been replaced by machinery . . . Each man works only two hours a day, and only according to his ability. Therefore, of the twenty-two hours left in the day, eight will be used for sleep, six for amusement, eight for study and inventive efforts which require concentration . . . When the time comes that each can take according to his need, every human being will have an exalted, pure, and exemplary character . . . there will be no deserted, dirty, or decrepit places on the face of the earth; for the world will be a grand park. When this time comes, man will have a head—because of the overuse of his brain—as big as a five-pound melon, while his body will be small and delicate (because all his needs of communication will be taken care of by machines). This is not a utopian idealization. There is already some evidence of its realization in countries which possess better and more skillful machines. Such a state of affairs is naturally the contribution of machinery.[16]

15. In *HCN*, 5:2 (1918), 158–60.
16. Ibid., 159.

吳稚暉先生題詞

自蒸之機發明而世界一變，自油之機發明而世界再變。十九世紀蒸之機所帶領出時代，二十世紀者油之機帶領出時代也。神哉摩託，聖哉摩託。

稚暉

His concern with the future industrial society earned Wu Chih-hui a reputation as one who believed in "saving the country with motors" (*"mo-t'o chiu-kuo"*). By 1933, fifteen years after the first appearance of this view, the idea and Wu Chih-hui's reputation as its first and most vocal supporter had lost no momentum. Japan's mechanized threat to Manchuria and Shanghai in 1931–32 heightened these sentiments. The widely-read *New China* (*Hsin Chung-hua*) ran a special issue in 1933 under the title, "Saving the Country with Motors."[17] Its editors acknowledged Wu as the honored progenitor of the idea; the issue carried a lead article by him. True to his favorite habit of keeping people guessing, as well as amused, at his intent, Wu Chih-hui wrote not in the popular *pai-hua* but in highly literary *wen-yen* on a timely, modern subject. Moreover, he adorned the frontispiece of the journal with a citation in praise of motors set in the ancient seal script for which he was so famous. In the old garb (see p. 40), this message read, "The world changed since the invention of the steam engine. The world changed again when the petroleum-driven engines were invented. The nineteenth century is an age governed by the steam engine; the twentieth century is an age ruled by the petroleum-driven engine. How miraculous, the motor! How sacred, the motor!"

Wu Chih-hui's love for this form of civilization is rooted in his belief in the omnipotence of science and its principles. This philosophical commitment led Wu to a strong advocacy of philosophical materialism. Materialistic views and scientific monism, a tide in late eighteenth and early nineteenth-century European thought (with de la Mettrie's *L'Homme Machine* and Holbach's *Système de la Nature*), now appeared in China to be served by its most insistent proponent, Wu Chih-hui.

Wu set the tone of this belief in the mechanical nature of the universe, based on Newtonian physics, by stating in 1909 that "in this world, there is nothing but matter, and there is no such thing as spirit which comes before matter." He continued:

> Spirit is but a by-product of the formation of matter. With 110 pounds of pure water, 60 pounds of colloidal solution, 4 pounds,

17. See *HCH*, 1:13 (1933). Wu's article presenting much the same views on the necessity for a weak country like China to have planes propelled by modern motors appears on pp. 1–4.

> 3 ounces of protein, 4 pounds 5 ounces of cellulose, and 12 ounces of otein in a suitable combination, the result is an 147-pound "I." This formation of matter and substance goes under the name of "I," unwittingly follows the laws of this material world, and plays around for a while. . . . This playing around . . . lasts only until the separation of the component parts and substances which formed the "I." As to just what are sadness and happiness . . . what is perfect, what is reality, I do not care. For, only after the combination of water, colloidal solution, fat, and other substances, is there spirit. From this spirit, which arises only after such a combination of matter, comes thought which in turn cannot be said to precede matter. All arbitrary hypotheses and willful constructs of imagination are but reflections of matter; they are nothing but ephemeral falsehoods and errors.[18]

In the beginning, for Wu Chih-hui, was not the word, but immutable matter. All that is not matter is unthinkable. Hence, no ideology—be it religious, social, or political—could claim validity, since it would merely be a by-product of the material configuration of substances. Man's only consciousness is of the existence of matter. Wu is following the materialistic and deterministic axioms, supported by the assumption that man in no way differs from the rest of nature as represented by the physical sciences. Hence, human society can be studied as a science, which is a method—the best method—for locating relation and causation in matter.

For Wu the conviction that science and its method were applicable to the analysis of human society did not lead him into the rigid Marxian conception; it led him into an utopian belief in the "science of nongovernment." [19] Had he pushed his assumptions to their logical conclusions, Wu would have turned to a dogmatic dialectical materialism. But when Wu faced the problem of social development and progress, he became a fuzzy idealist, and his rigid philosophical beliefs became flexible. Man, part of nature, now rose above the natural order which he could manipulate and conquer for his own benefit.

18. "Yü yu-jen lun wu-li shih-chieh chi pu-k'o-ssu-i shu" (A Letter to a Friend on the Physical World and Imponderables), *WCC*, bk. 4, 1

19. See his "I cheng-hsüeh chih fei-cheng-hsüeh" (Use Political Science to Study the Science of Nongovernment), *T'ai-p'ing yang* (The Pacific Ocean), *1*:2 (1917), 1–2 of the correspondence section.

This inconsistency can be explained in terms of the situation of modern Chinese needs and by Wu's primary concern to see China emerge from intellectual and technological obscurantism. To him, the all-important first step was to rid Chinese youth of fanciful and idealistic notions which favored the spiritualistic civilization. He wanted the youth to be creative with their hands, building a civilization based on the knowledge and in the spirit of science. How to find this creativity in a world of material determinism? Wu Chih-hui, like any other material determinist, contended that creative force and thought arose only from a material need; in the end, matter was the determining factor and criterion of need. Nevertheless, the conflict between his conception of man as being different only in degree from the rest of the natural world and his emotional appeal to man's creativity is not resolved.

Wu Chih-hui's pronouncements on science and its attributes, stated in popular terms and made in order to arouse a lethargic civilization, received widespread exposure in 1924. He was approached by the *Republican Daily (Min-kuo jih-pao)* to contribute articles to its supplement, *Science Weekly (K'e-hsüeh chou-pao)*. A popular magazine, the *Science Weekly* was started by a group of young students of the Science Research Society of the Peking Teachers' College. Wu finally accepted the editorship of the weekly. With its motto, "the study of the content of science and the realization of the value of science," the periodical, under the guidance of the prolific "old vanguard" (he was now sixty years old), launched its attack on what Wu called the "ugly delicacy of eastern civilization." Its scientistic tenor can be seen in the preface:

> Science has had an embryonic beginning in all civilized countries of the world, but ever since the Renaissance it has shone with sudden brilliance in Europe. During the last hundred years, it has affected all forms of scholarly endeavor in an ever intensifying degree. Areas of mystery—philosophy, esthetics which deals with feeling, the kaleidoscopic psyche, and the multifarious nature of society—have one by one ascended to the stage of science and made progress. Human thought, though easily capable of becoming careless and ad hoc, can, after scientific training, give ordered observation of and logical treatment to all things

> in the environment. Moreover, [as a result of scientific training] human thought will acquire a clearer and more accurate understanding of the universe, thus formulating the proper philosophy of life.
>
> In the past, people had been entirely too dominated by the forces of nature, and the dark epoch of divine authority has thus been possible. As science weakened the worship of divine authority, human thought could be liberated on a large scale. With it came such notions as independence, self-respect, and the coming of utopia. Is there any explanation for the prosperity and strength of Europe and America other than science? [20]

Wu Chih-hui gave three reasons for this love of science: logic informs us that where common sense is at best formed from vague impressions, science is precise and accurate; we humans do not wish to be furry, four-footed animals, but to use human labor to conquer natural forces, and besides, science is the basic method for this human labor; if the completion of all ideal morality is desired, only science is omnipotent. If one does not subscribe to these views, he can be considered as too lazy to be "man." [21] Soon after, Wu wrote, "Science itself is basically a kind of life force, forever beneficial to mankind . . . The progress of the world follows the progress of material goods. Science is . . . the most effective method in the production of goods. What is meant by progress of the world following the progress of material goods? I cannot make any answer to this if the inquirers believe in divine creation. But I would answer to the truthfulness of the statement if one accepts the [evolution theory of man]." [22]

Wu then believed that man could, through science, gain a picture of the universe hitherto unimagined by philosophers and unaccounted for by epistemologies. One must not be misled, however, by his seeming lack of interest in the philosophical aspects of science just because he showed an active interest in it as a tool. His own notions of real and reliable knowledge shows a philosophical commitment to science, its governing principles and scientific theories of evolution. Wu used

20. Wu, "K'e-hsüeh chou-pao fa-k'an-yü" (Preface to the Publication of the Science Weekly), *WWT*, 1, 74–75.

21. June 15, 1924 editorial in *K'e-hsüeh chou-pao* (*Science Weekly*). *WCC*, bk. 1, 70.

22. June 22, 1924 editorial in *Science Weekly*. Ibid., 83–84.

the term "science" in two ways. He made the humble appeal that science and the scientific knowledge and outlook be prerequisites for a civilization that aspired to be modern. He also used the word in a propagandistic and, in some cases, polemical sense, a tendency shared by all admirers of science in China. The principles of science, backed by the enormous prestige of the progress made through science, were used as a tool to criticize idealism. Idealism, in the years of China's struggle for progress, was suspect; progress had been predominantly achieved in material terms, and China's lag behind the rest of the world had been blamed on her material insufficiency. Idealism was identified with efforts which ignored reality: religion, metaphysics, esthetics, ethics, and many aspects of the national spiritual heritage.

CRITIQUE OF TRADITIONAL CIVILIZATION

Wu Chih-hui and his compatriots and contemporaries felt that religion was the dominant form of belief until the dawning of the scientific age. This sharp distinction between dominant beliefs may be valid for the West, but in China no such division existed. Our concern is not to trace the continuity of Chinese intellectual history, however, but to analyze the criticism which the scientific world-view leveled against the old world-view. The word "old" was associated with the religious age, and Wu's critique of traditional civilization was often directed at religion in general; his view of religion came from his socialist convictions. In his "The Problem of Religion" he wrote, "When religion reigned supreme, morality and virtue were obstructed in their development by hideous practices and hence were not imparted in good measure to humanity. When socialism is realized, the hideous practices will be eradicated, and the good morality and virtue will enjoy free development, capable in a large degree of being shared by all mankind."[23] This passage gives the premise of Wu's critique of all beliefs of the prescientific era. More particularly, religious belief to him was a form of mental intoxication which accepted with awe the seeming animation of natural objects and forces. The degree of intoxication would, according to him, recede as the process of evolution continued.

The materialistic determinist must deny all that is nonphysical, whether it be the spirit, values, or God. A worshipper of science must

23. "Tsung-chiao wen-t'i" (The Problem of Religion), *WCC*, bk. 6, 14.

find an explanation for man's belief in religion. This account must be complete, since any residual doubt of the proof or continuation of the belief in "unfounded tenets" would render the philosophical basis of this school highly untenable. The only way to explain religious experience is to explain it away. Thus, by the materialist creed, religious consciousness becomes a form of matter in motion, religious values become the power and authority of arbitrary social rules, and religion is no more than naïve notions generally associated with primitive beliefs and ignorance.

Wu Chih-hui made full use of these assumptions in his critique of religion. His insistence on the necessity for the triumph of the scientific outlook over the religious world-view is particularly reminiscent of the positivism of Auguste Comte. Wu, like Comte, felt the need to find a new object of worship. Since science had revealed a universe in which man became the author of his own destiny, the natural object of worship should now be man. Wu's critique of religion and morality, and of idealism in general, can be seen as a conversion to the worship of humanity. As science provides increasing material welfare and new knowledge of the universe, all old beliefs—Chinese or Western—must give way to new beliefs substantiated by the proofs of science. Where science acts as a corrosive agent to old and arbitrary notions, the religious impulse and new morality must be sought in the "new" human beings, now emancipated from ignorance and the material pressures of need and want. Wu, like his European predecessors, found the solution in the socialist vision. Religion in the scientific age could only propose morality between man and man, not between man and God.[24]

The broad scientific critique of religion turned into a critique of traditional values. The question of whether traditional Chinese thought and philosophy constituted any form or force of religion was conveniently avoided. Instead, for practical purposes, Chinese culture, along with other Asian cultures, especially the Indian, came to be termed "spiritualistic." In the years when science was taking hold of the Chinese imagination, the term "spiritualistic" was suspect and disreputable. The supporters of science, therefore, came forward to criticize the alleged spirituality of their own culture. (It must be kept

24. "Tsung-chiao tao-te yü she-hui-chu-i" (Religion, Morality, and Socialism). Ibid., 5.

in mind that the designation of spiritual civilization as belonging to the East and material civilizaton as belonging to the West was originated by growing numbers of Western thinkers who, after World War I, praised the superiority of Eastern spirituality over the Western preoccupation with material things. A number of traditionalists in China then began to use the term in a positive sense.)

Nothing could be more incongruous than the coexistence of the Confucian emphasis on the achievement of harmony within nature and the scientific world-view, predicated on the fact that nature can be abstracted and manipulated. Since it seemed necessary to eradicate the presuppositions of traditional thought, we must understand what the scientific thinkers found undesirable in the traditional culture and a hindrance to the introduction of the scientific outlook. Scientism in China must be seen as the efforts of the supporters of science to discredit their own culture, and the destructiveness of their opinions on Chinese culture is an indication of the degree of their devotion to the scientific spirit. Yet, since cultural discontinuity resulted, some Chinese thinkers, though perfectly committed to the new civilization, tried to find sanctions for science in the Chinese past. This intellectual dilemma seems not to have bothered Wu Chih-hui. He criticized traditional beliefs and values with unembarrassed severity, for he was convinced of the worth of submitting totally to the mechanistic view of life and society.

A good introduction to the manner in which modern Chinese intellectuals viewed their culture is their own assessment of their inheritance; Wu considered it sterile:

> The ancient Chinese were characteristically simple farmers. They were not an imaginative people and were incapable of establishing religious systems. They prayed and worshipped fetishes, as their descendants do to this day. They worked hard and were contented with their lot.
>
> It was only after the rise of several great sages from their midst, such as Confucius and Mencius, that they were emboldened to become an urbane people. And they succeeded in founding states and empires. But this life never suited the vast majority of the agricultural population who wanted only good crops and no government interference. Probably out of respect

for this class, the Confucian thinkers, too, had to preach the blissfulness of contentment and joyous acceptance of fate.

But the introduction of Buddhism from India created a new atmosphere. It gave China a religion. At first, the Chinese Buddhists merely interpreted the Indian religion in terms of the nihilistic philosophy of Lao-tzu and Chuang-tzu, and the new religion only furnished fresh material for leisurely and harmless gossip. It had not yet acquired for itself the element of governmental authority.

As time went on, however, Confucian thought became unconsciously influenced by the religion of India. The Confucianists of Sung, and Chu Hsi (d. 1200 A.D.) in particular, unwittingly incorporated much of Buddhism into their new interpretation of Confucius and Mencius, and they succeeded in remaking the old political principles of the country squires of old. The harmless gossip of the ancient farmers and their rustic philosophers sitting on their faggot piles and sunning themselves in the wintry sun now became the authoritative codes of morals and of government.

Buddhism was a religion which teaches man to forsake this world and prepare for life in the otherworld. But, when Chu Hsi and his coworkers unconsciously adopted this religion of the other world and superimposed its ideas upon the moral and political codes for life in this world, then the new codes became terrors and made Chinese society a tragedy. How lifeless has Chinese society become since the twelfth and thirteenth centuries! [25]

Wu firmly believed that it was this otherworldly element in Chinese culture that led Western observers to see the so-called "spirituality" in East Asian cultures. Such spirituality harbors ignorance and superstition; nothing could have been more offensive to Wu. It was serious that much Buddhism had crept into the Neo-Confucian philosophy of the Sung and Ming periods. What was originally an earthy system of socio-political ethics was now colored by religious sanctions; idealist thought was being perpetuated. When this Neo-Confucian

25. "A New Belief," *WWT,* I, 278–79, 286. Passage quoted is Hu Shih's English translation in *China's Own Critics* (Peiping, 1931), pp. 64–65.

emphasis was applied to all spheres of life and maintained as the only system of thought, a stifled culture, hostile to free movement and adventures of the mind, appeared.

The best literary example of Neo-Confucian influence was the vogue of the *pa-ku* (eight-legged) essay. Wu Chih-hui underscored the reliance of the intellectuals on this type of essay to make a living, since this was the only form accepted by the imperial civil service examinations. The term *pa-ku* had come to signify sterility. Wu, who reveled in the use of metaphors, borrowed it to attack another form of rigidity of practice and outlook; he named it the *yang-pa-ku* (foreign eight-leggedism). To this group belonged those who, through a false sense of national pride, tried to find Chinese antecedents for everything the West possessed. Wu singled out Liang Ch'i-ch'ao as typical of the group which used Western learning only as a tool to glorify China's past; they utilized the scientific method to study the past and then claimed that this very approach had been developed and possessed in early China. Wu believed that this national heritage, though deserving of study, should not be stressed in China before the materialistic culture had taken root. What then was this national heritage that was so offensive to Wu?

> This odorous thing, the national heritage, thrives along with concubinage and opium. Concubinage and opium in turn thrive together with status—and wealth—consciousness. When national learning was at a height, all politics were rotten. This is because Confucius, Mencius, Lao-tzu, and Mo-tzu were products of the chaotic world of the Spring and Autumn and the Warring States. They must be thrown into the latrine for thirty years . . . What is national heritage and what bearing has it on our present world? It is nothing more than a relic of the world, worthy of preservation and nothing more.[26]

The task of preserving such a heritage, he believed, should be in the hands of a few scholars appointed by high academic bodies. The subject matter of the heritage should not tax the minds of youth and should not be made the content of education. Wu even reprimanded

26. "Chen yang-pa-ku-hua chih Li-hsüeh" (A Critique of the Thought of Foreign Eight-Leggedism), *WWT, 1,* 157–58.

Hu Shih for unconsciously starting the trend of "tidying up the national heritage." [27]

Wu Chih-hui's conversion to science was complete; it was matched in sincerity by his critique of his own culture. He pinpointed the main reason for China's lack of a scientific spirit and tradition when he wrote "The Disease of Corruption of the Chinese." The main cause of China's ills was the misuse of education. Education in the past, Wu contended, was used for candidacy in the government after a series of examinations; moreover, since there was no huge reward for all the trouble of preparing oneself for the examinations, many Chinese resorted to selling mines and railroads (they became compradores and concessionaires) to justify a few years of inconsequential study.[28]

For Wu, those who praised spiritual civilization and showed excessive pride in China's national culture also classified science as materialistic civilization itself. According to this group, science as a value system, built entirely on material progress and welfare, was responsible for bloody affairs such as World War I. Wu unabashedly pinpointed for criticism Tagore of India[29] and Carsun Chang, the first to consolidate the antiscience forces in the Debate of 1923. To Wu, they shunned the so-called material world but they preferred trains to donkeys; they liked to ride in steamboats but turned up their noses at sampans, and they even craved electric fans and electric lights. Wu clearly had no sympathy for people who enjoyed the fruits of material advance and at the same time proposed the superiority of their own spiritual culture. Moreover, they blamed science and materialistic civilization for wars. Wu Chih-hui preferred to see the cause of such

27. Hu Shih's *An Outline of Chinese Philosophy* (in Chinese) and *The Development of the Logical Method in Ancient China* were intended to show the scientific method in examining China's past, as well as locate the development of scientific thinking then.

28. "Chung-kuo-jen chih fu-pai-ping" (The Disease of Corruption of the Chinese), *WCC*, bk. 6, 137.

29. Tagore visited China in 1923–24 to lecture under the auspices of the National University of Peking. Wu quoted him as saying that his purpose was "to promote Eastern thought. . . . The majority of Asia's youth has wiped out Asian traditional civilization and pursued the thought of Western cultures. This is a big mistake . . . Western civilization is particularly inclined toward the materialistic, and is greatly lacking in matters concerning the heart and the soul." See Wu, "Wan-kao T'a-ko-erh" (My Sincere Advice to Tagore), *WWT*, *1*, 32. What Tagore advised, Wu contended, was a "form of remedy which had already killed India."

conflict in the fact that less materially equipped cultures sparked jealousy and competition among the materially advanced nations. The responsibility for war, then, rested with the Chinese and any others who did not contribute their share to world (material) civilization. Only when universal education on the highest level was achieved could there be any peace. In the meantime, wars would continue as long as the industrial society was impeded and obstructed by the ignorant and fanciful speculations of spiritualistic life.[30]

Wu heartily agreed that science was materialistic civilization itself. He saw spiritual values in the aim of materialistic civilization to free mankind from want and greed. Mankind's salvation was not through a return to former beliefs and values; its only hope was a progressive demand for ever increasing man's store of scientific knowledge.

Wu Chih-hui wrote from the point of view of a critic, commentator, and revolutionary. He did not pretend to be an academic philosopher. He preferred to call himself a "comtemplator in the countryside." He made full use of metaphor, mimickry, parody, insinuation, innuendo, and personification of ideas and objects. The objects of his criticism and also of his praise were treated less in the spirit of academic disputation than as entities in a huge ideological war. Wu wrote his most important philosophical essay as a participant in the Debate of 1923. Unlike other participants, he went directly to the core of the problem by stating his new philosophy of life based on science.

PHILOSOPHY OF LIFE BASED ON SCIENCE

Wu claimed to have had this faith in a new scientific outlook since 1919 when the term "philosophy of life" first came into vogue. In the highly academic verbiage of the debate, Wu accused the proponents, as well as the opponents, of science of not openly stating their life-views but only indulging in a circus of academic word flinging. Wu Chih-hui, the keen-sighted humorist, began his long essay, entitled "A New Belief."

> The attitude I have in writing this essay is that of an old man of the countryside, lying on a pile of faggots, basking in the sunlight and thinking aloud to myself, hoping for self-enlightenment to save my soul, and to explain my transitory sojourn in

30. *WWT*, 1, 157–58.

> this universe. Naturally I am unqualified to talk about philosophy, but, to be honest, I actually despise that sort of philosophy which wields words and causes one great confusion. Such philosophies only succeed in using highly intoxicating verbiage to fool and flatter one another with magical and transcendental symbols and terms—Buddhism, Taoism, Confucianism, Greek philosophy, scholasticism, empiricism, rationalism, criticism, or other "isms." All such efforts are but attempts to satisfy their original urge to find a suitable faith.[31]

With this attitude and ignoring the bounds of "academic etiquette," Wu Chih-hui proceeded to criticize with broad strokes the reluctance of the intellectuals to proclaim their faith built on science and more significantly, set forth his own view of the universe and new philosophy of life.

The Universe

Wu conceived of the universe as a mechanism forever in motion and forever generating energy. He stated his conception of its origin.

> In the beginning, which is no beginning, there is a funny, indescribable and unidentifiable "thing," which says to itself, "I am being suffocated by this constant compression which goes on for days and years keeping me from hearing evil, seeing evil, touching and smelling evil" . . . Then suddenly in the wink of an eye it burst . . . and exploded into billions of units and selves. This sudden change is very simple. It is none other than the unfathomable energy [of the black thing] forming innumerable little units; from these units to electrons; from electrons to atoms; from atoms to stars, planets, suns, moons, mountains, rivers, flowers, trees, insects, birds, fish, and men. You can call this change evolution, or, lightheartedly, mental illusion. At any rate, even today this change continues and will be so forever. There has yet to be one satisfactory thing which has remained unchanged. This is my view of the universe (p. 198).

To Wu Chih-hui, behind the manifold appearances lies the original "black thing"; behind the multiplicity of appearances, lies unity of

31. "A New Belief," *WWT, 1,* 189. Quotations in this section are from "A New Belief," *WWT, 1,* 168–303. The page numbers appear in the text.

essence. That he dared to indulge in such speculation which others might brand as metaphysics, he explained by saying that the "metaphysical ghost" (a favorite term of the Chinese intellectuals to designate someone who favored fanciful and metaphysical speculations, and the term by which Ting Wen-chiang described Carsun Chang in the 1923 Debate) which haunted him was one already "baptized by science" (p. 175). To him, the world is still but "a thing," whether one chose to call it phenomenal, spiritual, all-possessing, void, reasonable and orderly, self-contradictory, subjective, or objective. All he insisted was that this "thing" was a living thing, generating energy, whether one chose to call it a temporal-spatial or a transcendental world, a phenomenal or noumenal world (pp. 174–75, 178). Wu's world conception had no place for either God or devil, for either soul or so-called "spiritual monism." Indeed, by his definition these things could not exist. His argument was that even if, with the greatest magnanimity, we accept God to be just a part of the "thing," and given the ordinary respect for Him as a higher being, how could one account for the disparity between God and man when both are parts of the "thing?" Thus, claiming a respect for reason, Wu advised that one must eliminate God (pp. 176–77). Then, borrowing the terminology of Bergson and Nietzsche, whose contribution in dethroning God he fully appreciated but with whose nonmechanistic explanation of life's creative force he hardly agreed, Wu Chih-hui stated,

> The whole world is an immense living organism, with substance and energy; using other terms, we can call this energy "power." From this power comes will. This "will" tends toward "eternal movement," and from this movement man's mechanistic form of life is arranged for him . . . Henceforward, contact with alien matter produces sensory perception; acceptance and rejection in sensory perception produce sentiment; fear that sentiment may err produces reason. With careful employment of reason, we coerce certain kinds of sentiment to follow the regularity of nature; or, if we choose to show decision by reason, then we have subjective feeling. When this subjectivity is found to be in harmony with the heart and body, it is often left without examination and is relegated as basic nature. Therefore, every reaction is traceable to the nervous system in which it builds up mecha-

> nisms. This is why we have a brain that weighs three pounds and two ounces, and five thousand and forty-eight pieces of brain muscle (pp. 193–94).[32]

Such a view, then, precludes the soul and God. The universe changes and unfolds of itself not at random, but according to certain natural laws and principles. All men are featherless bipeds, without souls or entelechies, endowed with biological organs which cause him to breathe, move, work, and rest. This, then, leads to Wu Chih-hui's philosophy of life.

Man and His Life

The Chinese term, *jen-sheng-kuan,* as used by Wu means "outlook on man and his existence" and connotes more than just a set of personal philosophical precepts, for it encompasses the world, the universe, and humanity in general; its approximate Western equivalent is Weltanschauung or world-view. Wu proposed to examine first what this expression meant. Man to him was nothing more than a featherless biped, possessing a comparatively more elaborate nervous system than other animals (p. 201). As for life, he chose to conceive of it as a great theatrical act in which the actors were those featherless bipeds with large brains. In a humorous manner, Wu says, "The period of life occurs when the band strikes up and the curtain rises to great activities in singing, dancing, and gyrations of all sorts. In the womb, man could be said to be still backstage; when he enters the coffin, he has packed up and gone home. If one is born he is nonetheless picking an auspicious opening date; if he loses life, it is merely a temporary postponement of the act" (pp. 201–02). The proper understanding of human life is the realization that we are merely acting out the vigintillionth act of this cosmic drama, and no more (pp. 207–08). We are living between a beginning that is no beginning and an end that is no end, in an external world that is infinitely large and in an internal world that is infinitely small (p. 205). Now that one is on the stage of the universe (displacing God and super-

32. Wu uses the favorite colloquial reference to numbers of his home area. Ch'ang-chou people usually refer to the head as weighing 9½ lbs. Wu explained, since the brain occupies 1/3 of the total head, it weighs 3 lbs. 2 oz.

natural idols as chief actors), in Wu's opinion, one might as well put on a good show; if not, it would be only self-deception.

How then could man perform well? Wu's contention was that he should use both hands to labor, and, with guidance of scientific inventions, create civilization. All of these advances would perfect morals. Moreover, to be a good actor, one must have the three following capacities: to enjoy the fresh breeze and bright moon, to create divine works of art, and to embrace heaven and earth in one's heart. By these he meant three instincts: eating (basic problem of livelihood), mating (free love and free expression of basic desires), and searching for association (the inevitable social context within which man works and lives). None of the impulses can be considered good or bad, for each is, far be it from spiritual or mystical, a manifestation and function of the "black thing" in process of evolution (p. 213). Science will help clarify the problems of life in these vital spheres.

Eating is seen as the problem of the material supply of the human race. One must eat the fruits of his own labor, must not obstruct others in eating the fruits of their labor, and, most importantly, must allow others to eat the fruits of one's own labor. Only science can multiply goods for human needs. If these goods are denied man, he dies, taking the "exalted soul" with him. Besides, in addition to revealing and increasing basic goods for human needs, science can also minimize waste by turning ordinary waste into other products (pp. 223–31).

In the sphere of reproduction, a scientific understanding of man's biological needs will lead to an unfettered view of such social conventions and standards as marriage, chastity, and adultery. Scientific knowledge will give an accurate understanding of the natural facts which in the past have been overly romanticized, poeticized, and sanctified and have created great mental anguish and social disharmony (pp. 231–42).

Man is chiefly a social animal. In Wu's third vital area of human life, the right outlook is chiefly concerned with relations with everything that is "non-I" and must view heaven and earth with equanimity. He asserts that what the metaphysicians considered the major tool in interpersonal relationships was merely the four Mencian cardinal virtues: sympathy, shame, humility, and justice. These so-called cardinal virtues, in the past supposed to belong to sages, are what we, as scientific men, understand today as a priority, intuition, magnanimity, and conscience. Indeed, man in his social life must consider these qualities and exercise them. For Wu Chih-hui, these qualities must be supported by reason; they did not, as the "metaphysical specters" haunting him maintained, stem from some inner well of realization or from any divine source (pp. 249–64). He refuted all of them, if a priority meant a gift of the Divine, unsupported by the workings of the individual's psychology; if intuition meant an innate endowment, and not the product of experience and trained reason; if magnanimity meant a product of feeling and sentiment, and not one proceeding from an immeasurable concern with humanity; and if conscience meant something which only God could endow. Only the progressive increase of scientific knowledge could invest these qualities with proper and unbiased meanings. They must be possessed and exercised by each member of the whole cast of actors in the cosmic drama.

Wu Chih-hui gave his readers the articles of his new faith which, as he had stated at the beginning of his long essay, was a nonreligious kind of faith:

1. I firmly believe that there is no spirit beyond matter. Such things as spirit or soul are merely terms to cloud reality; they have a narcotic effect on man. There are only two courses of action in this world: one is to help in the material improvement of heaven and earth—this is the progressive philosophy of *life;* the other is to leave everything alone and take refuge in spiritual wellbeing—this is the retrogressive philosophy of *death.*

2. I firmly believe that the universe is just a state of eternal motion. We can believe only in the evolutionary nature of the universe and should not speculate as to when the process is to stop or what it will evolve into. The only certain progress is the improvement of material civilization; it is the only safe and beneficial way.

3. and 4. In general, the ancients are inferior to the moderns, and the moderns are inferior to the men of the future. This is not a statement on the linear tendency of humans toward good and perfection. In matters of evil, just the same, the ancients are not as evil as the moderns, and the moderns not as evil as the men of the future. The power of knowledge can affect progress toward good as well as toward

evil. This axiom explains why the universe, though tending toward the point of perfection, will never reach such a point. People often forget about this axiom and become tired and fed up with the world, thereby causing a retrogression.[33]

5. I believe that the more material civilization improves, the fuller will be the supply of goods, the surer will be the direction that leads to the unity of mankind, and the easier will be the solution to difficult problems. I firmly believe that with industrial civilization helping material civilization the world will be unified; from there one can expect the great harmony.

6. I believe that morality is a product of culture; there is no such thing as low morals in a high culture. The early religions of the major civilizations were all illusory talk; they bred a philosophy of death. China has already received Mr. Science (dealing with knowledge), and Mr. Democracy (dealing with public morality). What we now lack is a private morality, which we shall call Miss Morality.

7. I believe that "all things in the universe" can be explained by science. But we cannot explain the "possibility" of everything. Indeed, if we could, it would be just like saying we can know the beginning that is no beginning and the end that is no end, the infinite greatness of the external world and the infinite smallness of the internal world. On the other hand, it is one thing to say a thing is not possible and another to say that it is probable. We must, then, work through the probability of things in order to solve the question of possibility. This is the true scientific spirit (pp. 265–86).

Hence Wu Chih-hui, in his own words, "ruled out the name of God and banished the soul and spirit" (p. 192). In this new conception, the formulation of a philosophy of life must be governed by the following four tenets:

the philosophy of life is not a philosophy of death;
the philosophy of life is not a selfish regard for one's own life;
the philosophy of life is a regard for the totality of life;
only from this philosophy of life will there be a philosophy of the universe (p. 304).

33. Italics added. On this topic, Wu had written more elaborately in an article, "Erh-pai-chao p'ing-min ta wen-t'i tsui ch'ing-pien ti chieh-chüeh-fa" (The Easiest Way to Solve the Problem of Two Hundred Million People), *TFTC,* 21:2 (special publication, 1924), sect. 3, L1–L30. The gist of this article had been set forth in 1916 in *Chung-hua hsin-pao* (*China's New Journal*).

Though Wu wrote forcefully on the new world-view and life-view, in the end he warned that even if one did fulfill all the requirements, one could be sure of having reached only a small part of the vast and infinite truth of the universe. Nevertheless, he reiterated, the only way to be sure to have performed well on this world stage was to have exemplified the proper philosophy of life; the only sure guide toward this goal, the advocate of scientism stressed, is a new faith in the "omnipotence of science" (K'e-hsüeh wan-neng) (p. 307).

Chapter 3 *THE DIALECTICAL MATERIALIST: CH'EN TU-HSIU* (1879–1942)

Although Ch'en Tu-hsiu is known chiefly for his political transition from republicanism to Marxism, his appreciation for science as a modern value did not change. In fact, his basic philosophical understanding of science and its implication served as an important link between his early enchantment with social democracy and his later belief in the materialistic laws of historical development. His conception of science came from philosophical materialism. In the years after 1919, when he gradually changed to Marxism, Ch'en pushed the premises of philosophical materialism with its note of determinism one step further to the emphasis on economic laws and invariable "scientific" laws of societal development. In other words, with the passage to dialectical materialism, Ch'en's views were now completely scientistic. Born in 1879 in the town of Huaining in Anhwei province, Ch'en remembered a childhood unpleasant in most respects, except for a kind mother.[1] The child was brought up under the rule of a tyrannical grandfather; his father died a few months after Ch'en's birth. By a puzzling coincidence, according to Ch'en, the grandfather had two major obsessions—cleanliness and light-footedness on the one hand, and opium-smoking on the other. To young Ch'en Tu-hsiu, no two

1. *Shih-an tzu-chuan* (Autobiography) (Shanghai, 1938). This seems to be Ch'en's only autobiography. It is a short account of impressions of his childhood and youth. For more information see Benjamin Schwartz, "Biographical Sketch, Ch'en Tu-hsiu, Pre-Communist Phase," *Papers on China,* Harvard Regional Studies, 2 (Cambridge, 1948). There is a short, but often inaccurate, biographical account of Ch'en in Robert S. Elegant's, *China's Red Masters* (New York, 1951), pp. 28–51.

qualities in such unique combination were more unlike. The vehemence with which Ch'en told of this aspect of his life reveals the degree to which it affected his later thought. The tyrannical insistence on quiet, cleanliness, and proper conduct represented to Ch'en the artificiality of the Confucian code of ethics, while opium smoking represented not only filth but an exceedingly antisocial attitude, in which the partakers of opium reveled in their own ethereal world (a good deal of "socializing" here) while they remained oblivious to everything beyond the den.

Ch'en studied the Chinese classics with his grandfather from the age of six to eight or nine. The floggings he received for failure to recite the passages made permanent scars on his young mind which understood only that the need for such recitations was superficial. Were it not for his mother's desire that he study diligently in order to pass the civil service examinations, more specifically the second degree, which his father had spent a whole lifetime in vain to obtain, he would not have applied himself to his studies. Often she would weep, and this moved Ch'en. Ch'en insisted that, though his mother was governed by the virtues of the examination system, he himself never doubted for a minute the futility of such a system and the narrow careers it helped establish.

In 1896, a year after the Sino-Japanese War, when he was seventeen years old, Ch'en sat for the district examinations in the first degree (*hsiu-ts'ai*). Much to the joy of his mother, Ch'en scored a first, even though he gave a very muddled answer to an illogical question. For Ch'en this episode crystallized all the more the uselessness of the examination system.[2] The next year, still not entirely freed from the wish to please his widowed mother, Ch'en went to Nanking for the second examination, the passing of which automatically qualified the candidate for an official position. The hall was congested and in dilapidated condition; the days were hot, and the place was small. The sight of the pale scholars, filing docilely into the examination grounds, complying with governmental specifications, and willing to sit in cell-like cubicles with no other hope than to become officials turned Ch'en's thoughts to the country's future and to his own presence there. He decided against taking the examinations. He said afterwards, "The daydreaming of two hours decided my personal

2. *Autobiography*, pp. 13, 19.

deeds and actions for the next few decades."[3] His early distaste for classical literature, now combined with personal experience in the stifling atmosphere of the examination halls in which this literature had been perpetuated for centuries, turned into a categorical contempt for the entire classical past of Chinese civilization.

Ch'en's decision was irrevocable. He turned to the works of K'ang Yu-wei and Liang Ch'i-ch'ao, two reformers whose efforts were later to be known as the Hundred Days' Reform. In a tearful farewell, he turned away from home and mother and set out for Chekiang province where the Truth-Seeking Academy (Ch'iu-shih shu-yüan) was then offering courses in foreign languages and naval architecture.

In his twenty-first year, 1900, Ch'en Tu-hsiu went to Tokyo which was at that time a haven for ambitious Chinese youths who could not afford faraway places and revolutionaries seeking refuge from Manchu political retaliation. At the Higher Normal School and later at Waseda University, Ch'en met many other radicals who belonged to patriotic and revolutionary societies. He seemed, however, to have already been converted to social democracy and could not find himself in sympathy with the nationalism of most of his acquaintances. Sun Yat-sen's campaign against the Manchus was couched in the terminology of the superiority of the Chinese race. This to Ch'en was a form of narrow nationalism; it may explain why he did not join any of the revolutionary groups. He left for France in 1907.

France enthralled Ch'en. He felt that he had found the grand summation of modern civilization. A Francophilia seized him and led him in 1915 to write an article in the first issue of the *New Youth* (which he alone managed and edited from 1915 to 1917) entitled "The French People and Modern Civilization."[4] He praised the French for their three, most significant gifts to modern civilization: democracy (as seen in Lafayette and Seignobos), evolutionary theory (in Lamarck), and socialism (in Babeuf and, later, Saint-Simon and Fourier). Ch'en's fascination with France lasted until 1919, when he, and many Chinese, interpreted the Versailles decision to grant Japan's demand for the Shantung Peninsula as a betrayal by the democracies of their own pronouncements on behalf of national self-determination. From this point on, Ch'en turned against everything Western (at least

3. Ibid., pp. 31–34.
4. *HCN, 1:1* (1915), 2nd article.

Western European and Anglo-American influence) with the same vehemence with which he embraced it in the beginning. He then turned to the messianic message of Communism.

Upon his return from Europe in 1910, Ch'en was fully convinced that the Oriental outlook and the Occidental outlook were entirely incompatible. Given his complete dedication to modern civilization, Ch'en's course of action was now clear: he campaigned for the total riddance of the traditional intellectual and political hold on the individual. Possessing a vague and rosy view of modern civilization, Ch'en nursed the faith that, as a later commentator put it, "the sheer process of enlightenment and the transplantation of democratic political forms would perform miracles on Chinese soil." [5] It is no surprise that Ch'en embarked upon the task of tearing down the old order immediately upon his return to China. This aspect of his career must be viewed with his role as a "modernist." He felt the "rightness" of being in the mainstream of modern civilization; an impatient modernist, he showed neither conciliatory nor compromising attitudes in advising China's youth on the modern course of action.

A short period of governmental and educational life saw Ch'en rapidly involved with forces opposed to Yüan Shih-k'ai's monarchical ambitions. Yüan's political moves against his opponents had sent many, including Ch'en, to Japan for refuge. After his return from Japan, Ch'en Tu-hsiu assumed the role of an educator-journalist which was to stamp him as a representative of the new wave of thought (*hsin ssu-ch'ao*) that swept over China in the decade following 1915. Ch'en and some friends started a journal whose title may have sounded like that of numerous other journals; but the *New Youth* turned out to be the leading publication during the years of quest and search from 1915 to the early '20s. It mirrored the mentality of a decade, from the revolution in language and literature, the revolution in thought, and the cry for abandoning the obscurantist Confucian value system to an insistent demand for political reform. The journal came to be identified with Ch'en's life. He guided its publication until the "betrayal" at Versailles, all the while promoting the democratic idea of government and intellectual enlightenment for the Chinese. When Ch'en turned to Communism, the journal did the

5. Benjamin Schwartz, *Chinese Communism and the Rise of Mao* (Cambridge, 1951), p. 10.

same. *New Youth* was not only the vehicle for introducing much of Western thought but also the means through which China's traditional culture was dealt its severest blow. The *New Youth* alone was not responsible for discrediting the old; indeed the social and political conditions of China ever since the mid-nineteenth century had been corrosive in themselves. The decisive language and burning intent of the contributors did influence those who were still vague and uncommitted about the direction of China's new culture. Ch'en Tu-hsiu stood at the forefront of the new forces, demanding not mere change but revolution in both thought and action. He has been hailed as modern China's most destructive intellectual who aimed at tearing down the two-thousand-year-old Confucian order, while Hu Shih's introduction and clarification of Western ideas in China may be called the constructive component.[6] Ch'en's destructive attitude toward the old-world values is seen in his use of slogans, of which the most noted is "Democracy in politics, and Science in the realm of ideas."[7]

CONCEPTION OF SCIENCE

As a publicist and propagator of ideas, Ch'en Tu-hsiu seemed never to have had the time or the temperament to give a coherent statement of his philosophical beliefs. His impatience caused him to be less interested in the logical presentation of philosophical convictions and more concerned with the forceful impression these ideas made on minds impatiently searching for respectable orientations. Yet, much can be educed from his writings to show that Ch'en never deviated from materialistic determinism. In fact, he proceeded from that premise and reached its ultimate dogmatic conclusion when he embraced Communism.

Science for Ch'en Tu-hsiu was primarily a way to expose a lethargic, compromising, imprecise, and superficial mode of thought and way of life. A modern commentator on Ch'en has described this conception:

6. See Kuo Chan-po, *Chinese Intellectual History,* p. 102.

7. He insisted that these were the two most precious possessions of modern civilization. See his "Shih-chü tsa-kan" (Random Thoughts on the Current Situation), *HCN,* 3:4 (1917), p. 1 of 1st art. It is a reiteration of a favorite theme first set forth in "Ching-kao ch'ing-nien" (My Solemn Plea to Youth), *HCN,* 1:1 (1915), p. 6 of 1st art.

> Like them [the Russian nihilists], he saw in science a weapon, a corrosive to be used in dissolving traditional society. He did, of course, appreciate the dynamic role of science in conquering nature, but he was particularly conscious of it as a weapon against "superstitions." As in the case of the nihilists, his readings had led him to identify science with certain crude forms of naturalism. By stridently proclaiming on the authority of science that the material atom was the only ultimate reality, he was quickly able to dispose of the whole basis of the "religion of rites" [Confucianism], as well as of the mysticism of Buddhism and Taoism.[8]

Ch'en's intention of identifying science with progressive forces in order to arouse people from old habits of mind was clearly evident in his leading article, "My Solemn Plea to Youth," which commenced the publication of the *New Youth*. He exhorted China's youth to escape the traditional habit of being young in age but old in spirit and offered them his six precepts. Of the six, the last two deserve our attention here:[9] young minds should be first, utilitarian and not formalistic, and second, scientific and not speculative. To Ch'en, the utilitarianism of Mill and the positivism of Comte had revolutionized modern thought. The culmination of their systems was to be seen in the changes wrought in society, for instance, the rapid scientific advancement in Germany, where materialistic civilization had reached its height. Ch'en placed the focus on the problems of livelihood and greater usefulness; all that was formalistic, imaginary, and useless to practical life was rejected. This stress on utility and practicality leads naturally to an emphasis on a scientific, not speculative, outlook.

> What is science? It is our general conception of matter which, being at one with objective phenomena, is not redundant when examined by subjective reason. What is speculation? It not only overreaches objective phenomena but also banishes subjective reason; it is a superstructure in the air, with hypotheses but no proof; and all the rationality and intelligence in the world

8. Schwartz, *Chinese Communism*, pp. 9–10.

9. The first four are: young minds should be independent and not servile; progressive and not conservative, aggressive and not withdrawn; and internationalistic and not nationalistic.

> cannot understand the reason in it or comprehend its governing laws and principles.[10]

The division between the modern age and the ancient world was clear and decisive. Speculation belonged to past civilizations and remains with the still unenlightened creatures of the modern day. Preceding science and the positive mode of thought were speculative and illusory attitudes caused by religion, art, and literature. The role played by science in fostering European supremacy was for him no less important than the theory of the rights of man.

> Our men of learning do not understand science; thus they make use of *yin-yang* signs and beliefs in the five elements to confuse the world and delude the people and engage in speculations on geomancy . . . Our farmers do not understand science; thus they do not possess methods of selecting crops and applying insecticides. Our men of industry do not understand science; therefore goods lie wasted on the ground, while we receive every need in warfare and production from foreign countries. Our merchants do not understand science; hence they know only short term gains and make no provision for future profits. Our doctors do not understand science; they not only know nothing of human anatomy, but also know nothing of the analysis of medicines; as for bacterial poisoning and infections, they have not even heard of them . . . The height of their wondrous illusions is the theory of *ch'i* [primal force], which really applies to the professional acrobats and Taoist priests. We will never comprehend this *ch'i* even if we were to search everywhere in the universe. All of these fanciful notions and irrational beliefs can be corrected at their roots by science, because to explain truth by science we must prove everything with fact. Although this is slower than imagination and arbitrary judgment, every progressive step is taken on firm ground. It is different from those flights of fancy which in the end cannot advance one bit. The amount of truth in the universe is boundless, and the scientific realm's productive areas awaiting pioneering are enormous! Youth, to task! [11]

10. "My Solemn Plea to Youth," *HCN*, *1:1* (1915), p. 5 of 1st art.
11. Ibid., pp. 5–6 of 1st art.

Ch'en appreciated the value of modern science, so successfully applied in Western society. He was all too concerned with portraying the power of science and consequently left few writings to show the philosophical basis for his admiration of science. An article he wrote for the first volume of the *New Youth* is the earliest available instance of a slightly philosophical attitude. In "Policy and Direction for Modern Education," Ch'en points out that the first principle, basic to an understanding of human life, is realism. Science informs us that while our sense perceptions can err and the world of appearances is inconstant, matter alone is real and its qualities are constant. The only reality is the material atom and the only constant are the properties of that atom. The indestructibility of atom means that the world and the universe are eternal, which in turn means that the totality of life is endless. This immortality of the totality of life again implies that history is infinite in duration. One must, then, adopt the outlook of the scientist and not that of a selfish individual who looks at the vicissitudes of his daily life and deduces that the whole of human life is inconstant. The realistic conception of life, according to the scientist,

> is that view of life which sees in the individual's life in this world merely the existence of minute cells in the body following the inescapable law of succession of new cells to replace the old ones and of the interlocking nature of life and death. Matter is passed on to successive generations (indestructibility of the atom), and spirit is carried on in history (infinity of human nature). There is no continuation of the individual life beyond death, but the totality of life is never ending. In understanding the reason of life and death, we must not tire of life or be afraid of death; we must know that the reality of our existence is but a precious moment in the eternal life of the whole of humanity. Our life is neither constant nor inconstant, nor illusory, nor empty . . . If the life-view is realistic, then the ruling of the world by man can be achieved, and superstition can be exterminated.[12]

Important to note in Ch'en's credo of life is his summary belief in a crass materialism which views reality as matter in motion. With this

12. "Chin-jih chih chiao-yü fang-chen" (Policy and Direction for Modern Education), *HCN, 1:2* (1915), p. 3 of 1st art.

belief in immutable scientific laws, Ch'en did not hesitate to act as a purveyor of scientific monism.

> Aside from the existence and movement of matter in the universe, people believe that there are spirits which act as judges. This is why religion, ever since its establishment, has not yet vanished. On the other hand, according to the research of the astronomer, the mutual destruction, the mutual combination, attraction, and repulsion between and among the heavenly bodies all follow definite causal laws. According to the studies of the geologist, the formation of the globe and its development are all clear and orderly and can be explained by scientific laws. According to the biologist, anthropologist, and anatomist, all animals—from the lowest cell animal to the highest class, man who possesses brain and nerves—evolved in a fashion, the details of which can all be proved . . . In this manifold world, if indeed there is a spirit who is the judge, then there must be arbitrary and whimsical creation and destruction. But why has there been no such event for so long, and how is it that nothing [in this manifold universe] escapes the laws of science? How can those who believe in the existence of God answer me! [13]

Such a categorical submission to the blessings of modern civilization and the modern outlook, both products of the rapid progress of the physical and natural sciences, earned Ch'en and the *New Youth* much opposition. Attacks from the traditionalists became increasingly vociferous in 1918–19. Yet it was in this atmosphere of charges and counter charges that Ch'en was at his best. In his "Reply to the Charges Against Our Journal," he reaches the height of his use of "science and democracy" as symbols for attacking the old order of values.

> We, of course, admit that we are guilty of all the charges. But if we go to the root of the matter, we are not really guilty. We committed the alleged crimes entirely for the sake of supporting two gentlemen: Mr. Democracy and Mr. Science. In order to support Mr. Democracy, we must oppose Confucianism, the code of rituals, chastity, traditional ethics, and politics; in order to sup-

13. "K'e-hsüeh yü shen-sheng" (Science and the Divine), *THWT* (Shanghai, 1933), 2, 5.

> port Mr. Science, we must oppose traditional arts and crafts and traditional religion; in order to support Mr. Democracy and Mr. Science, we cannot but oppose the so-called national heritage and old-style literature . . . If not [if we have not committed any crimes], then please do not pick on our periodical but devote your energy and courage to opposing the two gentlemen, Mr. Democracy and Mr. Science.[14]

In his role as the "grand impresario of modern thought" in China, Ch'en was not unlike Voltaire, publicist and propagandist of the eighteenth century.

In using science to discredit untimely and ineffectual outlooks, Ch'en naturally tended to ignore the specifics of research and accomplishment and to concentrate on the more summary and general principles and laws. This tendency in Ch'en is revealed by the introduction to his articles, "The Thought of Two Great Scientists of the Modern Era":

> In the theory of hero-worship of the English historian, Carlyle, there are numerous famous names, but none of them can be compared with the scientist for two important reasons. First, the first half of the nineteenth century still had not escaped the destructive spirit of the eighteenth century; the intricate constructive aspects of science had not been widespread. Hence, the standard of the people's image of a hero differed from that of today. Second, during that time, science inclined toward the analytical and inductive aspects and not toward the synthetic and deductive methods, which could affect the heart and mind of people.[15]

Ch'en Tu-hsiu goes on to say that the twentieth-century scientific thinker should meet the demands of the times and detach himself from the "analytical" habit by becoming "a prophetic thinker who synthesizes all branches of knowledge." [16] This attitude is perhaps the strongest link between Ch'en's pre-Communist phase and his later

14. "Pen-chih tsui-an chih ta-pien shu" (A Reply to the Charges Against Our Journal) *HCN*, 6:1 (1919), 10–11.

15. *HCN*, 2:1 (1916), p. 1 of 10th art.; continued in *HCN*, 2:3 (1916), 7th art. The two scientists are Metchnikoff and Ostwart. Ch'en's work on them is introductory in nature, with partial translations of their writings.

16. Ibid.

role as a prophet of societal change based on the inevitable economic laws of change.

After Ch'en Tu-hsiu changed from a publicist of democracy and republicanism to a devotee of Marxism, his intellectual presuppositions about science took the logical step forward to identifying science with social science. Still paying lip service to the practical results of science, he was greatly attracted to the lessons which the scientific principles and laws gave for the study of human social behavior. The most pointed statement of this later conviction came during the Debate of 1923, when Ch'en, with Hu Shih, prefaced the vast collection of essays written for the occasion. In answer to Hu Shih's charge that he was merely voicing a kind of historical outlook and not answering the immediate question, whether science could support a philosophy of life, Ch'en showed his deep conviction in materialistic monism. Science for him had now became nothing more than the systematized and minute study of matter. When such methodology was applied to the human sphere, economics was seen as the most important force.[17] Since society is made up of human beings, and history is simply the record of society's manifestations, historical materialism should be, therefore, the basic mode of thought, having a bearing not only on history, but on life views and social views as well. Historical materialism, Ch'en maintained, did not necessarily belittle such things as culture, religion, ethics, and education—the idealistic manifestations of society; they must be viewed as structures grafted onto an economic base. They are not the base themselves.

These "superstructures," while important as tools for the progress of society, cannot move and change society and life. For historical and economic laws, alone, are the regulatory and inevitable determinants. We should not, then, be surprised to hear this scientific monist proclaim, "Once detached from the monism of matter, science runs the danger of going bankrupt." [18]

CRITIQUE OF TRADITIONAL CIVILIZATION

Ch'en Tu-hsiu's scathing critique of traditional Chinese culture stemmed from a deep-seated belief in the basic differences between

17. See his "Ta Shih-chih" (Answering Hu Shih), *KHYJSK*, *1*, pp. 36–37 of 2nd preface.

18. Ibid., p. 41.

the civilization he chose and the civilization he inherited. That Ch'en made his choice early and that he was not tied to the sentimentality of a concern for cultural continuity, can be seen in his early pronouncement, "Basic Intellectual Differences Between Peoples of East and West." [19] There are, he believed, three such differences: first, the basis of Western civilization is struggle, while that of the Eastern civilization is rest. Orientals, in Ch'en's opinion, are basically afraid of struggle and death, and they are thus slavish. Moreover, they possess a cheap shamelessness which becomes more pronounced when they claim the superiority of the civilization of the "religion of rites" (Confucianism). Second, Occidentals are individual-centered, and Orientals family-centered. In the light of the organization of modern society, the family system in China at once shows its poisonous effects. It destroys the individual's independence and dignity, it chokes freedom of thought, it robs the individual of his right to equality before the law, and it breeds sycophancy which insults the productive power of the individual. These ills, Ch'en maintained, are instrumental in making the Orientals backward and hence unruly, pitiful, and ineffectual. Third, the Occidentals have as their common outlooks the rule of law and utilitarianism, while the Orientals base their world-view on sentiment, feeling, and formalism. In this one-sided comparison and contrast of *modern* civilization of the West and *traditional* civilization of the East (that of China in particular), Ch'en Tu-hsiu's critique of Chinese civilization takes inspiration from the modern, Western critique of its own old world-view. Ch'en has equated the qualitative difference between Chinese and Western civilizations with the internal, temporal difference between the medieval and modern worlds of the West. Thus the objects of criticism, though under the large heading of "traditional versus modern," became those of the old religion and superstition, the old morality and ethics. The nature of such critiques necessarily took the form of the new spirit of scientific proof and considered the morality of the social self rather than the individual self. This spirit, destructive of the old, explains Ch'en's statement, "Only two roads are now open to us: first, the bright road to republicanism, science, and atheism; second, the dark road to tyranny, superstition, and theocracy. If we want to avoid an-

19. "Tung-hsi min-tsu ken-pen ssu-hsiang chih ch'a-i," *HCN, 1:4* (1915), 1st art.

other Boxer incident,[20] another humiliating memory such as the Von Ketteler Monument,[21] which road shall we choose?" [22]

Under Ch'en's attack, religion suffered the most; it served as a symbol for all forms of unfounded belief only to be purged in his modern civilization. Always insisting on free expression of the intellect, Ch'en approached superstition and all forms of worship (those of science, democracy, and, later, Communism not included) with vehemence.

> All useless things, worshipped by people, are rubbish and idols and should be destroyed . . . If such idols are not destroyed, humanity will never be freed from self-deceiving superstitions and irrational beliefs.
>
> If the existence of the gods and spirits of heaven and earth cannot be proved accurately, all forms of religion are nothing but deceitful idols: the god Amida is false; Jehovah is false; and the Supreme Lord of Heaven [head of the Taoist Pantheon] is false. All kinds of Gods, Buddhas, Immortals, Spirits revered by various religions are useless, cheating idols and must be destroyed! [23]

Although China had never had an established religion in the Western sense, the leaders of new thought came to consider Confucianism (in strict characterization, a system of ethics) not too short of being a religion. The question of whether the corpus of Confucian teachings was ethical or religious concerned the modern thinkers less than whether or not this primarily ethical system should be worshipped as a state cult. In the years immediately following the founding of the Republic, conservative thinkers succeeded in having a clause endorsing Confucian teachings as the basis for a national education inserted

20. The forces behind the Boxer movement, according to Ch'en, had been the superstitious notions of Taoism, the supernatural fantasies of Buddhism, and the authoritarian servility of Confucianism.

21. The Von Ketteler Monument, in memory of the German Minister who was killed at the time of the Boxer Rebellion, was long considered by patriotic Chinese to be a national affront. The disgrace of this statue on Chinese soil, according to Ch'en, was brought on by the Chinese themselves, their ignorance, and their lack of enlightenment.

22. "K'e-lin-te pei" (The Von Ketteler Monument), *HCN*, 5:5 (1918), 458.

23. "Ou-hsiang p'o-huai lun" (On the Destruction of Idols), *HCN*, 5:2 (1918), 89. See also "Science and the Divine," *THWT*, 2, 5

in the proposed constitution.[24] Monarchical forces, in support of President Yüan Shih-k'ai's attempt to turn the Republic back into a monarchy, also worked for the re-establishment of Confucianism as the state religion. On February 8, 1914, Yüan issued a presidential decree, saying, "The doctrines of Confucius and the classical literature are without equal among mankind. The offering of incense and sacrifice is historic, and it is appropriate for the Republic to follow the old customs." [25] It became clear from the start that this was not a popular issue with avant-garde thinkers, now ready to launch the New Culture and New Thought movements. Hence, when K'ang Yu-wei, the reformer of the late nineteenth century, repeated in 1915 and 1916 the same sentiments as those of Yüan Shih-k'ai himself, the *New Youth* responded with a scathing criticism. Ch'en Tu-hsiu led the denunciation of reactionary views. He ridiculed those who tried to make a religion out of an ethical system, especially when this ethical system could hardly be considered in harmony with the times. Ch'en was not against ethics in general. He opposed the absolute ethics demanded by Confucian doctrines. There should be no body of transcendental doctrine which defies changing society. Ethics is socially conditioned, and to turn it into a form of religion just because its progenitor was considered a sage would be the most flagrant manifestation of illogical daydreaming. Furthermore, Ch'en contended, modern life is based on economics, the rise of which was made possible by the principle of individual independence. Ch'en maintained that this law of society could not be refuted. The individualism of modern ethics and the sanctity of private property in modern economics mutually prove the correctness and validity of the other. He saw progress in the fact that ethics followed economic development and social change; denial of this fact would ignore the need for progress in social order and material civilization.

> Confucius was born and lived during feudal times, and the ethics he advocated were feudal. What he taught and handed down as the religion of rites was but an attitude toward life, and this feudal religion of rites was nothing but a feudal attitude of life.

24. "Temple of Heaven Draft (1913)," *China Year Book 1914* (London, 1915), pp. 490–99.
25. Quoted in John K. Shryock, *The Origin and Development of the State Cult of Confucius* (New York, 1932), p. 216.

> His politics were feudal politics. The feudal ethics, religion of rites, attitude toward life, and politics had as their central reference the power and reputation of a small aristocracy; it had no connection whatsoever with the life and happiness of the large majority of common citizens.
>
> Morality is a thing which must not be considered as unchanging truth. Rather, it must change as the organization of society and attitude toward life change. We cannot say that morality, once established, should remain unchanged forever.[26]

Ch'en Tu-hsiu's critique of religion is intimately linked to his criticism of the traditional culture, for religion represented the old civilization. He saw in the deference paid Confucius and his teachings an unsavory disregard for rationality. Added to this were the superstition and the supernaturalism of the Taoists and Buddhists (as exemplified by the Neo-Confucianism of the Sung and Ming periods), the perfect example of people steeped in universal principles of the past while, in superstition and ignorance, thinking their principles capable of defying temporal change. Ch'en Tu-hsiu showed a categorical distaste for anything that belonged in the past and criticized it just because it was old-fashioned. But he did point out why beliefs lodged in the past were undesirable and why modern modes of thought were good for China. He was, one may say, a true example of a total convert to the linear (as opposed to cyclical) conception of history. He thought that Confucianism was degenerate and unfit for modern minds. It could, however, be studied by scholars—but not practiced socially. In reply to a Peking editorial, "The Need to Study Confucianism," the title of which might better have been "The Need to *Support* Confucianism," Ch'en Tu-hsiu saw three ways of looking at this body of teachings: first, the worth of Confucianism must be judged according to its suitability to the needs of modern society: second, Confucianism should be studied only from documents and commentaries, and not according to its spirit; third, Confucianism should be studied from the sayings and writings of Confucius as he intended them for the age in which he lived.[27] Ch'en thus unceremoniously debunked Confucianism's

26. "K'ung-tzu chih tao yü hsien-tai sheng-huo" (The Confucian Way and Modern Life), *HCN,* 2:4 (1916), pp. 2–7 of 1st art.

27. See his "K'ung-chiao yen-chiu" (The Study of Confucianism), *THWT,* 1, 625–27.

claim to be an immutable ethical and social system. He had no sentimental concern with cultural continuity. The sooner the people gave up their nostalgia for China's cultural past, the better equipped they would be to appreciate and embrace the present.

Ch'en Tu-hsiu, like Wu Chih-hui, considered modern Confucianists as supporters of "national heritage" (*kuo-ts'ui*). Against this concept did Ch'en and his colleagues direct their most vehement attacks on the whole of China's traditional order. Ch'en Tu-hsiu's opinions on national heritage were revealed best in "Scholarship and the National Heritage." Learning was extremely important: it spelled the difference between culture and barbarity, helped mold higher morality, added the meaning and provisions of life, and separated human beings from beasts. This attitude toward learning which linked it with the cultivation of respect for national heritage was, according to Ch'en, one of the main reasons for China's lack of progress.

> Chinese learning blossomed during the Later Chou [period] and compared favorably with the Greek classical past of Europe. The only difference is that European learning enjoyed a steady progress from Greek times to the present; especially so in the past few hundred years in which all sciences sprouted, a thing the ancients did not dream of. On the other hand, Chinese learning has decayed ever since the last years of the Chou . . . If we directly adopt and make use of the recent scholarship and learning of Europe, the labor will be less, but the reward will be greater than if we tried to learn from the examples of the first sprouting of learning of the Later Chou and Greek times.[28]

Ch'en Tu-hsiu then enumerated his reservations regarding scholarship and learning: one must not revere the sages; the sage admirers contended that all opinions must be brought into harmony with those of the sages, who, after all, could not be compared with the omniscient and omnipotent God of Christianity. One must not worship the past; those who did so maintained that if one did not learn from the past he was worthless. But how did one know whether the ancients learned from and emulated their past? One must not worship the country;

28. "Hsüeh-shu yü kuo-ts'ui" (Scholarship and the National Heritage), *THWT*, 2, 52.

oppressive nationalism could only lessen public morality; narrow culturalism would not increase morality, as the supporters of the national heritage contended.

Like Wu Chih-hui, Ch'en Tu-hsiu maintained that three types of men supported the national heritage: one type considered the foreign learning of Europe and of the West inferior to the ways of the Chinese sages; they constituted the most befuddled and illogical people. The second type believed Western learning good and satisfactory but saw no reason why people should forsake Chinese tradition to follow some new pursuit. This group did not realize that the only presentable qualities which China possessed were literature, history, and art, private possessions of a unique civilization which all humanity cannot share. Even as private possessions, Ch'en maintained, they would not compare favorably with those of the West. China's history and historiography understood neither cause and effect nor evolution; her literature was not in natural accord with the language; and her arts of music, painting, and sculpture were extremely superficial. The third type of admirer of the national heritage held that European learning offered what the Chinese had long possessed. Hence they compared the classics with modern science, exhibiting not only China's glory but also the admirer's dubious claim that his learning encompassed two cultures. Such people did not realize that they were not adding to knowledge, but simply going through the act of reinterpretation.[29]

Ch'en saw in the inherited Confucian orientation the chief impediments to China's progress. The traditional Chinese life-view hampered the individual from developing his personality freely. The rigid Confucian social pattern strangled the development of Chinese society along Western lines. Worship of an ethical system was no less than a form of religion, and Ch'en was not sympathetic to the Chinese counterpart of religion or religious practices. It has been suggested by Benjamin Schwartz that Ch'en's premises for his critique of traditional values had wellsprings in his Chinese heritage, that he himself was never freed completely from the influence of Chinese culture, and that, because of this, he was deeply imbedded in the social and ethical orientation of his forebears. This was shown by his search among

29. Ibid., 53–54.

Western values for those particularly germane to social philosophy and ethics.[30]

While this view of the predicates of Ch'en's approach to Western ideas is plausible and correct in many ways, it should not be taken as the only explanation. Ch'en, it should be recalled, was just as convinced of the values of the modern scientific spirit and the civilization that spirit had created. Ch'en's critique of traditional life-view and social philosophy also stemmed from this belief in the value of modern science. Ch'en's orientation in social thought may be less important than the *kind* of social philosophy which captured his devotion. This devotion to a decidedly scientific modernism in turn appeared with such a force that it serves as a major key to understanding Ch'en's thought and personality. Ch'en's role as the impatient propagandist for modern culture far outweighs his role as a social theorist. A conversion did take place in Ch'en, a conversion to belief in the nature and benefits of modern science, seen in his forthright demand that science replace religion.

The major reason, Ch'en maintained, for China's intellectual backwardness was her traditional addiction to categorical statements and to the spirit of compromise in argument. To him the Chinese were incapable of an analytical approach to problems because they lacked the Western sense of logic. Hence, his advice to his countrymen:

> I believe that in the future the true belief and course of action for humanity will be guided by the proper course of science. At such time all religions will be among the expendable items. The reasons for this are complicated, but they can be stated in outline. In the universe there are two kinds of law—natural law and man-made law. Natural law, to which science belongs, is all-pervasive, eternal and inevitable. Man-made law, to which belong religion, ethics, and rules, is partial, temporary, and rational. The mere facts that if we do not get enough to eat we are hungry, and when we grow old we die, are eternal and final as characteristic of the whole of the animate world and not partial and temporary . . . The future evolution and progress of mankind must

30. See B. Schwartz, "Ch'en Tu-hsiu and the Acceptance of the Modern West," *Journal of the History of Ideas*, 12 (1951), 72.

be based on the budding science of today; we must seek gradually to improve man-made laws so that they conform with the results of natural laws. Only when this is done can life and the universe be in perfect union. This is our greatest and most final purpose! [31]

Ch'en Tu-hsiu believed the results of modern science to be still insufficient to replace religion, but that is quite different from saying it would never be able to do so. He never doubted the ability of science to break through new areas of knowledge, revealing the secrets of the universe that once were thought knowable only by God. The deterministic aspect of the older science (in contrast to the new theories of indeterminacy which emanated from modern physics) caught Ch'en's imagination and he made of it a substitute religion, a new form of belief for modern man. We find him confirming, "Therefore, I am in favor of replacing religion with science and of cultivating slowly our realistic faith, which is definitely attainable by *science*. If we rely on religious superstition for true understanding, we choose a quick, though futile, way." [32]

Ch'en's critique of traditional civilization, especially its modes of thought and life-view, remained scientistic. He used Western ideas as weapons to assail the intellectual foundations of traditional thought. His scientism is seen in his uncritical, yet total, acceptance of the scientific spirit and heritage of a foreign civilization. It is precisely in Ch'en's lack of a profound understanding of science, however, that we see his scientistic strain most clearly. We see it also in his use of science as the slogan in the unrelenting attack on tradition. His appreciation of the implications of modern science, on the other hand (the new scientific humanism), can hardly be questioned, and his philosophy of life speaks for his sincerity.

PHILOSOPHY OF LIFE BASED ON SCIENCE

The problem of the philosophy of life, with Ch'en Tu-hsiu as with most of his contemporaries, was an impelling one. They all felt the need to educate the young in a new outlook, a new faith, which they themselves had found in contact with Western cultures. Indeed, some

31. "Tsai lun K'ung-chiao wen-t'i" (Again on the Problem of Confucianism), *HCN*, 2:5 (1917), p. 1 of 1st art.

32. Ibid.

of these new philosophies of life were new metaphysics based on the findings of science. Ch'en revealed this clearly in his intention that the *New Youth* be a vehicle for arousing political and social morality and for providing a new intellectual framework. Such popular journals as the *New Youth* were signs pointing to the rapidly decreasing prestige of the traditional world-view. Concurrently, the intense demand by publicists like Ch'en Tu-hsiu for substitute frameworks shows the degree to which the ideas of democracy, science, and evolution had permeated the Chinese mind. The understanding of these new "virtues," however (often the case in cross-cultural borrowing), was not deep, nor did it have to be. Ch'en Tu-hsiu exemplified all these tendencies in a forthright, though naïve, earnestness.

For Ch'en, the two primary questions about human life were the "why" and "how" of existence. He answered these questions most explicitly in his "The True Meaning of Life," in which he saw three attempts to solve the riddle of life. First, there was the religious attempt: the Buddhist explaining the world as only an illusion and the life in it as not consisting of life; and the Christian asserting that man was created by God from dust and that when he died he returned to dust. Second, there was the philosophers' explanation: Confucius and Mencius deemed the greatest ideal in life the attainment of the reputation of being a great moralist or a statesman; Lao-tzu and Chuang-tzu considered everything proper merely if all things conformed to nature's way; the school of Mo-ti stressed selfsacrifice for the welfare of others; the Yang Chu school emphasized egotistical will to the neglect of morality and concern for others. Third, the approach to life with which Ch'en was in full accord, was the scientist's explanation: human beings are forms of matter in the natural order, and not endowed with soul or spirit; while a man lives, all forms of feeling—bitterness, happiness, good, and bad—can be explained by the laws of the material world; when man dies, all forms of matter decompose, causing the final destruction of the various forms of sensations and values; there could be no such thing as a transcendental memory or transcendental sensation.[33]

Ch'en thought the religious approach to life wholly untenable. Buddhism's denial of life would not sustain life in the active world; Christianity's insistence on a Creator represented illusory belief; for

33. "Jen-sheng chen-i" (The True Meaning of Life), *HCN*, 4:2 (1918), 90.

the creation of the Creator could not be proved.[34] Ch'en considered the philosopher's life-view only partially acceptable. The Confucian-Mencian emphasis on the ultimate peace and order of mankind as dependent on the cultivation of personal ethics represented for Ch'en only a part of what one ought to do in society; it did not contain the true meaning of life. The philosophy of Mo-ti and that of Yang Chu and Nietzsche represented two simple structures of philosophy, inapplicable in an extremely complex and "civilized" structure of modern times. The escapist Taoist philosophy was equally undesirable, and Ch'en blamed the backwardness of the Chinese people on this embracing of nihilistic relativism. Only the scientific view of life was reliable and subject to proof. Ch'en maintained that only when one recognized individual life as but a fraction of a larger life could one be capable of a larger, unselfish concern for humanity. Thus, in one way, sensations and memory did live on beyond individual existence; they were the sum total of the achievement of individuals passed on to posterity. Ch'en Tu-hsiu then chose immortality and perfection of mankind as a whole in favor of salvation of the individual in the world. It was on a basis of the findings of the physical, chemical, and biological sciences that Ch'en Tu-hsiu outlined his conception of the proper philosophy of life.

> Individual life experiences an irregular life-death cycle; social life, as a whole, lives on in truth and in eternity.
>
> The culture and happiness of a society are created by the individual, and he, therefore, should enjoy them.
>
> Society is an aggregate of individuals; without them there would be no society. Therefore, we should respect the individual will and happiness.
>
> Society is the aggregate life of all its individuals; when society is disbanded and the individuals die, there will be no continuing

34. Ch'en was against religion only in its doctrinal insistence. He was never opposed to Christianity in its emphasis on love and character as exemplified by Christ. In fact, he praised the teachings of Christ and quoted profusely from the Gospels to illustrate the central tenets of Christianity, namely, the spirit of sacrifice, the spirit of forgiveness, and the spirit of equality and universal love. (This same Ch'en said elsewhere that Jehovah was false. See p. 71.) He wrote, "This kind of basic teachings of Christianity has never been overthrown by the scientists and never will be." See "Chi-tu-chiao yü Chung-kuo-jen" (Christianity and the Chinese), *THWT*, I, 425–29.

> memory and sensation. Therefore, there must be respect for social organization and order.
>
> All forms of religion, law, morality, and politics are simply unavoidable means of keeping the society intact and are not the original intentions of the individuals for a happy life. They can be changed according to the times and conditions.
>
> Human happiness is self-created and not endowed by God or realizable by just leaving it to the natural course of things.
>
> The individual in society is comparable to a cell in the human body, having no certainty of life or death but only [the experience of] the new succeeding the old. This is a law of nature, and there should not be fear or alarm.
>
> If one wants to enjoy happiness, he must not be afraid of suffering. The suffering of the present sometimes can mean the happiness of the future . . . The severest epidemic often causes great scientific progress.
>
> In all, what is the reason and the goal of existence? I dare say: while there is life, one should work hard to create happiness in order to enjoy it. Not only that, one should imprint this happiness on society, so that posterity can enjoy it also. Generation after generation till the infinite! [35]

The proponent of the sufficiency of the scientific life-views falls into the same difficulty that confronts the materialistic determinist who fights for social reform aimed at freeing the individual. Ch'en never did resolve the difficulty of considering the human being merely as a form of matter in the natural order, following laws of natural motion and susceptible to control and manipulation by science, while at the same time insisting that the individual human being was able to create happiness and enjoy it—that is able to be in control of matter, as well as science. He did not try to resolve this problem in the years before he turned to Communist doctrines. Until then Ch'en Tu-hsiu's insistence on man as nothing more than matter in motion was as unrelenting as his crusade for free development of the individual.

Ch'en used both ideas to discredit old society and thought—science to turn the Chinese mind from a concern with bookish and

35. "The True Meaning of Life," *HCN*, 4:2 (1918), 92–93.

ethical matters to an analytical inquiry of nature, and democracy to turn the institution-centered Chinese into individual-centered people. The incongruity of the two probably never occurred to Ch'en. Thus, when he did change politics, the philosophical implications of Communist doctrines were more in line with his earlier beliefs in scientific determinism. His conception of science never went beyond a vague understanding of Newtonian physics and a smattering of evolutionary theory. What interested him was the respectability of science in general. His preoccupation with the reliability of the scientific method and his inadequate knowledge and understanding of science itself led to a rigid belief, the materialistic and dogmatic variety of scientism. Ch'en's understanding of science never changed. It found even more encouragement when, for political reasons, he turned to dialectical materialism. The believer in the immutable laws of nature regulating not only matter but also human beings did not find it difficult, after his political conversion, to say, "We believe that only objective, material causes can account for social evolution, explain history, and determine the philosophy of life." The occasion of this utterance was the 1923 Debate. Ch'en prefaced the essays with his famous diatribe against all the participants for their lack of understanding of the lessons science had for society and life. While this phase of Ch'en's thought, in which science was synonymous with social science, must be viewed in the context of the stormy debate, there was an occasion two years before, in 1921, when Ch'en hinted at his later position.

> From now on our duty towards learning and thought must be the analysis of human affairs and matter in order to establish unequivocal facts [about the two areas, social science and science]. This then is my idea of science; it can also be called a philosophy. If, however, we were to detach ourselves from the analysis of human affairs and matter and indulge in the empty speculations of metaphysics, wishing to find a quick but illusory method to solve problems of the universe and life, we would be entertaining fanciful dreams that characterized the past. We must wake up! Let me ask you: outside of human affairs and matter, is there still any universe or life? [36]

36. "Ta Chieh-p'ing" (Answering Chieh-p'ing) dated June 1, 1921, *THWT*, 3, 273.

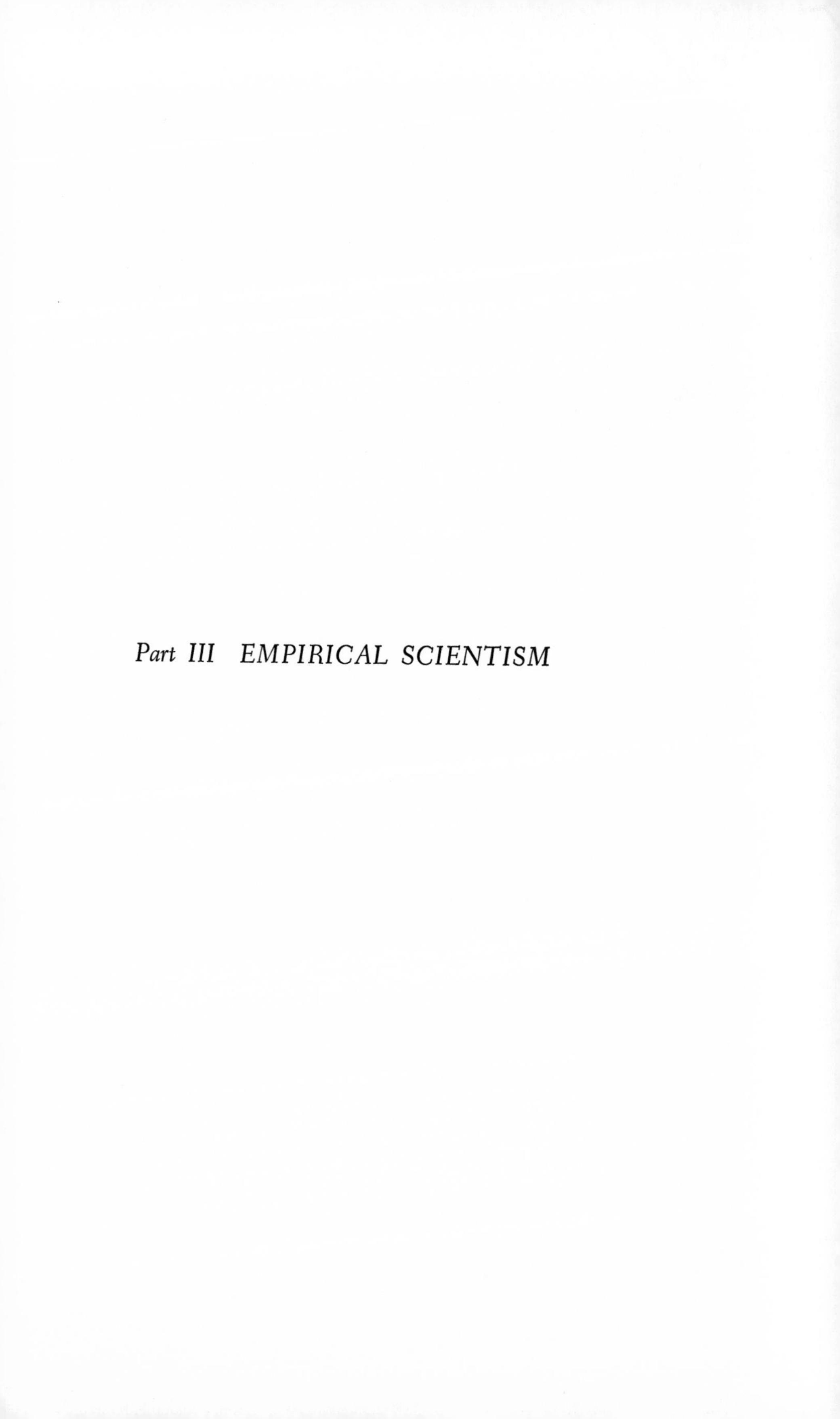

Part III EMPIRICAL SCIENTISM

Chapter 4 THE PRAGMATIST: HU SHIH (1891–1962)

Empirical philosophy is best represented in China by Hu Shih, who is known, more specifically, as the foremost proponent of pragmatism. From the time of the New Culture until the advent of Communism in China, he exerted a steady influence on Chinese thought.[1] Hu's insistence on China's adoption of empiricist philosophy was based on his belief in the validity of its two main props—the empirical method and the critical attitude. Hu Shih's belief in the scientific method came within his Western intellectual heritage; his support of science was in line with the empiricist tradition of the West. The story of Hu Shih's empirical scientism must start with his intellectual biography.

Hu Shih, by his writings and his words, actively influenced both public and academic life in China for almost half a century. It would be impossible to make even cursory mention of the many facets of his productive life, save in a full biography.[2] Our attention will be

1. Hu Shih's influence on China has been a topic of much debate. Some argue that his pragmatism definitely lost influence in the '30s when Marxism came into vogue. In terms of a single person's impact on China, Hu Shih must rank in the forefront until 1949, when the political situation robbed him of a base of operation. The vast amount of anti-Hu Shih literature by the Communist Chinese regime is an indication—even though it may be a negative one—that Hu's influence is strong.

2. Biographical data of Hu Shih's early years are contained in two works by the author himself. *Ssu-shih tzu-shu* (Autobiography at Forty) (Shanghai, 1933) is an unfinished account of his childhood and early formation of ideas until 1910 when he left for America. *Ts'ang-hui-shih ta-chi* (Notebooks of the Hidden Brilliance Study) (4 vols. Shanghai, 1939) is the famous diary of his student days in America, 1910–17. In 1947 the Commercial Press published a reprint, entitled *Hu Shih liu-*

focused on the incidents and occasions which have direct bearing on the formative years of his intellectual development in the area of scientism and materialism.

Between 1895 and 1904 Hu Shih attended a village school, where he memorized the canons of the classical education and several minor classics along the themes of moral behavior and filial piety. Normally the education of a Chinese youth did not constitute more than rote memorization of these texts, but Hu Shih's mother offered his tutor three times the normal tuition fee (six silver pieces) if he would explain the meaning of the memorized words to Hu Shih. Such early exposure to the meaning of the long passages, which for others remained obscure and tedious, established in the young boy a thirst and appreciation for literature. His comprehension of the difficult passages which were often permeated with literary illusions from historical classics and romances cultivated in Hu Shih a love for all forms of Chinese literary endeavor. He soon developed a keen taste for stories, particularly in the vernacular. This early literary excursion, thanks to a loving mother ambitious for her son to acquit himself well, played no small part in preparing Hu Shih for his prominent role in the literary revolution which he and Ch'en Tu-hsiu launched.[3]

A second important episode concerns Hu Shih's early conversion to atheism. When he was about eleven Hu came across in *A Comprehensive Mirror for Aid in Government* by Ssu-ma Kuang, a passage by Fan Chen[4] opposing Buddhism. Hu Shih quoted Fan as saying: "The body is the material basis of the spirit, and the spirit is the functioning of the body. The spirit is to the body what sharpness is to a knife. We have never known the existence of sharpness after the destruction of the knife. How can we admit the survival of the spirit when the body is gone?" The argument of this fifth-century philosopher who championed the destructibility of the spirit in opposition to the whole Imperial Court captured the inquisitive and youthful Hu Shih, who, some thirty years later, commented on Ssu-ma Kuang's inclusion of this passage by Fan Chen, "He [Ssu-ma] would have

hsüeh jih-chi (Hu Shih's Diary of Student Days Abroad), also in 4 volumes. This diary is a mine of information on Hu Shih's learning in America and also on the generation of Chinese overseas students, their dreams and projects.

3. *Autobiography at Forty*, pp. 43–53.

4. Philosopher of Ch'i and Liang periods noted for his championing against adoption of Buddhism by the Chinese court. Died about 510 A.D.

found it difficult to believe that, eight hundred years later, these thirty-five [Chinese] words awakened a boy of eleven or twelve, and affected his thought for the rest of his life." [5] Hu found his trip abroad and first-hand contact with the philosophical tradition of the modern West in harmony with these two incidents in his early life. The recognition of the need for a vernacular literature in China led him to prepare the ground for it while still in the United States; the antireligious attitude of empiricism and of such Western thinkers as Huxley and Dewey reinforced Hu Shih's early skepticism.[6]

Another early experience prepared him for the ideas he was to learn abroad. A wave of enthusiasm for the theory of evolution swept over China and was made possible by Yen Fu's translation of Thomas Huxley's *Evolution and Ethics,* which appeared in 1898. Young Hu Shih was affected by it.

> Rich men gave money for new editions to be made for wider distribution (there being no copyright law then), because it was thought that the Darwinian hypothesis, especially in its social and political application, was a welcome stimulus to a nation suffering from age-long inertia and stagnation.
>
> In the course of a few years many of the evolutionary terms and phrases became proverbial expressions in the journalistic writings of the times. Numerous persons adopted them in naming themselves and their children, thereby reminding themselves of the perils of elimination in the struggle for existence, national as well as individual.
>
> Even my own name bears witness to the great vogue of evolutionism in China. I remember distinctly the morning when I asked my second brother to suggest a literary name for me. After only a moment's reflection, he said, "How about the word *shih* (fitness) in the phrase 'Survival of the Fittest'?" I agreed and, first using it as a *nom de plume,* finally adopted it in 1910 as my name.[7]

5. *Autobiography at Forty,* pp. 75–76.

6. Atheist Hu Shih, by his own admission, almost did turn to Christianity while he was in America. "In days of despondency I took much interest in the Christian religion and read the Bible almost through. In the summer of 1911, when I was a guest at a conference of the Chinese Christian Students' Association held at Pocono Pines, Pennsylvania, I almost decided to become a Christian." *Living Philosophies, A Series of Intimate Credos* (New York, 1931), p. 253.

7. Ibid., p. 248.

This slight acquaintance with Darwin and Spencer was easily linked with the naturalism of some of the ancient Chinese thinkers.[8] Hu seems at that time to have already come to a vague belief in a natural order of things in which all beings in the universe coexist with men on an equal basis. No species exists for the sake of another; there is a natural order, but within it there is no preordained superiority or inferiority.

In 1906, at the age of fifteen, while under the spell of evolutionism, Hu Shih was invited to submit an essay to a new periodical which carried the evolutionary name of *Struggle Trimonthly* (Ching-yeh hsün-pao),[9] founded by his fellow students at the China National Institute. He became its editor a year later. The periodical's purpose was to popularize new ideas among the uneducated masses. Hu Shih later wrote of this experience, "In many of my articles written for this magazine I strongly attacked the superstitions of the people and was frankly iconoclastic and atheistic."[10]

This intellectual awareness, although still somewhat unfocused, prepared Hu Shih for contact with other Western ideas in 1910 when he went to the United States. Sharing pessimism with other young Chinese over the desperate state of affairs in their own country, Hu Shih felt the need to serve his country in a technical mission. He began his university career as a student in the New York State College of Agriculture at Cornell University. His choice was guided by the desire to gain practical knowledge and by the fact that the Agriculture College did not charge tuition; but the student of agriculture was soon attracted by the courses in literature, philosophy, and political science. A change was made, and Hu Shih embarked on a brilliant career as a philosopher, literary leader, and statesman. "The Sage School of Philosophy at Cornell," wrote Hu Shih, "was a stronghold of Idealism. Under its guidance I read the more important

8. He cited from a spurious Taoist work a passage with which he agreed entirely in spirit, if not in authenticity. The passage dealt with a young boy's retort to a company of adults, insisting on the equality of man with the "lower" order of animals. This naïve naturalism was later to receive the stamp of approval of modern science.

9. Copies of this periodical are now rare. Some passages of Hu's articles in this publication can be found in his *Autobiography at Forty*, pp. 119–35.

10. *Living Philosophies*, p. 249.

works of the classical philosophers of ancient and modern times."[11] His philosophical preference was not satisfied until 1915, when he went to Columbia University. There, with the guidance and inspiration of John Dewey, he wrote his dissertation, "The Development of the Logical Method in Ancient China."[12]

This was a period of great intellectual stimulation through books and personal contact with men such as Dewey. During this time, Hu Shih arrived at a more mature expression of his earlier beliefs. His childhood fondness for stories in the vernacular led him to advocate, while still in America, a revolution in the Chinese language and literature. His proposal was immediately supported by Ch'en Tu-hsiu, who helped popularize it in the influential *New Youth.*

To trace Hu's intellectual lineage from its Western genesis would be a tortuous course, except for the fact that it was felicitously traced by Hu Shih himself. With immense clarity of mind, he methodically outlined his own intellectual development, a feat seldom accomplished in such honesty by modern Chinese thinkers. In "Introducing My Own Thought" (*Chieh-shao wo tzu-chi ti ssu-hsiang*), written in 1930 as a preface to his *Selected Essays,* he states, "The two persons who have influenced my thought most are Huxley and Mr. Dewey. Huxley taught me how to doubt; he taught me how not to put faith in anything that cannot be proved. Mr. Dewey taught me how to think; he taught me to think with strict regard to the antecedents and consequences of thought, to consider all schools of thought and concepts as mere hypotheses waiting for proof. These two men enabled me to understand the nature and function of the scientific method." In this essay, he also indicated his conception of the nature of pragmatism and its relationship with evolutionism. Ch'en Tu-hsiu, according to Hu Shih, had earlier alleged that pragmatism and dialectical materialism represented the two most important methods of thought in modern times and expressed the hope that they could be synthesized into one philosophy. Hu Shih believed this to be erroneous. The dialectical method, he maintained, evolved from Hegel's

11. Ibid., p. 252.

12. This work was published in 1922 by the Oriental Book Co. of Shanghai, and formed the basis of his *History of Chinese Philosophy, I* (in Chinese). It was not completed beyond the first volume.

philosophy and was a metaphysical philosophy of pre-evolutionary times. Pragmatism was a scientific method which appeared after the introduction of the Darwinian theory of evolution. Hu Shih, when he wrote his own intellectual biography, had parted ways with Ch'en Tu-hsiu, for the latter had turned to dialectical materialism.

> Actually, dialectical philosophy was also a form of evolutionism in pre-evolution theory times; according to its theory, the stage that is formed by the mutual cancellation of the positive and the negative shall go on manifesting itself continuously. Narrow Communism, however, seems to have forgotten this axiom, and hence it summarily envisages an ideal world communism, thinking that this can be achieved by means of class struggle . . . This sort of reduction of the complicated to the simple, this sort of basic denial of evolution, then, is the most blatant pre-Darwinian mode of positivistic and deterministic thought . . .
>
> [On the other hand] pragmatism, ever since Darwin's theory, could admit that the only real and reliable progress is that gradual, but continuous, process of improvement.[13]

What Dewey taught Hu Shih was, essentially, a philosophy which contemplates thinking as an art and technique. "[This technique of thinking] in its essence consists of a boldness in suggesting hypotheses coupled with a solicitous regard for control and verification. . . . This laboratory technique of thinking deserves the name of Creative Intelligence because it is truly creative in the exercise of imagination and ingenuity in seeking evidence, and devising experiment, and in the satisfactory results that flow from the successful fruition of thinking."[14] This is the most important gift Hu Shih brought back to China in 1917. Never once did he give up this attitude. In matters concerning the intellectual, political, and cultural destiny of China, he demanded persistently that China's youth approach all issues with the method of thinking which Hu inherited from Dewey and Huxley.[15]

Upon his return to China, Hu became professor of philosophy and

13. *HSWT*, 4th coll. (Taipei, 1953), bk. 4, 608–09.

14. *Living Philosophies*, p. 255.

15. Hu Shih's best known advice to China's youth to employ such an attitude of mind was contained in two articles: "Wen-t'i yü chu-i" (On Problem and Isms), *HSWT*, 1st coll., bk. 2, 147–98; and "Hsin ssu-ch'ao ti i-i" (The Significance of

chairman of the English Department at the National University of Peking (Peita). He held both positions until 1926. Early in this period he was a regular contributor to the *New Youth,* and, with Ch'en Tu-hsiu, championed the revolution of the Chinese language and literature. With V. K. Ting he edited and contributed to *The Effort* (Nu-li) in 1922. Its first issue concentrated on political ideas, but the later issues were devoted to cultural and intellectual topics. The next year saw him enter the Debate in support of science and the scientific philosophy of life. Throughout the '20s Hu Shih commented critically on political matters and on problems of civilization in general. After 1921, when Ch'en Tu-hsiu and others founded the Chinese Communist Party, Hu Shih found himself in basic disagreement with Ch'en's politics and philosophy of Communism. From 1926 to 1930 he was on a leave of absence from Peita to visit England, America, and Shanghai, returning in 1931 to become Dean of the College of Arts. Our inquiry into Hu Shih's scientism ceases with this stage of his chronology after which his writing, though not differing in essence, assumed a different hue in subject matter and scope. He wrote more on political issues, as illustrated by his chief editorship of *The Independent Critic* (Tu-li p'ing-lun), a weekly to which V. K. Ting also contributed. Although there was a lively debate in the '30s in which Hu Shih played a part, and which revolved around the problem of wholesale adoption versus a China-centered adoption of Western civilization, it is a question which was discussed in essence during the '20s.

Hu Shih not only adopted Dewey's pragmatic philosophy with its emphasis on the method of inquiry and Huxley's demand for evidence but also shared wholeheartedly their essential enthusiasm for science and the scientific method and their characteristic antagonism toward religion.

CONCEPTION OF SCIENCE

Science, for Hu Shih, is the whole realm of observational and experimental methods, attitudes of doubt, and criticism. We find Hu Shih formulating his new philosophy of life: "this new philoso-

---

the New Thought), ibid., bk. 4, 151–64. He advised, for reconstructing Chinese civilization, the adoption of the pragmatic method to examine problems rather than superficial "isms." He showed a sincere regard for the gradualistic mode of cultural change.

phy of life is a huge hypothesis built on the scientific knowledge of the past two or three hundred years; we can call this the Scientific Philosophy of Life." [16]

The empiricist position toward science, as toward any intellectual pursuit, is much less rigid than materialism and determinism. It shares with determinism the assumptions and presuppositions of the scientific tradition. Empiricism pushed to its logical extreme, with its basic disinclination toward final conclusions, resulted in the crippling skepticism of Hume. Hu did not go this far, largely because the achievements of science in the post-Humian period gave practical, if not theoretical, grounds for the belief that extreme skepticism was not an unavoidable conclusion of empiricism. Thus did science, itself, rejuvenate empiricism. Darwin had solved the problems of epistemology and morality, stumbling blocks for Locke and Hume, by stating that the human intellect was merely an evolutionary development of animal intelligence, that morality was traceable simply to pleasure and pain in animals.[17] All these prerequisites for complete acceptance of the empiricist creed were quite in harmony with the essentially anti-religious attitude of the later empiricists.

When he was ready to preach pragmatic empiricism, Hu Shih was also to demand complete acceptance of the principles which the sciences had discovered. It was reasonable to urge the adoption of the "scientific" spirit along with pragmatism. Hu's conception is scientistic not so much in his conclusions as in his wholesale adoption of the scientific heritage of the West. The history of science stood as proof of the reliability of its principles and methods. Science is worthy of being worshipped.[18] And so he did not hesitate to say, "From our study of the times and our need, we cannot but conclude that the greatest [need] of all is the application of the scientific method to the problems of life." [19]

16. "K'e-hsüeh yü jen-sheng-kuan hsü" (Preface to the Debate on Science and Philosophy of Life), *KHYJSK*, 1, p. 27 of 2nd preface.

17. See his acknowledgment of contribution of Darwinian theory of evolution to his pragmatism in "Shih-yen chu-i" (On Pragmatism), *HSWT*, 1st coll., bk. 2, 80–83.

18. On March 15, 1958 in New Haven, Connecticut, Hu Shih told the author that his attitude toward science was science-worship.

19. See his "Wu-shih-nien lai chih shih-chieh che-hsüeh" (World Philosophy of the Past Fifty Years), *HSWT*, 2nd coll., bk. 2, 287. Originally written Sept. 5, 1922 for the Shen Pao symposium, *Tsui-chin chih wu-shih-nien* (Shanghai, 1923).

Hu Shih first adored the method of science; to him it was nothing more (or less) than "the respect for facts and evidence." In application it was nothing more than a "boldness in setting up hypotheses and a minuteness in seeking evidence."[20] He first proclaimed this in 1920 in "The Research Method of the Scholars of the Ch'ing Period," reiterated it in 1928 in "Method and Materials of Study," and held it throughout his life. He revealed it again in 1958 in a lecture entitled "The Development of a Scientific Method in Chinese Intellectual History."[21] Implied in this pragmatic regard for evidence is the assumption that there is a natural order in the world, whose every aspect is real and subject to scientific analysis. Hu's belief that the spirit of the scientific method existed in China's past involves the problem of Chinese cultural continuity. The attempt to lend Confucian sanction to scientific thought and method may represent a discovery of an uninterrupted lineage of scientific development in China. It may also cover up a severance in thought.

Credit has usually been given to the early Ch'ing (1644–1911) school, whose scholars turned to the concrete task of examining by minute and logical methods the Neo-Confucian texts. They came to the conclusion that true Confucian learning was to be found in the original texts of the classics of the Han Dynasty (hence their other name, Han Learning), rather than those of the Sung-Ming period. With the motive to discredit Neo-Confucianism and the diligence to prove their case, the Ch'ing scholars arrived at a method of textual criticism, historical research, and philological reconstruction that was truly critical. Regard for evidential thinking was high, and the demand for proof was a major criterion in establishing or overthrowing theories. But this is not to identify the Ch'ing scholars with Western science—from Bacon to the present day. The scholars paid no attention to the riddle of nature and stayed within the sphere of the Confucian doctrinal outlook on the social and ethical world. J. R. Levenson comments, "The empirical attitudes of these early Ch'ing thinkers, while in harmony with the scientific critique of idealism, are neither scientific themselves nor necessarily conducive to the birth of science. In European history, divergence from idealism could take

20. "Ch'ing-tai hsüeh-che ti chih-hsüeh fang-fa" (The Research Method of the Scholars of the Ch'ing Period), *HSWT*, 1st coll., bk. 2, 242.

21. This was the first Hume lecture at Yale, delivered on March 14, 1958.

the form of the pre-scientific nominalism of Peter Abelard (1079–1142) as well as the form of Sir Francis Bacon's (1561–1626) inductive empirical science; our Chinese thinkers' affinity was with Abelard, not with Bacon." [22]

The advocates of a Chinese antecedent of modern science, however, turned to the method of these empiricists as the link between Ch'ing science and modern science. But since the subject matter stayed within the Confucian framework, Chinese "science" can hardly be said to have shared much with the outlook of modern science. The results of the scientific spirit in China and the West show the real divergence in origins: in China the end product was refreshing critical thinking and method; in the West the result was modern civilization.

Hu Shih's equation of the modern scientific method with the Ch'ing scholars' empiricism seems strained. The superficiality of this equation was evident when Hu himself apologetically brought out the essential difference between Chinese and Western civilization. He said that what started out as a difference in degree became, in due course, a difference in kind.[23] Whether or not China had given historical evidence of a scientific method, what mattered was the fact that she had shown a definite cultural preference. Hu realized this and, although he insisted that there was a similarity of method, accepted the sharp distinction between the Western tradition and traditional Chinese culture.

But mere possession of the evidential method, particularly if applied only to bookish matter, was not enough for Hu Shih. This attitude is evident in his "Method and Materials of Study." [24] From 1600 to 1900, Hu maintained, the scientific method did indeed develop both in China and the West. The result in China was successful researches into philology, semantics, textual criticism, higher criticism, and archaeology. "Although the method is scientific, the materials have never been anything but literary. Even though the scientific method can stimulate great brilliance on bookish matters, these ancient texts have perpetually constricted the scientific method. Therefore, in these

22. J. R. Levenson, "The Abortiveness of Ch'ing Empiricism," *FEQ*, 13 (1954), 158–59.

23. Hu Shih, *The Chinese Renaissance* (Chicago, 1934), p. 65.

24. "Chih-hsüeh ti fang-fa yü ts'ai-liao" (Method and Materials of Study), *HSWT*, 3rd coll., bk. 2, 187–205.

three hundred years, the method was the method of literary things, the brilliance, a few torches among the ponderous volumes." Hu Shih believed that this bookish knowledge, while sharpening evidential thinking, dispensed with the precious training in experimentation.

Although Hu Shih was a leader in the movement for the systematic treatment of the national heritage along scientific lines, he admonished youth to look elsewhere.

> We hope that they [the youth] come to an early realization and concentrate on the knowledge and methods of the natural sciences. This is the road of hope, whereas the other road, that among old books and papers, leads nowhere. Even the best talents and intelligence of the last three hundred years, spent and wasted among books, did not produce any good results; we must, therefore, adopt another approach. Only after you [the youth] have achieved good results in the laboratory can you speak of and use your energies to tidy up our national heritage.[25]

Science, then, for Hu Shih is mainly method. It begins with observation and returns to observation. His conception of this method differs both from Ch'en Tu-hsiu's categorical acceptance of merely the deductive role of science and its implications and from Wu Chihhui's summary embrace of technology. Hu was in harmony with modern scientists when he said:

> Recent scientists and philosophers are gradually realizing that both hypotheses and experimentation are indispensable to the scientific method, that the scientific method is not only inductive, but also relies on the mutual application of the deductive and inductive approaches. It can be at one time inductive, at another deductive, and suddenly inductive again; at times it proceeds from the parts to the whole, at others it proceeds from the hypothesis of the whole to the component factual data; both are indispensable.[26]

While this understanding of the proper function of science is dispassionate, Hu Shih's designation of the scientific method as the only

25. Ibid., pp. 190, 197, 205.
26. "The Research Method of the Ch'ing Scholars," *HSWT*, 1st coll., bk. 2, 206.

way to truth and indisputable knowledge was not made in the same cool tone. "We may not easily and lightly admit that God is omnipotent, but we certainly can believe that the scientific method is omnipotent and that man's future is inestimably large." [27] Hu was enchanted with the cultural assumptions of modern civilization conditioned by the theoretical, as well as the practical, success of science.

The other aspect of Hu Shih's conception of science derives from his general conception of modern civilization. "The primary characteristic of modern civilization is the spirit of science," declared Hu Shih in "Our Attitude Toward the Modern Civilization of the West" in 1926. Here, as elsewhere, his pragmatic beliefs are evident. Science, with its method for exact verification, is analogous, if not synonymous in Hu Shih's mind, to the pragmatic test in philosophy. This pragmatic conception of science, reminiscent of James, is intended as a theory of establishing the truth of statements. Hu Shih, then, maintained that the basic spirit of science is the search for truth. This belief as such, taken as the *only* way to truth in all aspects of life (with truth taken in both the absolute and pragmatic senses), constitutes an assumption which gives science proper more power than it is capable of possessing. Clearly then, Hu Shih intended science to mean, as did so many of his Western contemporaries, systematized knowledge. The scientific method (or critical method, as Hu Shih would have it) could support a theory about, as well as an attitude toward, truth and reality. Science is vaguely equated with "reason." To substantiate these attitudes, Hu Shih wrote:

> The basic spirit of science is in the search for truth. Man in this world is oppressed by his environment, conditioned by customs and habits, and constricted by superstition. Only truth can free him, give him strength, and give him wisdom and intelligence; only truth can help him eradicate the strictures imposed by environment . . . Scientific civilization teaches us how to train our senses and intelligence to search gradually and progressively for truth . . . This is the only way to truth.[28]

27. "Wo-men tui-yü Hsi-yang chin-tai wen-ming ti t'ai-tu" (Our Attitude Toward the Modern Civilization of the West), *HSWT,* 3rd coll., bk. 1, 4. It originally appeared in *TFTC,* 23:17 (1916), 73–82. Hu Shih's English adaptation of this is in "The Civilizations of the East and of the West," *Whither Mankind,* ed. C. A. Beard (New York, 1928), pp. 25–41.

28. Ibid., 8–9.

Hu Shih was willing to enlarge the role of science. Its implications to Hu are first the method and then a general principle, which contemplates everything that is systematic and rationally arrived at as scientific. The knowledge gained from such a process is scientific knowledge, certain and verifiable. Strictly in terms of his philosophical endeavors, we can say that Hu saw science as a method of finding truth and pragmatism as an attitude of mind. Hu Shih generally saw science as systematic reasoning which teaches man and trains his faculties toward progress. This conception of science as systematized knowledge, reminiscent of Spencer, was evident when Hu insisted that science was not alien to the Chinese mind. "There was no open resistance to the new science from the West, which from the very beginning was hailed by the Chinese as a useful extension of the Chinese ideal to investigate the reason of all things. The only resistance was an unconscious one, the resistance of the old literary, bookish habits." [29]

His more general conception of science must be viewed in the context of his pragmatic-rational critique of traditional civilization. The totality of Hu Shih's conviction can be seen most fully in the way he dealt with cross-cultural values and assumptions. The encomia lavished upon the new civilization had to be accompanied by a critical presentation of the old.

CRITIQUE OF TRADITIONAL CIVILIZATION

Hu Shih's critique of traditional civilization was "based on the scientific knowledge of the past two or three hundred years" and is revealed clearly in "Our Attitude Toward the Modern Civilization of the West." [30] The enthusiasm with which Hu eulogized modern Western civilization in this article reflects a total rejection of unenlightened civilization. This essay was prompted by the allegation after World War I that Western civilization was materialistic and Eastern civilization spiritualistic. This had been an issue in the 1923 Debate. Now in 1926 he coherently set forth his position in this long article.

When Liang Ch'i-ch'ao criticized the bankruptcy of science after World War I, Hu immediately came to the defense of Western scientific civilization. "There is nothing more baseless and poisonous

29. Hu Shih, *The Chinese Renaissance,* p. 72.
30. See p. 96 n.

than the derision that Western civilization is materialistic and the praise that Eastern civilization is spiritualistic." Any civilization, according to Hu, is materialistic—it has all natural forces and materials—and spiritualistic—the wisdom, ability, knowledge, sentiments, and ideals of a people. Civilization is the product of the exercise of man's thought and intelligence upon the substance and energy of nature. Modern Western civilization, based on the tenets that the aim of life is the search for happiness, that poverty is a sin, and that disease and suffering are evil, is the kind of civilization which uses material things to enrich life. Western civilization was far from materialistic.

> Can we truthfully say that this civilization which utilizes things in order to enrich life neglects the needs of the human spirit and aspirations?
>
> We can boldly proclaim: the modern civilization of the West absolutely does not neglect the needs of the human spirit. Moreover, we can boldly say: the degree to which the modern civilization of the West can satisfy the needs of the human heart and soul is something which the old Eastern civilization cannot even contemplate. From this point of view, the modern civilization of the West is definitely not materialistic; it is idealistic and spiritual.[31]

The desire to know is the greatest spiritual need of man. Not only does Eastern civilization reject the move to satisfy this urge; it often tries to stifle it. Eastern civilization's shrinking from difficulties is a form of laziness. According to Hu, when the Westerner would search for truth, believing it to be inexhaustible, the Easterner would say, "Truth is infinite, how can such infinity satisfy the desire of the human being to know?" Hu answered: "Even if truth is infinite, does this mean that because of it science should recede? . . . This then is one of the basic differences between civilizations of the East and the West. One is self-deceptive and unthinking; the other searches continuously and unrelentingly for truth."

To the charge that Western civilization is materialistic because it embraces science and technology and neglects religion and ethics, Hu Shih retorted:

31. "Our Attitude Toward the West," *HSWT*, 3rd coll., bk. 1, 3, 7–8.

> On the surface, modern civilization has not yet severed its relationship with the old religion, and hence it has not openly established its new religion and morality. But those of us who study history must point out that modern civilization does have its new religion and new morality. The advance of science has raised the level of human knowledge and has enabled man's method of the search for knowledge to be more elaborate, thus improving his power of judgment. For these reasons, the old religious superstitions have been gradually reduced to the minimum; even that most minimal religious belief—the existence of God and the immortality of the soul—has become a doubtful matter.[32]

This new religion and morality differed from the old in its *rationalization* (li-chih-hua), *humanization* (jen-hua), and *socialization* (she-hui-hua). The development and expansion of man's knowledge through science has increased man's self-confidence and changed his heaven-oriented, fatalistic outlook into a faith in himself. Because of more material enjoyment (brought about by science) man could begin to consider the needs of others. An expanded sense of empathy coupled with increased ability produces an unprecedented, new social morality. Hu contends this *rationalization* is substantially Huxley's doubting attitude awaiting evidence. *Humanization* is the victory of scientific method over God in a contest of ability to solve all problems of life. The *socialization* of morality is a product of the industrial revolution, best proved by the rise of the utilitarian attitude, "greatest happiness for the greatest number of people." [33]

Hu Shih is now ready to draw the real difference between materialistic and spiritualistic civilizations and to join criticism of traditional civilization with praise of modern Western civilization. The differentiation, criticism, and praise must be viewed together.

> There is not much spirituality in those civilizations which bound the feet of their women for a thousand years without a protest from their philosophers, tolerated the practice of suttee . . . have maintained the horrible caste system for thousands of years, or to this day use human beings as beasts of burden.

32. Ibid., 10–11.
33. Ibid., 11–16.

The term "material civilization" should carry no reproach. All civilizations began with toolmaking, and all toolmaking is a creation of the intelligence of man, using matter and energy for the satisfaction of a want, a desire, an esthetic feeling, or intellectual curiosity. All tools of civilization are material embodiments of an idea or ideas, and the wheelbarrow of the East is no less material that the motor car or aeroplane of the West.

The real difference between the Oriental and Occidental civilizations lies in the historical fact that, while the West has in the past few centuries created a new age of science and technology by the development of scientific research and the discovery of steam, gas, and electricity as new sources of power, the East has lagged behind in science, and human labor has long remained its source of power. It is a difference in degree which in the course of time has amounted to a difference in kind.

There is true spirituality in this Western civilization of science and technology. Science is truly spiritual in its ceaseless search for truth, in its rigid discipline and methodology, in its moral courage to doubt and to accept nothing without sufficient evidence, and the rapturous and ecstatic joy which frequently rewards the patient creative researcher when he succeeds in solving a difficult problem . . . And all technological progress may be of high moral and spiritual value when it is considered as the use of human intelligence to create tools and machines whereby to relieve unnecessary pain and toil of Man, to multiply his productive power, and to enrich his life. Where Man has to sweat blood in order to earn a bare subsistence, there is little life left, let alone culture and spirituality.

There is true spirituality in what may be called the new religion of democracy . . .

That civilization which makes the fullest possible use of human ingenuity and intelligence in the search for truth in order to control nature and transform matter for the service of Man, to liberate the human spirit from ignorance, superstition, and slavery to the forces of nature, and to reform social and political institutions for the benefit of the greatest number—such a civilization is highly idealistic and truly spiritual.[34]

It is obvious that Hu Shih, unlike Ch'en Tu-hsiu, did not employ the destructive method in his critique of traditional civilization. Rather, he introduced and presented unstintingly the ideas and values of the civilization to be adopted. With a deeper understanding of the modern West than Ch'en, but not as categorical as Wu Chih-hui, Hu Shih in fact did not need to use polemics against the undesirable tradition and traditionalists. He extolled scientific and technological civilization, much in the same manner as Wu Chih-hui, but Hu's philosophical premise stemmed from his concept of utility. His many-faceted presentation of the virtues of modern civilization as benefited by science did not require a tirade against traditional forces.

Hu Shih's constructive criticism appears again in the question of the national heritage. Ch'en and Wu were in favor of placing the national heritage in the museum attended by a few well-qualified antiquarians. Hu Shih was less inclined to a summary disposal of the national heritage as something decrepit and corruptive. His pragmatic views again influenced his pronouncements and led him to a critical examination of this problem. Dewey's tutelage in instrumental logic gave Hu a technique which he "found to be true not only of the discoveries in the experimental sciences, but also of the best researches in the historical sciences, such as textual criticism, philological reconstruction, and higher criticism." He continued, "Curiously enough, this instrumental logic has turned me into a historical research worker. I have learned to think genetically, and this genetic habit of thinking has been the key to success in all my subsequent work in the history of thought and literature."[35] Hu approached the problem of national

34. Paraphrased from Hu Shih, "An Oriental Looks at the Modern Western Civilization," *Modern Education and Human Values,* 5 (1954), 50–54. This is another adaptation in English of the original Chinese article. It incorporates several other short articles on the subject written previously: "Ch'ing ta-chia lai chao-chao ching-tzu" (Let Us All Look at Ourselves in the Mirror), *HSWT,* 3rd coll., bk. 1, 39–50; and five articles under the title "Man-yu ti kan-hsiang" (Impressions of My Journey), ibid., 51–72. The latter articles all harp on the theme that Eastern civilization is not spiritual at all, or if it is, that spirituality is parasitic. On the other hand, modern Western civilization is really spiritualistic because it substitutes human energy with mechanical power, a creation of human intelligence.

35. *Living Philosophies,* pp. 255–56.

heritage armed with the scientific method; he wished to reveal "the true character" of long-held beliefs and to curtail the tendency toward an unhistorical attitude to what may be called pure fantasies. In a humorous letter, "The National Heritage and Ghost-catching," he writes, "I firmly believe that among the 'piles of old paper' there are innumerable old ghosts who are capable of gobbling up people, misleading them, and poisonous enough to harm them." [36] This process of turning darkness to brightness, revealing the miraculous and mystical as the commonplace, and dethroning the gods and sages is what Hu Shih called the "reassessment of all values."

The national heritage, strongly detested by Ch'en and Wu, was not so offensive to Hu Shih. He objected to the attention paid the national heritage by men who had had no scientific training. Only the scientific reconstruction of past values, with a view to eliciting clearly the genetic sequence and historical perspective in which these values took shape, could be tolerated. Hu Shih himself sums up this position in his well-known essay "The Significance of the New Thought," where he asserts that the attitude of the new thought toward old values should be critical and have three major emphases: it must set itself against indiscriminate acceptance of authority; it must oppose compromise; and it must insist on systematic reconstruction of the national heritage.[37] The first two aspects, according to Hu, were the traditional habits of mind of the Chinese thinkers and scholars; such uncritical and compromising spirits had fostered a national scholarship which showed no signs of order, system, or clarity. In turn, such a body of literature perpetuated the attitudes which brought them into existence. Herein lies Hu Shih's greatest contribution to the study of China's past in modern times.

The purpose of Hu Shih's constructive critique was to show the utilitarian benefits of contemporary Western civilization to a people who had not known the benefits of science and technology. Using examples of what direct application of the scientific method in matters of technology and values could do for time-worn civilizations, he argued in favor of the superiority of scientific civilization. His pragmatic concern with gradual change, as opposed to Ch'en Tu-hsiu's

36. "Cheng-li kuo-ku yü ta-kuei," *HSWT,* 3rd coll., bk. 2, 211. The "old ghosts" refer to superstitious beliefs and legends.

37. "The Significance of the New Thought," *HSWT,* 1st coll., bk. 4, 161–62.

impatience with and Wu Chih-hui's summary disregard for tradition, aimed at the eventual replacement of the traditional by the modern civilization. He presented to changing China a totality of the cultural assumptions of the modern West and asked for its gradual acceptance.

Hu's critique of traditional civilization points out no specific defects; it deals with two general themes: the underlying materialism of Eastern civilization and its distasteful moral and religious orientation. With no real refinement of argument, Hu Shih says, "if the priests of the Medieval Age were justly canonized as saints, Galileo, Watt, Stephenson, Morse, Bell, Edison and Ford certainly deserve to be honored as gods and enshrined with Prometheus and Cadmus." And again, "The difference between the Eastern and Western civilizations is simply a degree of success or failure in the process of breaking away from medieval ideas and institutions which once ruled the whole civilized world." [38] By not pausing to tear down the traditional façade and substance and by portraying the new religion and new morality, Hu Shih again uses the constructive scientific critique. Just as Ch'en and Wu felt compelled to substitute science for the old religious way of life, Hu Shih proposed to substitute his new religion, that of Social Immortality. The very statement of the need for a new religion was, in itself, a serious indictment of old ethical and religious beliefs.

PHILOSOPHY OF LIFE BASED ON SCIENCE

Hu Shih began forming his new credo, which he called the Religion of Immortality, in 1918.

> As I reviewed the life of my dead mother, whose activities had never gone beyond the trivial details of the home but whose influence could be clearly seen on the faces of those men and women who came to mourn her death . . . I came to the conviction that *everything* is immortal. This line of reasoning led me to what may be called the religion of Social Immortality, because it is essentially based on the idea that the individual self which is the product of the accumulated effect of the social self, leaves an indelible mark of everything it is and everything it does upon that larger Self which may be termed Society, or Humanity, or the Greater Being . . . This Great Self lives forever as the everlast-

38. Hu Shih, *Whither Mankind,* pp. 27, 31–32.

> ing monumental testimony of the triumphs and failures of the numberless individual selves.[39]

Hu Shih contended that the ancient Chinese doctrine of the Three Immortalities, Virtue, Deed, and Word (te, kung, yen) were good in themselves but selfish, because only the sage and the learned man were supposed to possess them.[40] His new religion included all people, great and small, good and evil.[41]

> And it is this recognition of the immortality of evil as well as of good that constitutes the moral sanction of the doctrine. The decay of a dead body may found a religion [Buddhism], but it may also plague a whole continent. A chance remark of a barmaid may lead to the sudden enlightenment of a Zen monk, but a wrong theory of political or social reconstruction may cause centuries of bloodshed. The discovery of a microscopic bacillus may benefit millions of people, but a tiny sputum from a consumptive may kill multitudes and generations.[42]

The religion of the Confucianist is built around a parental and ancestral concept which guides Man's conduct. The meditative religions, divine-right sects, and others, worship idols. All these, Hu Shih believed, could not affect or fulfill spiritual need, and so they were incapable of guiding one's life's conduct. Only the religion of Social Immortality was adequate. Its credo was: "The individual self has a tremendous responsibility to the infinite past as well as to the infinite future of the Greater Self. We shall always remind ourselves of how we can best utilize the individual self so that he fulfills his duty toward the memory as well as the future of the Greater Self." [43]

During the 1923 Debate, while advocating a new philosophy of life devoid of old religious and ethical connotations, Hu commented, "In the China of today where religious worship has been comparatively free, if we deeply believe in the scientific evidence available

39. *Living Philosophies,* pp. 257, 259.

40. These three immortalities appear in the *Tso-chuan.* See Hu Shih's treatment of them in "Pu-hsiu, wo ti tsung-chiao" (Immortality, My Religion), *HSWT,* 1st coll., bk. 4, 107–09.

41. Ibid., 116.

42. *Living Philosophies,* p. 259.

43. "Immortality, My Religion," 118.

now, we can only deny the existence of God and the immortality of the soul. If this is the case, then we might as well proclaim ourselves atheists. This type of faith cannot be called dogmatic because it is based on evidence."[44] Evidence is knowledge built upon the natural and physical sciences. Because Hu believed that advances in scientific knowledge had in the past caused people's philosophy of life to change (the Copernican theory and the Darwinian theories, for instance), he contended that a proper philosophy could be realized with the correct degree of publicity and education. Furthermore, one basis for all philosophies of life could be found, "to use the sober, dispassionate, and unbiased attitude of the scientist, namely, the commonly accepted 'Scientific Philosophy of Life,' as the common denominator of the philosophy of life of all mankind."[45]

Life is forever changing, as Hu saw it, according to environment; therefore, one must use a scientific attitude to study life. The scientific philosophy of life must provide the basis of a life-view and rules for conduct according to this life-view. Hu enumerated ten instances from the natural and physical sciences[46] (these were ridiculed by foreign missionaries as "Hu Shih's Decalogue") from which he arrived at the conclusion that space is infinitely large and time unending, hence there is no need for the concept of a Creator or a benign Ruler; that Man, an infinitesimal part of this order, differs from the world of animals only in degree and not in kind; that organisms and societies evolve; that all phenomena are explainable by the law of cause and effect; that morality and religion are subject to change; and that matter is in motion and not static. This view of life sees the individual as small in comparison to total mankind. It suppresses the egotistical self in favor of the magnanimous whole.[47]

Hu Shih proposed and insisted on the adoption of scientific spirit, attitude, and method for ethics, as well. There must be doubt, so that uncritical postulates will not be formed; there must be a mode of conduct based on factual data, so that one is not guided by sensational values and slogans; there must be a demand for evidence—if there is belief in God, there must be proof that God exists; and the foremost

44. "Preface to the Debate on Science and the Philosophy of Life," *KHYJSK, 1*, 14–15 of 2nd preface.

45. Ibid., 23.

46. Listed in detail in Chapter 6. See pp. 155–56.

47. "Preface to the Debate," 25–27.

goal in life is truth. "The constant search for truth does not imply a complete success because truth is infinite and the universe is infinite. That we must keep on searching is merely to fulfill our obligation, hoping that we can add an iota to the total whole . . . Therefore, only science possesses the unselfish and cooperative spirit." [48]

Hu Shih called this the naturalistic conception of life and the universe. In this universe of infinite space and time, "Man, the two-handed animal whose average height is about five and a half feet and whose age rarely exceeds a hundred years, is truly an infinitesimal microbe. In this naturalistic universe, where the motions of the heavens follow the laws of nature, where the great law of causality governs the life of man, and the tragic struggle for existence directs all his activities—in such a universe man's freedom is indeed restricted." [49]

This statement would seem to stamp Hu Shih as a believer in the type of linear causation postulated by Ch'en Tu-hsiu or seem to share some of the deterministic implications of Wu Chih-hui's philosophy. Yet it is at this point that Hu Shih broke away from the other two philosophers. His lifelong devotion to individual freedom, which he found epitomized in Ibsen,[50] rescued him from a total submission to a monistic and mechanistic explanation of man and his place in the universe. Ibsen represented the quintessence of nineteenth-century European individualism. "This individualism on the one hand teaches us to emulate Nora to create a whole individual; on the other hand, it teaches us to learn from Dr. Stockmann in order to become independent, to dare to say the truth, and to fight against the evil forces of society." [51] Hu Shih caustically replied to the charge that he was a reactionary following the virtues of the Victorian Age by maintaining that the Chinese culture was so far from the Victorian Age that the comparison was nonsensical. The individualism of the eighteenth and nineteenth centuries in Europe, which produced numberless individualists who loved freedom more than bread and truth more than life, made possible the modern civilization of the present day.

48. "K'e-hsüeh ti jen-sheng-kuan" (The Scientific Philosophy of Life), *Hu Shih wen-hsüan* (Selected Essays of Hu Shih) (Hong Kong, 1958), p. 77.

49. He would have called it "scientific" but did not do so to avoid controversy. See "Preface to the Debate," pp. 27–28.

50. See his "I-po-sheng chu-i" (Ibsenism), *HSWT,* 1st coll., bk. 4, 13–38.

51. "Chieh-shao wo tzu-chi ti ssu-hsiang (Introducing My Own Thought) *HSWT,* 4th coll., bk. 4, 613.

This view led him, on another occasion, to formulate what he called the "non-egotistical new life." Because society is the sum total of various forces, we must be ready to fight and change such forces when necessary. Because social change is necessarily gradual, one must search, experiment, and wait for evidence. Because society contains egotism, one must accept struggle.[52] In other words, everywhere in life, Man must exercise to the utmost his "creative intelligence." Hu Shih's faith in individual freedom explains why his seemingly monistic scientific philosophy of life now assumed a different course.

> Yet this tiny bimanual animal has his proper place and value in this naturalistic world. Using two hands and a large brain, he actually has created many tools, devised many methods, and created some culture. He has not only tamed many animals but also studied and discovered many laws of nature, utilizing them to help him master the natural forces, so much so that he can summon electricity to propel his vehicles and ether to deliver his messages.
>
> The increase of his wisdom and knowledge has meant the extension of his power. In addition, it has expanded his vision and heightened his imagination. In the past, he has worshipped all forms of matter and animals and feared the gods and spirits. Now, however, he is gradually realizing that the infinity of space only enriches his appreciation of the natural universe, that the timelessness of time only helps him to understand more the tremendous hardship his ancestors faced in building up this human inheritance, and that the regularity of nature's ways only increases man's power to dominate it.
>
> Even the totality and the universality of the law of causation cannot really constrict his freedom; the law of causality not only enables him to explain the past and predict the future, but also gives him the means of using his intelligence to create new causes and obtain new results. The struggle for existence does not necessarily turn him into a cold and brutish animal; on the contrary, it might even increase his sympathy for his fellow creatures, make him put more faith in the need for cooperation, and focus all the

52. "Fei ko-jen chu-i ti hsin sheng-huo" (A Nonindividualistic New Life), *HSWT*, 1st coll., bk. 4, 184–86.

> more his realization of the importance of rigorous human endeavor in the reduction of cruelty and waste . . . In sum, this naturalistic conception of life need not exclude beauty, poetry, a sense of moral obligation, or the opportunity to fully utilize the "creative intelligence" of man.[53]

Hu Shih believed in pluralism. Man is not totally enslaved to regulatory natural, social, or economic laws. For beyond the laws of nature, man can still exercise his own creative faculties to contribute to the social whole. This belief in pluralism helped Hu Shih escape the determinism often implied in the concept of causation.

Hu Shih presented this life-view which began and ended with science and embraced the sum total of the cultural assumptions of the modern West at the Debate of 1923. Presented in this way, the life-view was to be accepted or rejected, not really to be debated. After all, those who reject it must first answer Hu Shih's question: "Shall we say, 'After us, the deluge?' or shall we say, 'After us, the millennium?' "[54]

53. "Preface to the Debate," 28–29. Hu Shih's own English version of this passage appears in *Living Philosophies,* pp. 262–63.

54. *Living Philosophies,* p. 260.

Chapter 5 THREE SCIENTISTS

Among the pioneers institutionalizing science in modern China were three men who felt called upon to champion the supremacy of science in the area of human values. Their writings appeared often in nonscientific journals and commented widely on the cultural implications of science as the method of transforming Chinese culture and thought. The points of view of all three, in varying degrees, resembled the thought of Hu Shih. Ting Wen-chiang, an internationally known geologist, and Jen Hung-chün, a mathematician, were close friends of Hu Shih; they were in personal—as well as intellectual—rapport. T'ang Yüeh, a psychologist and pragmatist, seems not to have shared in this intimate friendship, but he was much in agreement with their thought. These Western-trained scientists sought, by wide and persistent publication and—in Ting's case—by personal example, to impart to China the scientific spirit they so cherished. Their double role of cultural purveyors and scientists brought them under furious attack by the traditionalists in the Debate of 1923.

Ting Wen-chiang (1887–1936), better known as V. K. Ting, was one of China's leading geologists. In his biography of V. K. Ting, Hu Shih says, "Tsai-chün [his other name] is the most Westernized Chinese and is most under the influence of science. From this basic standpoint, no one can compare with him. This is so perhaps because he went abroad when he was only fifteen and early came under the influence of the English." [1] Ting's friends and contemporaries dubbed

1. Hu Shih, "Ting Tsai-chün che-ke-jen" (This Man Ting Tsai-chün), *Chin-jen chuan-chi wen-hsüan* (Biographical Essays on Recent Men), ed. Chang Yüeh-jui (Changsha, 1938), pp. 93–94. The most complete biography to date of Ting (d.

his mode of living "scientific." He had to have eight hours of sleep; he was obsessed with being hygienic, always insisting on washing his eating utensils in boiling water at public restaurants; he did not drink, but always used the liquor to rinse his chopsticks (a wasteful habit to his good friend Hu Shih); he despised lavishness, but emphasized the need for comfort and rest; he never acted against the doctor's orders.

V. K. Ting was born into a well-to-do gentry family of Kiangsu province. As a child he was regarded as somewhat of a genius. Between the ages of five and fifteen he acquired a firm foundation in classical literature and language. His later literary efforts could be traced to the labor of these years. In 1902, he left for Japan and in 1904, for England. Financial difficulties beset him soon after he enrolled at Cambridge, and he moved to Glasgow in 1907. He flirted with medical training before completing his program at Glasgow with a degree in both geology and biology.

Upon his return to China in 1911, he was a pioneer in the field of geology, then a neglected discipline.[2] His tenure as the head of the Bureau of Geological Survey of the Ministry of Agriculture and Commerce from 1916 to 1921 turned the Bureau into a truly scientific research institute. Its deserved reputation is largely due to the vision of its director who saw geology as more than a narrow study of rocks. Professor Amadeus W. Grabau, a well-known paleontologist whom Ting had invited to teach in China, best described Ting's contribution in this field of science:

> Dr. Ting's conception of geology is extremely vast; it is not limited to the materials composing the globe, such as metallic substance and rocks, but includes the forces of those materials which shape and change matter as well as the degree of such changes. This vision includes as worthy subjects for research such things as the shape, constitution, and the history of the globe; it takes into account all forms of matter, both land and marine, which

---

1936) is by Hu Shih, "Ting Wen-chiang ti chuan-chi" (Biography of Ting Wen-chiang), *Annals of Academia Sinica*, 3 (Taipei, 1956), pp. 1–123, presented on the twentieth anniversary of Ting's death. In the earlier publication are other valuable biographical data by Chu Chia-hua, Hollington K. Tong, T. F. Tsiang, Tung Tso-pin, C. L. Lo, and Li Chi. Other data on Ting's life, written by his friends at the time of his death, appear in *TLPL*. No. 188 carried 18 articles; later articles appeared in nos. 189, 193, 196, 208, and 211.

2. Hu Shih, "Ting Tsai-chün," pp. 14–22, 27–32.

> have existed since time immemorial; all degrees of the evolution of life-forms . . . are considered [by him] to be within the realm of geological study.[3]

Besides his impeccable professional record, Ting was celebrated for the rigid standard he set for himself as well as for others. For the younger people he exemplified hard work and honesty. The Anglo-Saxon idea of the rule of law was personified by this geologist in his own country, where such a concept did not exist. For this reason V. K. Ting's way of life was appreciated for the most part by students who had encountered the concept outside of China.

He also brought the wide vision of his particular field of research. He was well-known for his temporary excursion into politics,[4] and he wrote significantly, though not too extensively, on his philosophy and the more popular aspects of science. Three times in his life he pronounced his life-view based on science. In 1911, when he was twenty-five, Ting published a textbook of biology in which he explained a world- and life-view based on science. In 1922, at his instigation and with the help of Hu Shih, the *Effort Weekly* appeared, first as a voice of political criticism and later as a vehicle for the ideas of science and democracy. This weekly served as one forum for the arguments of the 1923 Debate. In his response to Carsun Chang's attack on science, Ting reiterated his new world-view, his new religion. In 1934 he wrote "My Belief," and stressed the same view for the third time—the religion of self-sacrifice taught by scientific habits and outlook.

For Jen Hung-chün (1886–1961) and T'ang Yüeh (b. 1891), biographical data does not exist in quantity or collected fashion. They did not leave as forceful an impression on modern Chinese thought as Wu Chih-hui, Ch'en Tu-hsiu, Hu Shih, and V. K. Ting. Their importance lies in having commented and written on many aspects of Chinese culture in this time of change. They wrote in response to major events and debates and gave the reading public the impression that they were not just laboratory scientists. These men went beyond the serious work of definite scientific contribution to vindicate the very cause of science.

3. Ibid., p. 28.

4. This was in 1925 when he served as Special Commissioner of Shanghai for the politician-warlord, Sun Ch'uan-fang. Ting had been remorseful that he had miscalculated Sun as having the strength to unite China. For details, see ibid., pp. 59–71.

Both Jen and T'ang were American-trained, the former in mathematics, the latter in psychology. They shared with other Chinese students abroad high hopes and noble purpose which the recent (1911) revolution in China had produced. When T'ang arrived at Cornell University in 1914, he joined Jen Hung-chün, who had already made friends with Hu Shih. That year Hu Shih discussed, in the company of Jen, T'ang and Mei Kuang-ti (a man who was to be a formidable foe of Hu's literary views), his thoughts of introducing *pai-hua* as an agent for the cultural transformation of China.[5] Jen Hung-chün remained faithful to Hu Shih's cause. The mathematician often wrote poetry in the vernacular, in friendly exchange with Hu Shih. The two men were close in mind and temperament with Ch'en Heng-che, woman pioneer of the new culture of China, friendly critic of Hu's poetry, and a poet in her own right.[6] Jen introduced Hu Shih to her in Poughkeepsie in 1917 and married this gifted woman himself.

Jen Hung-chün brought back to China the *Science Journal,* the publication of the Society which he and others had founded at Cornell in 1914. It became the leading publication of theoretical and applied science in China, and it enjoyed a long run until threats of war and internal political change brought it to an end. Jen was alternately the chairman of the executive council of the Science Society of China, publisher of the journal, and its editor in chief. Along with other scientists, such as Yang Ch'uan and Wang Hsing-kung, Jen wrote on the more popular aspects of science, vindicating its worth as *a* value, if not *the* value, of the modern age. He became better known in this role than as a mathematician. Jen also served as professor at Peita and in various administrative positions, including the presidency of Ch'eng-tu University during World War II, and on numerous governmental commissions.

T'ang Yüeh was, since his student days, an unwavering believer in the need for cultural renovation along modern principles, although he

5. See an intimate description by Hu Shih, "Pi shang Liang-shan—wen-hsüeh ke-ming ti k'ai-shih" (Compelled into Rebellion—The Beginnings of the Literary Revolution), *TFTC,* 31:1 (1934), 15–31.

6. See mention of exchange of poems and letters between Hu, Ch'en, and Jen in Hu Shih, *Notebook of the Hidden Brilliance Study,* 4; Hu's poem on their friendship, "Wo-men san-ke p'eng-yu," in his *Ch'ang-shih chi* (A Collection of Experiments) (Shanghai, 1922, 1925), pp. 81–83.

retained a semi-literary style of language to convey his thoughts. He did not belong to the inner circle of friends composed of Hu Shih, V. K. Ting, Jen Hung-chün, Ch'en Heng-che, Fu Ssu-nien, T'ao Meng-ho, and Ch'ien Hsüan-t'ung. He was, however, regarded by them as a sympathetic voice.

He returned to China in the early '20s, in time to join the 1923 Debate, which was the occasion for most of his writing on psychology and the new philosophy of life. These works are collected with later writings into two volumes of his selected essays.[7] Among his more notable activities were a term as chairman of the department of psychology at Tsing Hua University and, after 1929, the directorship of the Institute of Psychological Research of the Academia Sinica. In addition to his occasional writings, T'ang is noted for his translations. Both he and Hu Shih helped Hsü Ch'ung-ch'ing translate John Dewey's *Reconstruction in Philosophy*. He himself was responsible for parts or the whole of several of William James' works. He translated James' *Varieties of Religious Experience* and, from *Principles of Psychology,* the chapters, "On Emotion" and "Thought."

CRITIQUE OF TRADITION

The scientists' inherent empiricism was at the root of their criticism of China's tradition and their propagandizing for cultural change. This attitude did not produce the frenzied attacks on tradition we saw with Ch'en Tu-hsiu and Wu Chih-hui. But scientism was in all cases evident.

V. K. Ting, "the most Westernized Chinese" according to Hu Shih and others,[8] combined the phenomenalism of Karl Pearson, the eugenics of Francis Galton, and the general theories of Darwin and Huxley. Ting saw science as a wide-ranging attitude of mind, shaping and affecting man's outlook on life. Ting criticized tradition in light of the need to approach all of life's problems scientifically. No longer were judgments to be based on moral, religious, and ethical thinking; the good and bad became relative to time and space; they are not to be judged according to any preordained standard.

7. *TYWT,* 1st and 2nd coll. (Shanghai, 1925, 1929).
8. For example, see Fu Ssu-nien, "Wo so jen-shih ti Ting Wen-chiang hsien-sheng" (The Ting Wen-chiang that I knew), *Fu Meng-chen hsien-sheng chi* (Collected Works of Fu Meng-chen), 2, sect. B, bk. 6, 5.

Shortly before Ting engaged in the Debate of 1923, he demonstrated this spirit of scientific impartiality in a lengthy article on "Eugenics and Heredity," in which he argued that the reason for China's lack of progress was a lack of attention to the ecological and demographic problem of man and his environment. Vital and intense interest in this problem, Ting maintained, was behind the rapid progress of Western civilization. The West was solving its population problems by rational means, with an increasing awareness of eugenics and euthenics and the help of socialism. In China, the pressure of population on land had in the past led to upheavals which, Ting lamented, were the product of ignorance. He contended that the cold reason of the sciences, especially eugenics and ecology, could help China overcome her tremendously difficult problems of transition. Ting maintained that the only criteria for judging between new and old were the impartial and unerring laws of the science of evolution and heredity. China's custom of concubinage, for instance, according to Ting should not be discussed in terms of equality of men and women or monogamy. The scientific method demanded quantified analysis of the good and bad effects of concubinage on the newborn infant.[9]

Ting joined in the spirit of the '20s which turned to China's past with vehement criticism and unrequited doubt. In 1931, in an article on "How China Acquired Her Civilization," he wrote, "The Confucianist version of the Chinese history, with its *uncritical* acceptance of the legends and its *fanatical* belief in the Golden Age as represented by feudalism and semicommunal holding of land, is . . . untrue." [10] Ting was also to deny the spirituality of Chinese civilization in the 1923 Debate. The statement of his arch opponent, Carsun Chang, that cultivation of inner life helped to produce China's spiritual civilization triggered a heated retort from Ting. The centuries of emphasis on inner cultivation produced a delusion of superiority, while practical affairs were neglected to such an extent that China was repeatedly conquered by others.[11]

If one accepts the opinion that modern science, inclusive of its

9. "Che-ssu hsüeh yü p'u-tieh" (Eugenics and Heredity), *KT*, 3:5 (1921), 35–36.
10. In *Symposium on Chinese Culture*, ed. Sophia Zen (Shanghai, 1931), p. 1. Italics added.
11. See full translation and treatment in Chapter 6.

methods and spirit, is a product of the West, and that China in the past had not produced such a method and spirit to explain the world of nature despite some notable inventions, then Ting's espousal of science and the fact that his contemporaries called him the most modern Chinese is a departure from traditional thought and behavior. The past is invalidated by such acts. But Ting also loved his country in this time of cultural stress, and he showed his love not in wanting to recapture the past, but in his desire to "adapt ourselves to the conditions created by industrial civilization which is conquering the world." [12]

While Ting derided the impractical inner life of the past, Jen Hung-chün and T'ang Yüeh criticized tradition from many points of view. Jen firmly believed in science as a Western product, stating, "it is one thing to say that we have had some material which could be of use to science and quite another to say that science, as we understand it in the modern sense of the word, has already been in existence." [13] Jen said that the Chinese mind had confined itself to literary and classical studies because the traditional program of study emanated from Confucius and his school, which overemphasized the cultivation of the self in society and in institutions; traditional Chinese humanism had directed intellectual activities to established ideals and doctrines and not to the analysis of nature; the examination system was a means of bringing together intellectual attention and social ambition. "Looking through the two thousand years of intellectual history, we see a whole procession of scholars, literary writers, historians, and commentators on classical books, but not a single man who could be called, in the phrase of Francis Bacon, 'an interpreter of nature.' " [14]

As early as 1915, Jen remarked that China's intellectual history was one of retrogression. Since the first unification of China (Ch'in-Han period, 221 B.C.–A.D. 220), the study of current affairs was particularly arid. Instead, the gaze turned backward, toward emulation of an elaborate antiquity. The Chinese way of approaching the facts of life concentrated, moreover, on their reasonableness rather than on their reason. The method used to understand the world suited the realm

12. Ting, "How China Acquired Her Civilization," *Symposium,* p. 21.

13. Jen, "Science, Its Introduction and Development in China," *Symposium,* p. 143.

14. Ibid., pp. 143–45. See also his "K'e-hsüeh ching-shen lun" (On Scientific Spirit), *K'e-hsüeh t'ung-lun* (Essays on Science) (Shanghai, 1919).

of illusion more than the realm of reality.[15] Jen saw such tendencies as deterrents to the rise of science in China and believed that they accounted for the lack of any real systematic principles.

Jen did not think that China's lack of scientific development was due to a particular genius or the force and pressure of circumstance; China had not developed the *method* of science. This difference in method was Jen's chief point of discussion. He went on to unite the spirit and method of science. In "The Future of Thought in Our Country," he wrote,

> A general view of four thousand years of the history of Chinese thought reveals that it has been literary rather than scientific. The acceptance of an idea and the establishment of schools of thought have been formed on the basis of intuition, not material facts . . . [Chinese thought] has followed subjective observation and not objective analysis; it has exhausted the vicissitudes of human affairs and not studied the diversity of matter. The material [for thought] has been simple, and therefore the application of thought has not been widespread. Is it any wonder that [thought] has been static and dormant, not showing a single thread of light? [16]

Following Comte, Jen divided the development of human knowledge into three stages: the Age of Superstition, during which the elements of nature awed the people; the Age of Experience, during which a form of trial and error civilization took shape; and the Age of Science.[17] This analysis was, in itself, a modern notion. Jen's concern with the power and province of science impelled him to write numerous articles for the leading journal, *Science Journal* (K'e-hsüeh), of which he was longtime editor, on such topics as "Science and Education," "Science and Morality," and "Scientific Spirit." Like Ting, Jen's critique of the past was constructive. He declared that science, understood as an entire range of method and attitude, repre-

15. "Shuo Chung-kuo wu k'e-hsüeh chih yüan-yin" (On the Reasons for China's Lack of Science), ibid., p. 184.

16. "Wo-kuo hsüeh-shu ssu-hsiang chih chiang-lai" (The Future of Thought in Our Country), ibid., p. 192.

17. See his "Wu-shih-nien-lai chih shih-chieh k'e-hsüeh" (World Science of the Past Fifty Years), *Tsui-chin chih wu-shih-nien* (The Past Fifty Years), 1, p. 1 of 6th art.

sented all that is modern and respectable. Their age as well as their content made old education, learning, and cultural endeavors worthless.

While T'ang Yüeh cannot be considered strictly a scientist, he considered himself a scientist and a follower of empiricism. More specifically, T'ang, who contributed the greatest number of articles to the Debate of 1923, considered himself a scientist of the human psyche. Human behavior proved, to T'ang, the existence of the laws of causation and thus was psychology qualified to be a science. It revealed the inadequacy of philosophy alone. His critique followed the same mode as that of Ting and Jen but, since he was fond of philosophizing and not dedicatedly absorbed in pure research, his critique was less controlled and tended to be polemical. T'ang believed that science was a contribution of the modern West.[18] From this premise he spoke on China's past failures. The supremacy of the moderns over the ancients is most evident in a series of articles written in the early and middle '20s.

In "Several Weak Points in the Habit of Thought of Our Countrymen," T'ang indicts the Chinese on the grounds that they suffered from constricting notions of morality and class consciousness, were moved by sentiment and literature, approached things in a piecemeal and unsystematic way, tended to be vague and imprecise, favored categorical and empty, illusory thinking, and were too often concerned with verbal and stylistic authority.[19] T'ang believed that the "diseased roots" of traditional learning could be seen in the Chinese emphasis on bookishness and neglect of factual data, in the preference for translation and commentary above real research, and in the attention given literary style instead of intellectual content. He believed that if a people could produce significant thought, the literary style, no matter how coarse, could be tolerated.[20]

In such criticism of the intellectual tradition of China, T'ang resembled V. K. Ting and Jen Hung-chün and shared their deep belief in and a conscience born of science and modernism. Where Ting and

18. T'ang Yüeh, "Han-hsüeh shih k'e-hsüeh ma?" (Is the Han Learning Science?) *TYWT*, 1st coll., 249–74.

19. "Wu kuo-jen ssu-hsiang hsi-kuan ti chi-ke jo-tien" (Several Weak Points in the Habit of Thought of Our Countrymen), *TYWT*, 1st coll., 127–38.

20. "Chung-kuo hsüeh-shu ti tsui-ta ping-ken" (The Root of the Disease in Chinese Scholarship), *TYWT*, 2nd coll., 299.

Jen let their belief be implicit, T'ang expanded it into a social critique of China's past which resembles that of Wu Chih-hui, Ch'en Tu-hsiu, and other impresarios of modern culture. His "On a Sick Country" charged that China's ills, long and protracted, manifested themselves on all levels of society. People of the lower classes were too numerous and too poor, and they were also stupid. T'ang considered these conditions the result of overpopulation and poverty, poor planning and poor distribution of resources; he did not consider stupidity to be innate. The two most devastating upper-class ills were conceit and sycophancy. According to T'ang, the latter came from the four-thousand-year tradition that produced the bookishness of the examination system. The former perpetuated the institutions supported by notions of bookish learning and civil bureaucracy.[21] These upper-class diseases manifested themselves in the penchant for showing off literary skills and the desire for official position. All of this, T'ang maintained, combined to produce the illusion of a national heritage. This illusion persisted for lack of an enemy to challenge it. T'ang believed that the West provided a challenge, and he favored awakening his country from its illusion, to embrace modern civilization.[22]

T'ang tackled the problem of Han Learning,[23] the empirical scholarship of the early Ch'ing, used by Hu Shih, Liang Ch'i-ch'ao, and other intellectuals to prove that China had possessed spiritually, if not actually, a true scientific heritage. Science had a unique birth in the West, and with this birth began the methodological approach to nature. T'ang was ready to sacrifice intellectual continuity for science as a modern system of values. T'ang believed it proper and imperative that China adopt and propagate science now. His second volume of collected essays, *A New Leaf in the History of China* (Chung-kuo shih ti hsin-yeh), took the title of one article in the collection. T'ang denied the existence of democracy in China's past, as he denied the existence of science. What appeared to be a democratic institution, for example, the examination system in reality limited the field of study, forced the standards to become rigid, insured the service of persons too old and weak to accomplish anything, accommodated the

21. "Ping-kuo lun" (On a Sick Country), *TYWT*, 2nd coll., 277–88.

22. "Kuo-jen pu-k'o-pu hsing ti ta mi-meng" (The Great Illusion from which the Chinese Must Awaken Themselves), *TYWT*, 2nd coll., 306–07.

23. "Is Han Learning Science?", *TYWT*, 1st coll., 249–74.

bureaucracy and the leisure groups, and actually blocked individualism and creativity.[24] Neither science nor democracy then, the twin enobled concepts of Ch'en Tu-hsiu and the new culture, existed in China's past. T'ang ended his second collection of essays, not surprisingly, with a translation of "The Higher Values of Science," a chapter from Winterton C. Curtis' *Science and Human Affairs.*

V. K. Ting, Jen Hung-chün, and T'ang Yüeh all thought science would fill the technological (in its widest meaning) requirements of China and infuse the Chinese mind with a habit of thought which could find truth, knowledge, and life according to the language of modern science. Each man felt compelled to speak of science as a substitute for old habits of thought, old religion, and old morality.

CREDO OF LIFE

"Tsai-chün is truly the best and most useful representative of China in the new age. He is the purest product of the Europeanization of China. He is a huge machine using the fuel of scientific knowledge. He banishes subjectivity, serving scholarship and country, mankind's progress, and happiness." [25] So commented an admiring friend of V. K. Ting. In England during the early twentieth century, he studied biology and geology and came under the influence of reformist Darwinism which emphasized cooperation rather than competition. The lessons of social conscience and intellectual rigor (the latter through science) contributed to Ting's life-view. Ting wrote his textbook on biology in 1911. He used the ant to illustrate the collective superiority of the species due to individual sacrifice. From the fact that the queen and the workers renounced personal freedom to produce the ant colony, Ting drew the lesson that man ought to see the value of "sacrificing one's own benefit for that of the group, and sacrificing the group's benefit for that of the everlasting generations." This was the correct religious impulse and attitude; there was nothing divine in religion. One could feel religious by observing and understanding the laws of nature. He continued in his *Textbook on Biology:*

> Looking at the phenomena of animal life and the ways of evolution and natural selection, we know that what is considered supe-

24. *TYWT,* 2nd coll., 326–27.

25. Fu Ssu-nien, "The Ting Wen-chiang that I Knew," *Collected Works of Fu Meng-chen,* 2, sect. B, bk. 6, 5.

> rior, inferior, successful or unsuccessful, concerns not the individual but the entire genus, not one epoch but infinity. As the individual and the epoch's fortunes or misfortunes often collide with those of the race and infinity, the results of evolution and selection are such that all animals have the instinct to sacrifice the individual and the epoch for the race and infinity. If this were not so, there would be no existence to speak of. Man is the soul of all things . . . Ever since the emergence of knowledge in primitive times, there were those who possessed the religious impulse and those who did not. The former were superior and survived, the latter perished. As the generations accumulated, [this lesson] became the general view of religion of our time. Accordingly, religion is also a product of evolution, and it is wrong to say that religion deals with the way of the gods.[26]

Ting went on to define religion as "that natural impulse to sacrifice the self and the present in the interest of the entire human race and infinity. This impulse is shared by mankind and animals alike."

Ting held this belief throughout his life. He was to repeat it at critical stages in the development of modern Chinese thought. Each time his intent was apparent: that this modern view of life could and ought to be scientifically supported. With his scientific philosophy of life already implied in his textbook in 1911 and his "Eugenics and Heredity" in 1921, Ting explicitly said in the 1923 Debate that science could not be separated from the philosophy of life.

V. K. Ting's theory of knowledge was coextensive with his philosophy of life, for he postulated that the ever-expansiveness of science implied eventual union of science and philosophy. His theory of knowledge mainly derives from the phenomenalism of Karl Pearson and Ernst Mach, though Ting preferred to call it "skeptical idealism." It is a positive philosophy which considers the perceiving faculties to be united with what is perceived. Observation of natural phenomena can be reduced to the exercise of sensory perception; sensory perception can be reduced to sense stimulation. Therefore, all phenomena (material now reduced to psychological) come under the province of scientific ordering, study, and interpretation, based on our knowledge

26. Passages were quoted by Ting himself in *KHYJSK*, 2, 1st art., pp. 37–39.

of perception. Empirical scientism is manifested not only in the phenomenalist's assertion that there is no need to wonder about reality, but also in the veiled rational absolutism (despite their claim of empirical skepticism) that equates the objectivity of scientific study with a doctrinal finality. This absolutism comes from treating science as omnipotent and omniscient.

In the case of the empirical scientists, finality (which pervades the choice of a philosophy of life) is shown clearly by their desire for objectivity in the realm of scientific knowledge, which is almost commensurate with knowledge of life itself. This satisfying sense of finality can be viewed as the modern substitute for faith, for it was faith that made the scientists talk in terms of "credos," "beliefs," and the "new morality."

V. K. Ting gave a final summation of his credo shortly before his death in 1936. He combined beliefs, sacrifice and honesty, science and phenomenalism in private, as well as public, morality, on May 6, 1934, in the popular Tientsin newspaper *Ta-kung Pao,* in an article entitled simply "My Belief" (*Wo-ti hsin-yang*). The *Independent Critic* (Tu-li p'ing-lun), a journal known for its empirical outlook on politics, philosophy, and literature, quickly reprinted it.

Of primary importance to Ting was the cause of good behavior: it is the sentiment, "guided by scientific knowledge," which propels man to do good for society. Good behavior is defined, in the utilitarian spirit, as that which satisfies the greatest number of desires of the greatest number of people. As for knowledge, Ting commented, "I believe that conclusions not arrived at by the scientific method do not constitute knowledge at all. Within the realm of knowledge, the scientific method is omnipotent. Science is unlimited; all the myriad phenomena are material for science. All that is gained by the use of the scientific method, regardless of the nature of the materials [studied] is science . . . Things such as subjective philosophy and mysterious religion are not knowledge and are incapable of guiding us." [27]

Ting did not believe in God or a soul which exists separately from the body. Like Hu Shih, V. K. Ting made the impossible demand for proof that God could be seen, heard, and touched, and placed the burden of proof on the believers. The probability that God or soul did

27. *TLPL,* 100 (1934), 10

not exist was greater than the probability that they did exist. "Scientific maxims all deal with questions of probability." [28]

He praised mental and physical activities which banish mystery. Repeating his 1911 tenet, "true religion is the instinct to sacrifice the self for the good of the group," he saw in the scientific creed a religion without fear. The new religion to him imparted a reassuring sense of the useful and manageable, guaranteed by the power of science. His religion of sacrifice, truth, and truthfulness approached utopian proportions. "None can match the effort of the Soviet Union in banishing superstition, and yet none is so rich in religiosity as the Communist Party." [29] "From each according to his ability, and to each according to his need" was an ideal goal.

Ting denied that he was either a Communist or a believer in communist doctrine. His empirical creed kept him from this total commitment. Ting did not believe in revolution as the only way to attain the ideal, and especially did not accept the ability of "laws of history" to account for its success.

This empirical creed emphasized gradual and persistent reform by "drips and drops" (Hu Shih's oft-repeated expression). Both the vision of the good society and its needs are scientific. V. K. Ting felt compelled to have the expanding world of Chinese thought adopt his credo built on science. As any credo deals with a broad range of belief, the linking of it with methodologically derived knowledge leaves out much of the ineffable in life.

> In the realm of knowledge, science is all-embracing. The so-called "science," or "non-science" question is one of methodology and not one of material content. All phenomena and facts are materials for science. Science is merely the use of unerring methods. The so-called scientific method uses logical approaches to classify phenomena and facts systematically, to understand their interrelations, to seek their common laws, and to predict their future. Thus when we say that certain knowledge is true, it is the same as saying that it is scientific.[30]

28. Ibid.
29. Ibid., 11.
30. "K'e-hsüeh-hua ti chien-she" (Scientific Reconstruction), *TLPL, 151* (1935), 10.

This credo presupposes that the methods of science can answer all questions of life, from immutable matter to emotions and sentiments. All beliefs of the prescientific era became suspect. Ting's view combined an affirmation of the modern creed with an implied rejection of the old. The temper is scientistic.

Jen Hung-chün, too, took advantage of the 1923 Debate to expound his modern philosophy of life. He had already published several articles in the *Science Journal* in 1915 and 1916. Although these articles covered subjects and themes not directly describing his philosophy of life, they shaped the outlook of life which Jen proposed during the heated Debate.

In the first issue of the *Science Journal,* Jen defined science as systematic knowledge of facts supported by the specific methods of science. Jen found that China's intellectual past lacked science. He went on to praise the scientific method. "The nature of science lies not in the material, but in the method. The material does not differ from that of thousands of years ago. But today's science did not exist thousands of years ago, all because of the presence or absence of a method. Once there is a method, all things can be science." [31] He extolled mainly the inductive method, even though Jen, the mathematician, realized its inseparability from the deductive method. Jen could say, "because it [science] is systematic knowledge, it can have systematic development. In combining everything under one law, this law will again discover new facts. In systematizing new things, new laws will be discovered." [32]

Jen Hung-chün saw science primarily as the spirit and attitude for finding truth and achieving progress. Science for him was the foil of the modern age with which to point to an unprogressive past. In his "On Scientific Spirit," Jen boldly stated, "The past approach to learning was literary; today's approach is factual. Twentieth-century civilization is nothing but the result of the victory of factual learning over literary matters." [33] He then contended that the scientific spirit aims at the search for Truth, with Truth understood as an absolute term. "What the scientist knows has factual data as its basis, experiment as

31. "Shuo Chung-kuo wu k'e-hsüeh chih yüan-yin" (On the Reason for China's Lack of Science), *Essays on Science,* p. 189.

32. Ibid., p. 187.

33. "K'e-hsüeh ching-shen lun," *Essays on Science,* p. 1

its corrective, application as example, and experimental proof as its claim to finality. It does not accept subjectivism, established teachings, and words of ancients. Not only does it reject subjectivism, but if the established teachings and words of ancients clash with what I perceive as truth, then even if it means great difficulties and going through water and fire, I will fight them until death and without regret. This is what I call scientific spirit." [34]

Jen believed that science's importance for education lay not in the quantitative acquisition of knowledge, but in training in the correct methodology. More than that, it lay in the "cultivation of the impulse and attitude of mind." [35] A habit of study—classifying, establishing relationships, and discovering laws—would mean that one is mindful of facts, sees cause and effect, is undeceived by sentiment and unmoved by bias. This would contribute to the progress of learning and education and eventually result in a society built on a firm foundation.

Jen did not compromise his faith in the omnipotence of the scientific spirit when he said that the three great systems of thought in life were the literary, the philosophical, and the scientific. Human thought has been approached subjectively and objectively. The subjective was supported by feeling and sentiment; the objective (dealing with matter) was the source of all knowledge. What bridged the two worlds of matter and self, according to Jen, was philosophy,[36] scientific philosophy. Moreover, "spiritual learning cannot really be separated from matter." As the province of scientific discovery and description of material relations expands, said Jen, so will one's philosophy of life. Science gave Jen not only the priceless source of knowledge but also the spirit with which to expand the realm of factual understanding of the world so as to merge with mankind's general feelings of truth and honesty.[37] Jen's philosophy of life was, in identifying science with the modern age, a progressive one. It also contained much of the inherent impatience with which this modern age looked upon past generations.

By the time of the 1923 Debate, Jen could state boldly, "a science of

34. Ibid., pp. 3–4.

35. "K'e-hsüeh yü chiao-yü" (Science and Education), *K'e-hsüeh,* 1:12 (1915), 1352.

36. "Wo-kuo hsüeh-shu ssu-hsiang chih chiang-lai" (The Future of Thought in Our Country), *Essays on Science,* pp. 190–91

37. Ibid., 197–99.

the philosophy of life is an impossible thing, but a scientific philosophy of life is possible." [38] Admitting that there might be different philosophies, Jen saw that all shared a common point of departure, that is, a harmonizing of external and internal life. "Since the philosophy of life cannot be separated from the material world and be independent, then the more the knowledge of the material world increases, the more the inevitable change in the philosophy of life. In other words, if the increase of knowledge of the material world belongs to the scientific, then the philosophy of life based on science will increase proportionally." [39] He then used the theory of evolution as an example. Its impact on the changing philosophy of life was to place man in the world of nature, destroy the religious belief in creation, and disprove the metaphysical argument from design. For all of this it substituted the notion of the struggle for existence.

Jen believed that science itself could directly produce a philosophy of life.

> First, the aim of science is truth, and truth is boundless. Thus the students of science all have a brave, progressive . . . and ever-youthful philosophy of life. Possessed of this kind of philosophy, one can overcome the many temptations of the materialistic world. . . .
>
> Second, because of [the above], all prejudices and private wishes of the mind and heart could be banished, allowing the mind and heart to come into direct contact with the lofty spirit of the natural world . . . Possessed of this kind of philosophy of life, therefore, some scientists can actually abandon fame, prestige, and concerns of social class . . . Third, science studies relations among matter. Only when the relations are understood can laws be discovered. Such studying of relations and discovering of laws all give men an attitude of causation [sequential thinking] . . . Thus this philosophy of life aims at whatever conforms with reason and the demand for proof.[40]

38. "Jen-sheng-kuan ti k'e-hsüeh huo k'e-hsüeh ti jen-sheng-kuan" (A Science of the Philosophy of Life or A Scientific Philosophy of Life), *KHYJSK,* 1, p. 4 of 6th art.

39. Ibid.

40. Ibid., pp. 6–7 of 6th art.

This argument for the ability of science to affect and produce directly a philosophy is irrevocably based on the faith that science is omnipotent. By saying that science is but systematic knowledge and that only with the Scientific Age do we have reliable knowledge, Jen Hung-chün has discarded all knowledge before the rise of science as unreliable and dispensable. By identifying the knowledge gained from science with the totality of human experience needed for a successful philosophy of life, and by fusing the two with what he called the "scientific spirit," he was nevertheless endowing a laboratory attitude and the method of its studies with enormous power and prestige. For these reasons, his philosophy of life can be called "scientistic." This scientism is nowhere more clearly manifested than in his "What is a Scientist?", in which, again identifying scientific knowledge and further identifying the scientist with the ideal modern man, he states, "A scientist is one who talks factual knowledge and one who chooses as his goal the discovery of hitherto unknown principles." [41] Jen provides no definition of the nonscientist who pursues knowledge in a critical manner. Such a general definition of the scientist does justice neither to the actual working scientist nor to the man involved in objective and critical scholarship. In any event, this equation of criticalness with science and of objectivity with scientific verifiability can only be traced to the popularizing impulse of scientism.

At the time when Jen was beginning to write on the value of science, T'ang Yüeh also began his series of writings. He, too, participated in the 1923 Debate. The first clue to T'ang's philosophy of life appeared in "Science and Morality," an article he first wrote for the *Science Journal.* He declared, "It is one of the world's felicities to consider how science, through its truth-seeking methods, contributes to the increase of morality." [42] T'ang saw seven ways in which science could help the moral improvement of man. "Because of the lack of definite criteria, the esthetician and man of letters often tended to speak of beauty for beauty's sake . . . Science is, on the other hand, not so, always using the test of facts to judge the truth or falsity of a thing and the acceptance or rejection of an idea. Not a single thread of subjective opinion finds a place in it [scientific judgment] . . .

41. "Ho-wei k'e-hsüeh-chia" (What is a Scientist?), *HCN,* 6:3 (1919), 252.

42. T'ang Yüeh, "K'e-hsüeh yü te-hsing," *TYWT,* 1st coll., 116. Further quotations in this section are from the same article; page numbers are in the text.

Thus science nurtures sobriety and dissolves prejudices and conceit" (p. 116). Second, even though the sincerity of the old morality cannot be questioned it was an ignorant form, often witnessing unnecessary sacrifices, as seen in the son who amputates part of his body to make medicine for his aged dying father. "From the individual and his family to the country and the world, there must be for all endeavors a method that will examine and exhaust the reasons of things. Only after this [the perfection of a method] can the moralist know how to be good . . . The clarity and orderliness of transportation, hygiene, commerce, and government of modern times could not have achieved this degree of development were it not for science" (p. 117). Third, "the scientific spirit can overcome injustices and misunderstanding [T'ang uses the examples of Giordano Bruno and Galileo], and therefore it treasures truth and sacrifice, acting as the guide for modern civilization" (p. 118). The previous laws of custom and usage are full of compromise; scientific laws are objective and impartial. Therefore, "it is a scientific law that there is a common humanity [sic]. If man fully merges himself in such sentiments, then his law abiding impulse is strong . . . If the individual's law abiding impulse is strong, his society's unity is powerful" (p. 119). Fifth, laws of causation nurture one's sense of place and understanding of phenomena around him. Thus, an appreciation of the essence of science, which T'ang took to be the law of causation, would lead to increasingly accurate hindsight, an avoidance of the feeling of the accidental and fortuitous, and thus provide a pragmatic and practicable morality. Sixth, history proves that science can support morality. Here T'ang subscribes to Comte's view of the triadic development of human society. "Proof is the same as scientific evidence. Ever since biology's proving, among other things, that the group instinct is an important condition to the preservation of the race, man came to know that moral laws, unshaped by sages and not included within the powers of God, are natural laws" (p. 121). Thus *morality has a scientific basis*. Last, science promotes morality because the scientific spirit provides for a new religious feeling. To T'ang, even though morality can exist without dependence upon revealed religion, it would if it were to improve by leaps and bounds, require an exalted sentiment to sustain itself: "Is there anything better than the science-nurtured emotion to reap the benefits of religious faith and yet avoid the ills of superstitious worship?" T'ang equated this sentiment with Ernst Haeckel's "cosmic emotion" and called it the proper religion for modern man (p. 122).

This analysis of the correct philosophy of life grew out of T'ang Yüeh's knowledge and acceptance of psychology. One article for the 1923 Debate was entitled "Psychological Phenomena and the Law of Causation." By psychological phenomena he meant all behavioral and psychical phenomena. By the law of causation he meant that every effect has its cause. If A must precede B, then B will not happen without A. T'ang believed that we learn about causation from experience (thus fulfilling the quantitative and mechanical principles of science mentioned in Chapter 1) and that, if the causal relations are known, there is no need to know the specific details. Here he preferred Bertrand Russell's approach: causal relations do not mean that the same cause would produce the same effect, but that the same kind of cause will produce the same kind of effect. We often know causes and effects, but we cannot tell which is the effect and which the cause. This happens because nature is complicated. It does not mean that there are phenomena beyond causality.

All psychological phenomena can also be understood according to the scientific laws. A philosophy of life is the individual's attitude toward the myriad things (including man) of the world, and this attitude is conditioned by the individual's nervous system, experience, and knowledge. This system of nerves and the totality of sensation, T'ang maintained, together form the "cause" of the philosophy of life.[43]

It is not so much in his discussion of the principle of causation or in his discussion of psychological phenomena that T'ang's empirical scientism is revealed, but rather, in the strongly suggested notion of a law, with its implied dispassion and orderly shaping of man's view of himself and the world around him. The awareness of an operating law of cause and effect took precedence over the concern for the individual and unique character of every minute thing in life. Though suggesting determinism, T'ang's views come closer to empirical scientism than to material scientism, largely because he left much of human and material events to the testing of experimental research, guided by

43. "Hsin-li hsien-hsiang yü yin-kuo-lü" (Psychological Phenomena and the Laws of Causation), *KHYJSK*, 2, 2–12 of 2nd art.

the laws of cause and effect and not to be totally dictated by all laws of nature, as in material scientism.

In matters of faith in science, however, T'ang shared notions common to both empirical and material scientism. Immediately after the Debate, this psychologist-scientist talked resolutely on two occasions about psychology as a science, about machines, and human life. In his defense of psychology as a science, T'ang pointed to many misconceptions which arose, he said, from an uneasy feeling about the independence of psychology as a science and the principle of determinism which psychology follows. All sciences follow this principle, but philosophers cannot accept psychology's deterministic dismissal of free will.[44]

T'ang argued that the sciences merely give us conditional knowledge. The fact that there are more detailed and unknown conditions in psychological phenomena than material phenomena should not be construed to mean that invariable causal connections among such phenomena do not exist. Second, we can understand the psyche by seeing recurrent patterns and by predicting on the basis of this knowledge. Third, to the argument that the multiplicity of schools of psychology does not permit a unified science, T'ang answered that, since all schools deal with phenomena, all accept the law of causation as a common law.[45]

Symptomatic of the impatience of the times, T'ang argued more from proclamation and faith than from the cold reason and sobriety which an "understanding of the law of causation and the scientific spirit" would produce. In answering Fan Shou-k'ang's "Freedom of Will and Morality," T'ang showed this tendency when he wrote "Machines and Human Life," leaving many paradoxes. He argued that the law of causation, "a certain kind of cause will produce a certain kind of effect, and without this law there would be no science" does not exclude freedom of will. The individual was still under the law of causation when he decided to be with or against society, for "the same cause can produce two effects." The causes were there, he said, but the decision to react was determined by the self; hence freedom.

44. "Che-hsüeh-che chih yen-chung-ting—hsin-li-hsüeh" (Psychology—The Nail in the Philosopher's Eye), *TYWT*, 1, 205–06.

45. Ibid., 212–13.

T'ang saw the major difference between machines and human beings not in the fact that one followed causal laws and the other did not, but in the fact that human beings possessed will and sensation. Even then, T'ang minimized the differences between them. "Human behavior (the exercise of will is also behavior) is caused by the formation of his nature and is the same as mechanical behavior caused by the organization of the mechanism." Empirical caution went with the wind when T'ang went on to say "the general behavior of the machine is the responsibility of the individual mechanisms, just as the general behavior of mankind is the responsibility of the individual human being." [46]

T'ang believed that morality could be approached in the same way and with this same spirit. If the machine misbehaves, one goes to the machine to correct it. If the human being misbehaves, one goes to the internal factors of man to correct him. T'ang called his philosophy of life a mechanistic view of morality.[47] He even called it a form of scientific superstition, in that such beliefs cannot yet be proved beyond a doubt. The fact that one *believes* in the "most effective hypothesis" with a high degree of invariability is a form of superstition, but now an acceptable one. This identification of faith with belief in probable and hypothetical truths brings into full relief T'ang's scientistic credo of life which made him state, "I am a devout believer of science and a student of psychology." [48]

We see that the supposedly dispassionate men of science also felt called upon by the intellectual demands of the times to criticize and articulate the world-view gained from their studies and observations. All three studied here, voicing what can be taken as the majority opinion of "scientific" men, saw a clear break with the past, a break caused by the rise of the scientific method. V. K. Ting and Jen Hung-chün emphasized the power of this method to know everything and establish a new outlook, while T'ang Yüeh stressed the law of causation as the guiding intellectual principle. All three agreed upon the value of the "scientific spirit," with its laboratory habits of evidential, precise thinking which—Ting and Jen admitted—was necessary for mankind's moral and intellectual advancement and T'ang labeled a

46. "Chi-hsieh yü jen-sheng" (Machines and Human Life), *TYWT*, I, 223, 231.
47. Ibid., 236, 238.
48. Ibid., 222.

religion. All three treated truth as that which is discoverable and ascertainable by science, and excluded experiences and information acquired "unscientifically." The completely scientistic nature of their sentiments can best be seen in their failure to point out the highly abstract nature of scientific laws. In addition, they saw the methods, laws, and equations describing abstract reality with qualified precision as operative, or as ones which ought to be operative, in a world beyond the realm of science. This claim that science is commensurate with the totality of knowledge and experience angered thinkers who wished to preserve the importance of the ineffable in life. Against this background of concern the polemical Debate that ensued occurred, in the words of T'ang Yüeh, according to the "law of causation"—inevitably.

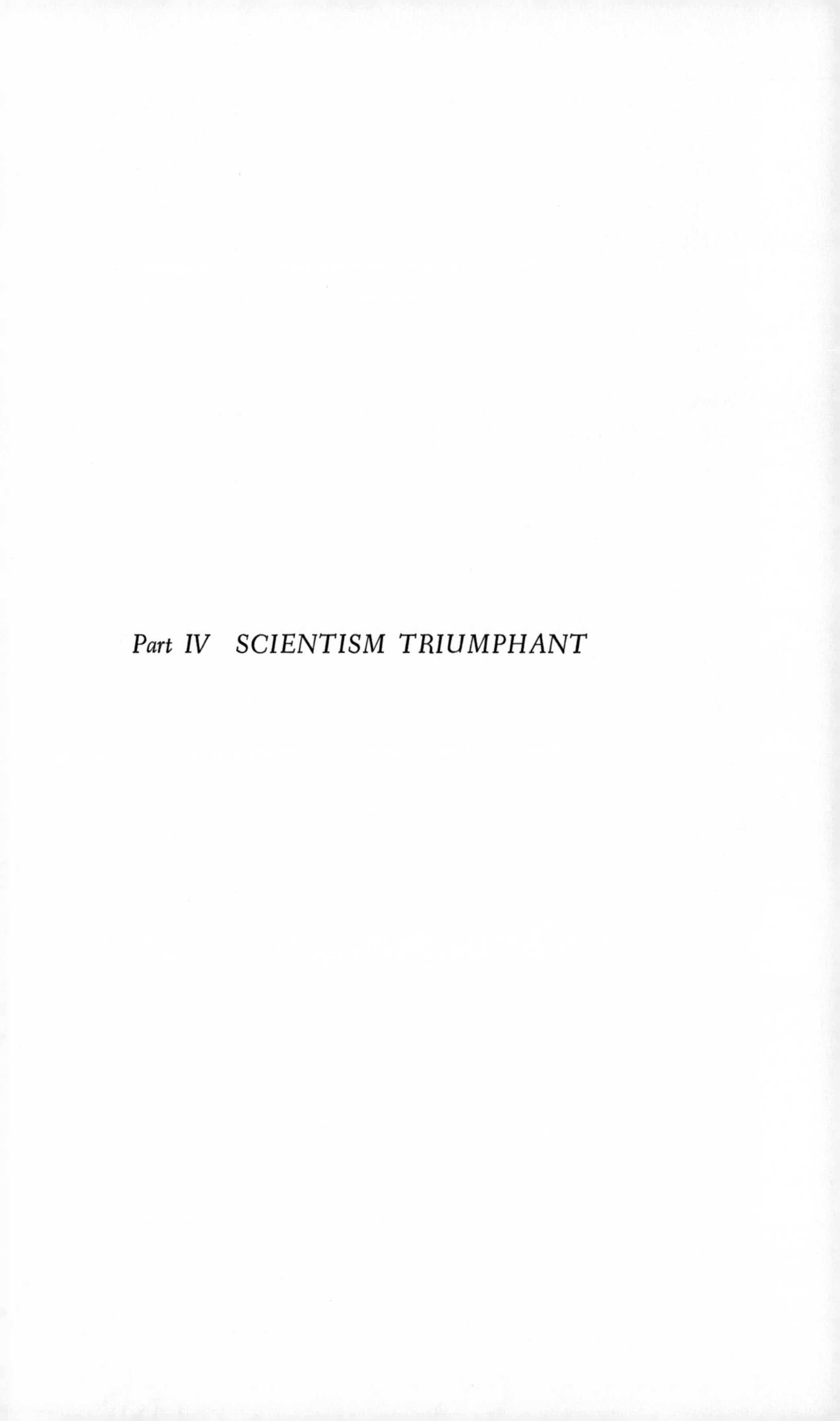

Part IV SCIENTISM TRIUMPHANT

Chapter 6 "SCIENCE" VERSUS "METAPHYSICS" IN THE DEBATE OF 1923

During the time when the term "science" became almost synonymous with modern civilization, the upholders of the traditional outlook became alarmed. Using the philosophy of life to designate a value system derived not from science but from religion, ethics, and esthetics,[1] the traditionalists challenged the monistic tendencies of the proponents of science. These forces consolidated when Professor Carsun Chang (Chang Chün-mai) of Tsing Hua University, in a speech on February 14, 1923, summoned the youth to turn away from a philosophy of life based on science. The supporters of science, with V. K. Ting as the leader, responded immediately. When the controversy was over, a polemic of some 250,000 words (not including the lengthy prefaces by Hu Shih and Ch'en Tu-hsiu) had been registered. Most of the sacred names in the different religions and the sages of various systems of philosophy were enlisted for support on one side or the other. The opponents of science were dubbed "metaphysicians" by the opposition, and sarcastic caricature of personages was given full play. The voluminous literature of the Debate was later collected into a symposium entitled *Science and the Philosophy of Life* (*K'e-hsüeh yü jen-sheng-kuan*). [2] It is important documentary evidence of the intellectual commitments of some twenty leading

1. The synonymity of the terms, philosophy of life, ethics, morality, religion, and esthetics in twentieth-century China is also emphasized by Brière in *Fifty Years of Chinese Philosophy*, pp. 88–89.

2. *KHYJSK*. Another edition of these essays, published in 1924 by T'ai-tung Book Co., Shanghai, prefaced by Carsun Chang, is entitled *The Battle of the Philosophies of Life* (*Jen-sheng-kuan chih chan*).

scholars and thinkers of modern China. Hu Shih, in characterizing the Debate, said, "Everyone joined in this discussion of Science and the Philosophy of Life. The length of the battlefront, the large number of its warriors, and the duration of the conflict all contributed to make this the first great battle in the thirty years since China's contact with Western culture." [3]

The Debate had actually been fermenting for four years before it broke into the open. Liang Ch'i-ch'ao, the prolific journalist, and Liang Sou-ming, professor of Indian and Confucian philosophies at the University of Peking, inspired the "metaphysicians" in the years between 1919 and 1923.

PRELUDE

At the end of World War I, Liang Ch'i-ch'ao, as a member of the Chinese Observers' Team in Europe, offered, upon his return to China, his assessment of the postwar European intellectual climate. His proclamation of the "bankruptcy of science" in modern civilization, as exemplified by the destruction of the War, was received enthusiastically by the antagonists of the New Thought Movement. It created a diversion from the insistence on science by Ch'en Tu-hsiu and other contributors to the *New Youth*. These comments were all the more remarkable when one recalls that Liang had urged strongly the acceptance of science as the "master teacher" of the world in the years from 1898 to 1912.[4] Now, in his *Reflections and Impressions of My European Journey* (*Ou-yu hsin-ying lu*) he spoke of the dream of the omnipotence of science, which immediately attracted numerous readers. Liang Ch'i-ch'ao indicates (in the following excerpt) many of the important themes which the participants of the Debate were to develop.

> [B]ecause of the development of science which in turn created the industrial revolution, the external life of modern man has experienced rapid and numerous changes, while his inner life has faltered and become unstable . . . Those materialist philosophers, sheltering themselves in the respectable aura of science,

3. *Nu-li chou-pao* (The Effort Weekly), no. 75 (1923).

4. See E. R. Hughes' quotation of one of Liang's 1902 articles in which he showed an unreserved enthusiasm for science in *The Invasion of China by the Western World* (New York, 1938), pp. 210–11.

have established a purely materialistic and mechanistic view of life. [They] horde all inner life and external life into the materialistic "laws of invariability [of change]." . . . Not only this, they also equate the psyche with the spirit and, in the name of experimental psychology, insist that the human spirit is but another form of matter and is thus governed by the laws of invariability. This way the freedom of will must also be denied. Without freedom of will whence comes the existence of good and evil? . . . This is the greatest danger-point of the modern intellectual world. Religion and traditional philosophy have been defeated and are in utter confusion, but this Mr. Science barges in and wants to build the great new law of the universe through experimentation. Not to speak only of this one great law, even those small laws are so newfangled that one day they are considered laws and the next they become erroneous opinions. Not only can new authority not be established, there can never be a revival of the old authority. Because of this, the whole society succumbs to doubt, depression, and fear; it resembles a ship lost in a fog without her compass . . . With things like these, hedonism and authoritarianism will receive further impetus to expand . . . Warlords and vicious financiers are all born of this process [of gobbling up the weak]. This World War is but a consummate outcome of it all.

Nevertheless, in this age of the all-powerfulness of science, the main trend of thought inclined in this direction [the belief that the materialistic universe could provide all]: those who sang the glory of science's omnipotence all wished that once science succeeded the golden world would appear. Now it must be admitted that the efforts have been rewarded; a hundred years of materialistic advance have multiplied the aggregate efforts of the past three thousand years. Mankind, however, not only did not receive happiness [as a result of science] but experienced many disasters which it brought. [We] are like travelers lost in the desert; we see a huge black shadow in the distance and strive to catch up with it, thinking that it could be relied on as a guide. But after we catch up a little, the shadow disappears and we are in utter despair. Who is this shadow? He is none other than Mr. Science.

> The Europeans have had a grand dream of the omnipotence of science, but now they are talking about its bankruptcy.[5]

Liang added a note of reservation at the end of the article: "The reader must not be mistaken [by this article] so as to belittle science; I absolutely do not recognize the bankruptcy of science, but then also I do not recognize the omnipotence of science." As to be anticipated, Liang Ch'i-ch'ao's more sober advice went unheeded. His attack on scientistic beliefs gave new life to the traditionalists; it also gave them starting points for their attack in the Debate. By indicating the gulf between inner life and external life, Liang furnished authority for them to insist on a pluralistic basis for the philosophy of life. By hinting that modern civilization was materialistic, he gave them their famous outcry that materialistic civilization was bad and spiritual civilization was good. Again, by accusing the materialistic emphasis of being responsible for the war and by proclaiming the bankruptcy of science, he enabled the "metaphysicians" to indict science as the culprit for all the bloodshed. Last, by showing pessimism because of overemphasis on science, Liang indicated the serious need for a reorientation of values.

Liang Ch'i-ch'ao, himself, was led to these conclusions by his conversations abroad.

> Since we came to Europe, this pessimistic note has filled our ears. I remember talking with a noted American correspondent by the name of Simon. He asked me, "What are you going to do after you return to China? Are you going to introduce to China some Western culture?" I said, "Of course." He heaved a sigh and said to me, "Alas, Western culture is already bankrupt." I asked him, "What are you going to do when you return to America?" He said, "When I go back, I shall shut the door and wait. I want to wait until you have introduced Chinese culture to save us." [6]

Europe's postwar pessimism brought a renewed belief in the value of China's own cultural heritage.

Liang Ch'i-ch'ao never explicitly stated that science was to be

5. Liang Ch'i-ch'ao, *Liang Jen-kung chin-chu* (Recent Writings of Liang Ch'i-ch'ao), 1st coll., 1 (1922), 19–23.

6. Ibid., p. 28. This translation is by Kiang Wen-han, *The Chinese Student Movement,* p. 42.

completely avoided. His postwar position was to urge moderation in China's response to the West. Liang, in fact, remained convinced of the benefits and merits of the scientific method and spirit. In 1922, about six months before the Debate, he wrote "Scientific Spirit and the Cultures of the East and the West" (*K'e-hsüeh ching-shen yü Tung-Hsi wen-hua*), in which he urged the Chinese to take the spirit and method of science seriously. This article also pointed to the drawbacks of the Chinese intellectual tradition—categorical designation of things, dogmatic disregard for proof, emptiness of content of study, a compromising attitude, and unsystematic treatment of knowledge—all of which could have been avoided if science had developed in China. After paying elaborate tribute to science, Liang closed the article with the statement that the scientific spirit could indeed be used to differentiate between old and new cultures but that it should not be used to discredit the Eastern civilization in favor of Western civilization.[7]

Despite Liang Ch'i-ch'ao's cautious warning, the idea that Eastern spiritual civilization was superior to Western materialistic civilization was abroad. The opponents of science in the Debate assumed this qualitative definition of the superiority of civilizations, while the scientistic thinkers made a temporal analysis, identifying Eastern civilization with an older form of heritage.

The antiscience debaters received authority for their claim from another person: Liang Sou-ming was then professor of Indian and Chinese philosophies at the University of Peking. In contrast to many others, Liang Sou-ming had never been abroad. In 1922 he published a famous book, entitled *East-West Cultures and Their Philosophies* (Tung-Hsi wen-hua chi ch'i che-hsüeh). For Liang Sou-ming, civilization was divided into three phases, corresponding to the three attitudes of life and portrayed by the three major civilizations of the Occident, China, and India. The Western attitude is characterized as striving forward and demanding progress, the Chinese approach is marked by man's desire to restrain his impulse for progress and to attain a balanced harmony of passions; the Indian outlook is noted as repre-

7. Liang Ch'i-ch'ao, "K'e-hsüeh ching-shen yü Tung-Hsi wen-hua," *Liang Jen-kung hsüeh-shu chiang-yen chi* (Collections of Liang Ch'i-ch'ao's Academic Writing), 2nd ser. (Shanghai, 1922), pp. 144–52. This was originally a speech to the Science Society of Nan-t'ung, Aug. 20, 1922.

senting man's attempt to rid himself of these desires and renounce his passions.[8]

Ruling out Indian civilization as entirely unfeasible, Liang Sou-ming did pay tribute to Occidental civilization; with its concepts of science and democracy, the West could have a serious impact on, and possibly a victory over, Oriental civilization. According to Liang, in face of this impact, the question should be whether Oriental civilization could be renovated, not whether it should be eradicated. If it could be renovated at all, it should be as a world-wide civilization for all mankind. "If it [Oriental civilization] cannot be established as a world civilization it should not exist at all. If it can exist, it should be applied not only to China, but be established as a world civilization." His culturism led to the conclusion (really a prediction): "the world civilization of the future will be rejuvenated Chinese civilization." [9]

Liang Sou-ming did not discard Occidental civilization entirely. To him science was something of merit to be conserved but also to be corrected. In the re-establishment of Chinese culture, "science would be helpful, but it must be cured of its utilitarianism and prevented from committing further crimes." Liang thought it necessary to invest the scientific spirit with the idealistic spirit of the neo-Confucianist Wang Yang-ming (1472–1528), so as to minimize covetousness and an excess of striving and want. "In short, it is necessary to reject Hindu civilization as useless, to revise radically the Occidental, and to return after criticism to our own tradition." [10]

Liang Ch'i-ch'ao and Liang Sou-ming's ideas provided much material for discussion. But it was science and the adoration of it in China which prompted all the exchanges.

THE DEBATE PROPER

Carsun Chang, a follower of the philosophies of Bergson, Eucken, and Driesch,[11] seized the trends indicated by Liang Ch'i-ch'ao and

8. Liang Sou-ming, *Tung-Hsi wen-hua chi ch'i che-hsüeh* (Shanghai, 1922), pp. 31, 71, 72.

9. Ibid., pp. 12, 199.

10. Ibid., p. 202.

11. He admitted an interest in philosophy after a call on Eucken with Liang Ch'i-ch'ao in Germany in 1919. However, he is best known as the popularizer of Bergson in China. See his self-confession in "Tsai lun jen-sheng-kuan yü k'e-hsüeh

Liang Sou-ming and, in a lecture to the students at Tsing Hua University entitled "The Philosophy of Life," indicted the tendency to regard science as all-powerful. He urged the students to turn back to a serious concern with spiritual values. No doubt he felt that the young minds were equating the respectability of science with its ability to furnish a philosophy of life.[12] For him, the philosophy of life was characterized by the inner world of the "I" vis-à-vis the external world of the "Non-I." Chang stressed that the philosophy of life was marked by its stress on subjectivity, intuitiveness, synthetic outlook, freedom of will, and uniqueness of personality; that the special attributes of science were its objectivity, logical method, analytical approach, belief in the laws of causality, and its basic assumption, the uniformity of nature.[13] Since the two were diametrically opposed to each other on all accounts, science then could never supply a philosophy of life for Chang.

The worshippers of science participating in the Debate, with the exception of Wu Chih-hui and Hu Shih, concentrated on the problem of whether science was sufficient in coping with such areas as feelings and values which enter into the philosophy of life, without defining clearly the nature of a scientific philosophy of life. In this first article, Chang also implied that, in addition to the qualitative difference between the philosophy of life as spiritually oriented, and science as impersonally oriented, there was yet a difference in civilized traditions. He stated:

> [N]o matter how developed science is, it can never solve the problems of the philosophy of life, which depends entirely on man himself and nothing more . . . the great thinkers of the past and present have all had significant contributions to this question of the philosophy of life. For instance, the school of Yang Chu accented the "I," Mo-tzu emphasized love, and Confucius and Mencius followed the doctrine of the Golden Mean.

---

ping ta Ting Wen-chiang (Again on the Philosophy of Life and Science, and also In Answer to V. K. Ting), *KHYJSK, 1*, p. 96 of 3rd art.

12. He had stressed this point earlier, blaming World War I on science and accusing the omnipotence given to science in China. See his "Ou-chou wen-hua wei-chi chi Chung-kuo hsin-wen-hua chih ch'ü-hsiang" (The European Crisis in Culture and the Direction of China's New Culture), *TFTC, 19*:3 (1922), 117–23.

13. "Jen-sheng-kuan" (The Philosophy of Life), *KHYJSK, 1*, pp. 1, 4–9 of 1st art.

> From Mencius and Confucius down to the *Li* school of Sung, Yuan, and Ming, the thinkers all gave priority to the cultivation of the inner life and hence brought about a spiritual civilization. Europe, on the other hand, for three hundred years concentrated on the control of nature by human power with the result that it produced a materialistic civilization.[14]

Chang's delineation of the battle line as the spiritual civilization of the East, confronting the challenge of the materialistic civilization of the West, played into the hands of the science supporters. Here was a serious weakness in Chang's view, as far as the outcome of the Debate was concerned. By saying that science could never support a philosophy of life, he defined science in a narrow, academic way. In doing so, of course, he revealed himself as unwilling to accept either the social implications of science for the modern age or the changes in Western thinking modern science had fostered. By calling science the cause of materialistic civilization and at the same time implying that spiritual civilization is superior, he left himself open to further attack. If Chang had confined his arguments to the metaphysical realm, the weakness would not have been so obvious. But he went on to offer solutions to the problems raised by consideration of any proper philosophy of life—namely those between spirit and matter, love between male and female, relations between the individual and society, and the relationship between nationalism and internationalism. By admitting that the philosophy of life needed a social context to be meaningful, and neglecting to examine science, whose role had undeniably brought so many social and intellectual changes (political changes also, when one considers the role that technological improvements in communication have played in nationalism), Chang was vulnerable to attack by the "scientolaters."

V. K. Ting, leading the attack on the traditionalists, added a mischievous note to the Debate by calling them "metaphysical ghosts." To him, as to his cohorts, concern with traditional spirituality, intuition, esthetics, morality, and religious feelings was a prime example of fanciful thinking as contrasted with evidential, and hence substantial, thinking. Science was popular because of the honesty of its method. Metaphysics, in the context of the counter attack, was used

14. Ibid., pp. 9–10 of 1st art.

in a derogatory sense to show that Chang Chün-mai and company were merely deceiving themselves by indulging in illusory inquiries. Ting commented, "Metaphysics is truly a shiftless ghost—having mystified Europe for more than two thousand years and finding existence difficult there in recent years, it has now [masqueraded itself] and come to China to show off and deceive people. If you don't believe this, please see Chang Chün-mai's Philosophy of Life." [15]

He questioned the contention that the philosophy of life could be separated from science, saying, "It is one thing to say that the philosophy of life cannot be unified for the present but quite another [to state] that it can never be unified" (p. 1). To Ting, unless there was factual evidence to the effect that philosophy of life could never be unified, it was the duty of the human race to try to unify it; and in doing so, man could only rely on the scientific method. Ting defined the scientific method as "none other than the classification of all natural data and the finding of order among them. After the classification and order are made clear, we use the simplest and clearest language to summarize the many phenomena, and call it a scientific law [or axiom]" (p. 3). Ting assailed Chang's rigid conception of science as an academic discipline and pointed out that Chang erred in thinking that "human life is a living matter and so cannot be treated as easily as dead matter by a single law of causation." [16] Ting cited sarcastically the realms of animals and plants which, far from being dead matter, were the subjects of such respectable disciplines as biology, zoology, and botany.

V. K. Ting denied that science could be separated from the philosophy of life and maintained that the so-called material sciences could not have meaningful differences from the so-called spiritual sciences. To illustrate this point, he presented his theory of knowledge. He believed that all real knowledge comes from sensory perception which, in turn, depends on the sense stimuli. Psychological phenomena such as emotions, thoughts, and concepts are simply products of sense stimuli and can all be studied scientifically. He used a bookcase as illustration. His eyes told him the color and shape of the

15. A long article by Ting, which appeared two months after Chang's initial charges in *Nu-li*, *48*, *49* (1923). See Ting, "Hsüan-hsüeh yü k'e-hsüeh" (Metaphysics and Science), *KHYJSK*, *1*, p. 1 of 2nd art. Pages of further citations from this long article of Ting are in the text.

16. Citing Chang in Ting, Ibid., p. 5.

bookcase, but his association and inference from former sensory experience gave him the idea that it was a bookcase (p. 7).

> [The] contents of psychological phenomena are all material for scientific study. The nature of matter that we know is but [that derived from] psychological sensory stimulation; perception leads to conception, and conception leads to inference. What science undertakes to study is nothing but these conceptions and inferences; whence comes the difference between the so-called spiritual sciences and material sciences? How can one also say that purely psychological phenomena cannot be governed by the scientific method ? (pp. 9–10.)

Ting labeled this theory of knowledge "Skeptical Idealism." In his opinion, all scientists and scientific thinkers who had studied philosophical problems (such as Huxley, Darwin, Spencer, William James, Karl Pearson, Dewey, and Mach) grasped this theory in more or less the same fashion. It is called "Idealism" because they believe that the sense stimuli are the sole basis of knowledge of the natural world. It is skeptical because they do not know the ultimate reality of a physical phenomenon save from what their sense organs tell them, and so regard it present but unknowable. On the other hand, Ting said, "This unknowable thing is what Berkeley called God, what Kant [sic] and Schopenhauer called Will, what Buchner called Substance, what Clifford called I. They never came to a common definition and method agreeable to all; each has his own mystery, while all insisted that the unknowable is knowable" (pp. 12–13). Ting obviously had no patience with the metaphysicians, but he was even more contemptuous of Chang Chün-mai and labeled him a "reincarnation of Western and Chinese metaphysical ghosts." He was accusing Chang of trying to combine the Bergsonian anti-intellectualist intuitionism of *élan vital* with the mind and conscience school of Sung and Ming philosophy in order to recall an outmoded idealistic metaphysics (p. 17). Though these are fervent accusations, Ting actually represents the dispassionate, rational, logical, scientific mind for which he was well known. For him, the sphere of metaphysical speculation shrinks as the power of science increases to such a degree that science will undoubtedly be the sole means for answering all problems of human life. "The aim of science is to eliminate from the philosophy of life preconceived and subjective ideas, the greatest enemy of the philosophy of life, [and] to search for the kind of truth that can be recognized by all. The method of science is to distinguish the falsity and truth of things, to classify all available data, and then to bring order to these data, and to use the simplest and clearest language to express them . . . Science is all-sufficient not so much in its subject matter as in its method and procedure" (p. 20).

By drawing epistemology into the argument, Ting perhaps committed an error, for he shifted the Debate to areas which had nothing to do with the original premises. Ting was to receive a ten-page retort from Chang Chün-mai on Skeptical Idealism. Much verbiage was expended on this subject[17] which, from the beginning, did not seem to have any finite and satisfactory solution.

Ting did not ignore Chang's implied charges that the spiritual civilization of the East was far better than the materialistic civilization of the West, and that the War was caused by science. He was especially sensitive to Chang's seeming equation of materialistic civilization with science; for him materialistic civilization could be considered only an effect of science, rather than its cause.

Ting's criticism of Chang's spiritual civilization is best illustrated by his own conception of the so-called spiritual civilization.

> Chang Chün-mai said, "From Confucius to Mencius to the thinkers of the *Li* schools of Sung and Ming times, the accent was on the cultivation of inner life with the result being a kind of "spiritual civilization." Let us now see the result of this kind of spiritual civilization in history.
>
> The Sung had more than just one of these *Li* scholars who advocated the art of inner control; the most obvious was the school of Lu Hsiang-shan. The scholars of the time, fortunately, still emphasized learning and had not yet become entirely addicted to empty talk. During the Southern Sung, though, it was alarming how the scholar-literati lacked ability and common sense. The result was that we were for a hundred years controlled by

17. Lin Tsai-p'ing, for instance, wrote a forty page article, "Tu Ting Tsai-chün ti hsüan-hsüeh yü k'e-hsüeh" (Having read V. K. Ting's "Metaphysics and Science"), *KHYJSK, 1,* 11th art., half of which was devoted to the problem of the theory of knowledge.

the barbarian Mongols, and the southern people were butchered by the millions, and the Han culture all but died . . . Toward the end of the Ming, the schools of Lu [Hsiang-shan] and Wang [Yang-ming] were popular everywhere. They were even more backward than the people of the Southern Sung. In their eyes, to study was a frivolous affair and a wasting away of the ambition, to attend to affairs was injurious to the dilettante ideal . . . The scholar-literati did not know the present or the past . . . like insane people they became completely ineffective in time of need. The two bandits of Shensi became the vanguards for the Manchus. The slaughtering in Szechuan by Chang Hsien-chung alone amounted to more than the total deaths in the first World War, not to speak of the atrocities of the Manchus in a few of the southern provinces. Let us ask ourselves fairly what price this spiritual civilization! (pp. 27–28.)

Ting answered the slogans of the bankruptcy of materialistic civilization:

Even if European civilization is bankrupt (actually this is not the case), the responsibility is absolutely not with science, because the main reason for bankruptcy is international struggle. As for the main responsibility for the war, it is politicians and educators who should be blamed. The majority of these two kinds of people are still not scientific.

The psychology of these people is very much like that of our Chang Chih-tung[18] in their consideration of a metaphysics as the substance and science merely as a means of application . . . They do not dare do away with science, for their industries still rely on science, and yet they incessantly try to circumvent science . . . This is the reason why their politics lack absolutely the scientific spirit, even though their industries make use of scientific invention . . . This is why the philosophy of life cannot be unified and war cannot be abolished . . . Now that the European nations have actually experienced bankruptcy because of warfare, those metaphysicians, politicians, and educators who

18. Chang Chih-tung's famous saying, "Chinese learning as substance and Western learning for application," characterizes the efforts of reform of an earlier age.

> should really bear the responsibility not only did not repent, but tried to attribute to the pure and respected name of science the sinful name of materialistic civilization (pp. 22–26).

In this article, Ting also stated that the scientific method had great benefit for the philosophy of life. He sincerely believed that the true scientific spirit was the best educator for a responsible life in this society and lived according to this belief.[19]

> Science is not only not external, it is the best tool for education and cultivation of the personality; the reason is that through the constant search for truth and the incessant desire to do away with prejudice, the men of science not only gain the ability to look for truth but also acquire the sincerity about truth. No matter what they are confronted with, they can study and analyze with dispassion, seeking the simple in the complicated and order in disorder. Their imagination increases the more their imagination is trained by logic; their perceptive power becomes more alive as this perceptive power is guided by experience. True awareness of the pleasure and happiness of life can be acquired only when the manifold relations of the universe, of the biological and psychological realms, are known. This kind of "vibrant" state of mind can be thoroughly enjoyed only by those who use the telescope to survey the vastness and infinity of the heavens and by those who use the microscope to peer into the minutia of the living world. How can this [state of mind] ever be dreamed of by those who sit meditatively talking about Zen, and by those who speculate metaphysically? (pp. 20–21.)

Quite to be expected, Chang Chün-mai retorted with a ninety-eight page article,[20] ten pages of which discussed the scientific theory of knowledge. Chang summoned the authority and respectability of such Western thinkers as Driesch, J. A. Thomson, Bergson, Urwick, H. G. Wells, Eucken, and Kant. He charged Ting with wholesale adoption of Karl Pearson's epistemology of phenomenalism, and he denied that knowledge was possible only through empirical science

19. See an elaboration by Hu Shih, "This Man Ting Tsai-chün," *Biographical Essays on Recent Men,* pp. 23–24.

20. "Again on the Philosophy of Life, and also In Answer to V. K. Ting," *KHYJSK, 1,* 3rd art

and that sense data were the only bases of knowledge. Chang quickly pointed out the weakness of the phenomenalists' position—it could not tell whether knowledge produced by science itself afforded any explanation of reality. Reality for Chang meant more than matter and sense data. Ting's contention in itself, charged Chang, showed that sensory perception could not be the only source of knowledge. He commented that the very choice of the sense data as the basis of knowledge to the exclusion of other means involved a standard of judgment, and standards of judgment were not within the scope of sensation. "If one cannot tell the difference between true and false, he cannot tell one sensation from another." [21] He cited J. A. Thomson, a scientist who admitted that the scientific method could not be the only road to knowledge, and that recognition must be given to philosophy, art, and religion.[22]

On May 30, Ting answered Chang's retort by again denying the existence of any clear delineation of the so-called spiritual sciences and the philosophy of life. According to Ting, this problem was understandable only when one discovered whether any actual difference existed between spirit and matter. Chang's separation of spirit and matter, according to Ting, could not be a mere contrast between the inner and the outer, between the I and the Non-I. His line of argument was simple: one could be spiritual when one, as I, faced the Non-I, but one could also be material if one were the Non-I and another person were in the position of the I.[23] This fallacious argument went unnoticed (the scientolater is treating man like matter now).

More important than his metaphysical arguments against Chang was Ting's statement of his religion, prompted by Chang's allegation that art, philosophy, and religion were all valid roads to knowledge. Ting was not against art, much less religion, but he opposed absolutely recognizing theology as religion.

The religious instinct resulted from the evolution of man's social nature, which is in constant conflict with the residue of the antisocial

21. Ibid., pp. 46, 56.

22. See also J. A. Thomson, *The Outline of Science*, 4 (N. Y., London, 1922), 1165–80.

23. Ting, "Hsüan-hsüeh yü k'e-hsüeh, ta Chang Chün-mai" (Metaphysics and Science, and the Answer to Carsun Chang), *KHYJSK*, 2, p. 37 of 1st art.

nature of an earlier age. Man is good or bad, depending on which instinct prevails. Besides, Ting maintained, human conflicts result from a difference in method rather than a difference in unchangeable nature. Their propensities for good or for bad are influenced by inherited gifts and then by social environment. For Ting the study of genetics is helpful in improving inherited gifts[24] and education is the all-important means of correcting and adjusting the individual to his environment. The greatest problem in education is to determine the kind of environment most conducive to making the development of the religious instinct suitable to human life. As the scientific method had proven itself so capable in the sciences, Ting maintained, it should be the chief tool in education to change the religious instinct from the blind to the self-revealing.[25]

These long and often polemical charges of the two main contenders in the Debate were but the invitation to battle, and almost all the influential thinkers of China took part. Liang Ch'i-ch'ao, who was responsible for the prelude to the Debate, appointed himself arbiter and laid down "international laws" governing the conduct of the Debate.[26] Few allowed him to perform this function, and so Liang himself contributed an article to the controversy. He assumed a middle position. "In the problem of life, there is a great part which can and must be solved by the scientific method. On the other hand, there is a small part—perhaps the most important part—which is above science." He stressed emotion as the major part of human life when he said, "All problems of life which have to do with reason must be solved by the scientific method. Those concerning feelings are absolutely beyond science."[27] Lin Tsai-p'ing, another participant, subscribed to the usefulness of the scientific method for human material needs but refused to admit that it had any control over Man.[28] These were weak allies for Carsun Chang. His only strong cohort was

24. Ting also wrote authoritatively on eugenics. See his "Che-ssu-hsüeh yü p'u-tieh" (Eugenics and Heredity), *KT*, 3:4, 5, 6 (1920, 1921), 37–44, 31–36, 7–15.

25. Ting, "The Answer to Carsun Chang," pp. 39–40.

26. Liang Ch'i-ch'ao, "Kuan-yü hsüan-hsüeh k'e-hsüeh lun-chan chih chan-shih kuo-chi kung-fa" (Concerning the International Law of the Battle of Metaphysics and Science), *KHYJSK*, 1, 4th art.

27. Liang Ch'i-ch'ao, "Jen-sheng-kuan yü k'e-hsüeh" (Philosophy of Life and Science), *KHYJSK*, 1, pp. 4, 9, of 8th art.

28. Lin Tsai-p'ing, *KHYJSK*, 1, 11th art.

Chang Tung-sun, a trained metaphysician. "Having been divorced from theology, philosophy assumes the new function of becoming a critic of science; [it] adopts the method of self-criticism and attempts to formulate higher principles which will synthesize all scientific principles . . . science is to describe, not to interpret the universe; it answers how, not why." [29]

An important participant, one of the few who tried to define science, the philosophy of life, and the relationship between the two, was an unassuming philosopher and psychologist, Fan Shou-k'ang. He seems to have been the only impartial participant in the Debate. He divided the sciences into the descriptive, especially biology and psychology, and the normative, such as ethics. The descriptive sciences told what life is, and the normative, what life ought to be. He believed that science could explain most of human life but not all of it. To him, the laws governing the facts of life were invariable, whereas those governing the ideals of life were normative and changeable. One is in the domain of science, and the other is not.[30] A philosophy of life should strike a balance between the two.

Wang Hsing-kung shared Fan's distinction between the two approaches to the philosophy of life. Unlike Fan, he further defined the content of science as merely two indispensable axioms: causality and the uniformity of nature. He argued that his definition of the philosophy of life (as composed of both the knowledge of the facts and the general outlook on life) could not escape these two axioms; hence, science is capable of solving all problems of human life.[31] Wang's strained and faulty argument illustrates well the prevailing scientism of the time.

Arrayed against the groups supporting Chang Chün-mai were such popular and notable names as Ch'en Tu-hsiu, Hu Shih, Wu Chih-hui, Jen Shu-yung, T'ang Yüeh, and Chu Ching-nung, with V. K. Ting and Wang Hsing-kung.

29. Chang Tung-sun, *K'e-hsüeh yü che-hsüeh* (Science and Philosophy) (Shanghai 1924). See English abstract by Lin Mou-sheng in "Symposium on Science and the Philosophy of Life—Abstracts and Reviews," *China Institute Bulletin*, 3:2 (1938), 48–50. Chang's book was a consummate criticism of the polemic.

30. Fan Shou-k'ang, "P'ing so-wei 'K'e-hsüeh yü hsüan-hsüeh chih cheng' " (A Critique of the so-called "Debate on Science and Metaphysics"), *KHYJSK*, 2, p. 14 of 16th art.

31. Wang Hsing-kung, "K'e-hsüeh yü jen-sheng-kuan" (Science and the Philosophy of Life), *KHYJSK*, 2, p. 16 of 10th art.

T'ang Yüeh's introductory contribution was entitled "Psychological Phenomena and the Law of Causation." [32] All phenomena, for him, are subject to the laws of causality. T'ang Yüeh implied that because all phenomena have their causes, they all come under the governance of science, which, after all, is concerned with the scheme of cause and effect and the order and relationships of matter.

T'ang was to be more explicit in his third article, "Dream-talks of a Derelict—Is Sentiment Above Science?" (Liang Ch'i-ch'ao had said that those who stated that science could explain sentiment were derelicts talking in their dreams.) T'ang called himself a derelict and explained that beauty and love (the two indispensable components of Liang's "human sentiment") could be analyzed scientifically. In this attempt T'ang adopted a truly scientistic attitude in making the reservation that "the fact that love and beauty can be analyzed has nothing to do with the degree of their value." [33] He was trying to counteract the general assumption that science deals with dead matter, and that whenever science intrudes its analysis, all things are deprived of their beauty.

T'ang was most concerned with reminding people that phenomena such as love and beauty were aspects of experience, whose data can be analyzed. These phenomena should not be held as sacred or mysterious, and hence above reason. "In matters relating to sentiment, we must rely on the extent of our reason and solve them with the scientific method. Our idea that sentiment is suprascientific comes from the immediacy of experience with sense data; but this experience is no different from all experience, and it is the starting point for science [to investigate it]." [34]

Jen Hung-chün came into the fray by declaring that whereas a science of the philosophy of life may be impossible, a scientific philosophy of life is well within reach. To him, the philosophy of life meant the pursuit of harmony between the material world and the inner world of the self. "The more the knowledge of the material world improves and becomes scientific, the more the philosophy of

32. "Hsin-li hsien-hsiang yü yin-kuo-lü," *KHYJSK,* 2, 2nd art. This was followed by four more. See Chapter 5 for a detailed treatment of his thought.

33. "I-ke i-jen ti shuo-meng," *KHYJSK,* 2, p. 2 of 9th art.

34. Ibid., p. 10 of 9th art. T'ang himself uses "givenness" elsewhere in the same article (p. 5) to mean sense datum. Science, to him, is a study of the relations between sense data and things.

life will become scientific and will be proportional to it. The most obvious example of this is the evolution theory of biology."[35] Jen stated further that not only could scientific progress indirectly change the philosophy of life, but that science could help create a kind of philosophy of life. Here he undoubtedly agreed with Ting, T'ang Yüeh, Hu Shih, and their cohorts, that although most of the scientists were nonbelievers in religion, their morality and ethics were often quite complete, their characters exemplary. The scientist's philosophy of life is influenced by his experience in scientific research. His concern with truth, causation, and factual data, according to Jen, should be applied to the philosophy of life. As a result of research, an ordered outlook on life, independent of supernatural and superstitious beliefs, becomes possible.

It is understandable that Carsun Chang's warnings about an overemphasis on the virtues of science provoked so many strong retorts from the scientists; that they should have aroused the ire of nonscientists such as Ch'en Tu-hsiu, Hu Shih, and Wu Chih-hui is evidence of the unpopularity of Chang's cause. Ch'en by this time had been totally converted to the doctrines of Communism and showed an impatience characteristic of men active in a political cause which demands a total ideological commitment. This man who had previously extolled the spirit of modern civilization and science, now as an active Communist, showed dogged devotion to the sociological conclusions of Marxism, and practically ignored its finer theoretical premises. For Ch'en, scientific laws were categorical economic laws. For specific theoretical justifications Ch'en substituted force in declaration of his belief in the social sciences. In his preface to the collection, Ch'en attacked the attitudes of almost all the participants, except that of Wu Chih-hui.[36] He saw the controversy as a belated repercussion of the spirited debates between science and metaphysics that took place over the years in Europe.

35. Jen Hung-chün, "A Science of the Philosophy of Life or a Scientific Philosophy of Life," *KHYJSK,* I, p. 4 of 6th art.

36. He attacked the metaphysicians as well as the supporters of science, the former for their dream-talks, the latter for an "inaccurate attitude" which did not advocate a scheme of linear causation. Hu Shih, his former colleague and friend in the movement for literary reform, parted ways with Ch'en before this debate was underway.

> Comte divided human society into three stages [religious, metaphysical, and scientific], and we are still in the stage of religious superstition, as can be proved by the large number of people who believe in such nonmaterial phenomena as ghosts, geomancy, incarnations and fortunetelling. We have also a large group resembling Chang Chün-mai, who believe in metaphysics, including the whole of the old scholar-literati and the majority of the new . . . Now, in the transition from the age of superstition to that of science, naturally there should be an intervening period of the absurd harangues of the metaphysician. No one can deny this societal reality [passage of society through Comte's stages]. Similarly, we cannot deny that the Comtian division of societal stages constitutes a law in the social sciences. This law can explain the differences in life-views of peoples between epochs and between societies.[37]

He criticized Carsun Chang's portrayal of the I and the Non-I to describe the spiritual and materialist worlds. Chang had enumerated nine differences between the two.[38] Ch'en found that the nine categories, contrary to Chang's contention, could all be supported by objective, immutable, and materialist laws. For instance, he contended that religious thought, belonging to the spiritual realm according to Chang, was entirely governed by the forces of time and society.

> According to the legends, all primitive societies worshipped natural objects, such as the sun, fire, high mountains, huge rocks, asps, and ferocious animals. Later on, in agricultural societies, people on the whole believed in polytheism, such as the clan spirit, ancestor spirits and agricultural gods. With the development of commerce and the progress of national unification came monotheism. When industry expanded and science advanced, atheism and antitheism followed.[39]

All problems and relations of the I and the Non-I are answerable by objective laws of the society, or more accurately, by the laws of economic development.

37. Ch'en Tu-hsiu, "Preface to Science and the Philosophy of Life," *KHYJSK, 1*, p. 4 of 1st preface.
38. See Chang's "The Philosophy of Life," *KHYJSK, 1*, pp. 2–4 of 1st art.
39. Ch'en, "Preface," *KHYJSK, 1*, 5–7.

Ch'en's critique of Liang Ch'i-ch'ao's contention that "questions of feeling and sentiment cannot be solved by science" was based on a stock determinist conviction that human feelings and emotional values are conditioned by socioeconomic laws and forces. The same criticism of dualism was applied to Fan Shou-k'ang, who believed that our knowledge needed for a philosophy of life was in part a priori and in part a posteriori. For Ch'en, the so-called a priori modes of knowing (conscience, intuition, and freedom of will, in Fan's terms) are not a priori—they are shaped by conditions of life and society. The socioeconomic conditions of various societies differ and create different moral standards and emotionally determined values, and individuals in different societies hold different things to be good and bad. Here the monistic Ch'en Tu-hsi adopted cultural relativism. There is no doubt, however, that he ultimately remained monistic. He himself said, "we believe that only objective, material causes can account for social evolution, can explain history, and can determine the philosophy of life." [40]

While Ch'en believed in monism, his former friend and colleague Hu Shih believed in pluralism. Hu said of Ch'en, in his preface to the Debate, "while we accept historical materialism as an important instrument of historical research, we must realize that thought, knowledge, education are also 'objective causes' and can also change society, explain history, and determine the philosophy of life." [41] Hu Shih thought that almost all the speakers neglected the very important question of what exactly the scientific philosophy of life was. He ridiculed Carsun Chang's metaphysics[42] but praised Wu Chih-hui for having unabashedly presented his conception of life. In Hu Shih's eulogistic appraisal of Wu's conception of life, "A New Belief's Conception of the Universe and the Philosophy of Life," [43] one may see

40. Ibid., 8–9.

41. Hu Shih, "Preface to the Debate on Science and the Philosophy of Life," *KHYJSK*, 1, p. 31 of 2nd preface.

42. As a participant, Hu wrote a satire, "Chang Chün-mai yü Sun hsing-che" (Carsun Chang and the Monkey King), *KHYJSK*, 1, 5th art. The monkey, according to that popular novel, the *Hsi-yu-chi* (Record of Western Travels), had an aerial speed of 18,000 miles per minute. Chang was described as the monkey—he made metaphysical somersaults. Hu claimed he had captured this monkey, who thought he had vaulted into never-never land.

43. The last article is by far the longest in *KHYJSK*, 2. Wu had de-emphasized the self-imposed superiority of man, and characterized human life as merely a "stage act of a bimanous animal." See Chapter 2.

what Hu Shih himself thought should be the proper outlook on life. He wrote of Wu:

> In one stroke he dispenses with God, banishes the soul, and punctures the myth that "man is the most spiritual of all things." His is the real challenge. We want to see those who believe in God defend Him against Mr. Wu. We want to see those who believe in the soul come out to defend it against Mr. Wu. We want to see those who believe in the mystery of life come out to defend it against the philosophy of life as "a stage act of two-handed animals." We want to see those who deem love as something mysterious come out and fight against the conception that love is "entirely a physiological function, and contains no mystery whatever . . ."
>
> Those of you who embrace science! In the battles to come, please study first Wu Chih-hui's "A New Belief's Conception of the Universe and the Philosophy of Life." If you agree with it, you must defend him just as Huxley defended Darwin. If you cannot agree with him entirely, please revise it, just as subsequent biologists revised Darwinism.[44]

Like Wu, Hu Shih had, before the Debate, contributed much to demonstrate his belief in science and the type of world-view to be built on it. The controversy afforded him an opportunity to elaborate his views. He was convinced that changes in the philosophy of life followed experience and common sense; hence propaganda (in the good sense of the word) and education could lend common ground for building mankind's philosophy of life. He argued that if religion, through its theism and belief in the immortality of the soul, could have united the European philosophy of life for more than a thousand years, the scientific world-view should, by analogy, also be able to achieve a basic and minimum unity through education and propaganda. Thus he believed that the imminent task was to spread and popularize this new outlook on life. With some borrowing from Wu, he set forth his new philosophy of life:

> 1. On the basis of knowledge of astronomy and physics, one should appreciate the infinity of space.

44. Hu Shih, "Preface," *KHYJSK,* 1, p. 20 of 2nd preface.

2. On the basis of knowledge of geology and paleontology, one should know the infinity of time.
3. On the basis of all the sciences, one should be aware that the universe and all things in it move and change according to natural laws—in the Chinese sense of the term, "being so of themselves"—and do not depend on a so-called supernatural Ruler or Creator.
4. On the basis of knowledge of the biological sciences, one should realize the waste and ruthlessness of the struggle for existence in the biological realm, hence the indefensibility of the hypothesis that there is a benevolent Ruler.
5. On the basis of the sciences of biology, physiology, and psychology, one should be aware that man is but another form of animal and is differentiated from other animals only in degree [of development] and not in kind [of species].
6. On the basis of the biological sciences and the sciences of anthropology, genetics, and sociology, one should understand the historical evolution of living organisms and human society, and the causes for such an evolution.
7. On the basis of the sciences of biology and psychology, one should learn that all psychological phenomena have causes.
8. On the basis of knowledge of biology and sociology, one should know that ethics and religion are always in evolution, and that the causes for this evolution can all be located by scientific methods.
9. On the basis of the new knowledge of physics and chemistry, one can find out that matter is not dead, but live; not static, but dynamic.
10. On the basis of knowledge of biology and sociology, one should realize that the individual—the Smaller Self—is susceptible to death, but humanity as a whole—the Larger Self—is undying and immortal; that religion, the highest religion, is "to live for the sake of the whole species and posterity," and that those religions which seek heaven and the Pure Land for after death are religions of the most selfish kind.[45]

45. Ibid., 25–27. This is an expansion of his earlier article, "Pu-hsiu," discussed in Chapter 4.

Such a philosophy of life, according to Hu Shih, is a hypothesis built on three hundred years of scientific knowledge. Hu Shih would have called it a scientific philosophy of life, but for reasons of argument he called it a naturalistic philosophy of life.

Thus the atheist Hu Shih also in one stroke wiped out the existence of God and the immortality of the soul. And, like Wu Chih-hui, he presented a concrete philosophy of life based on knowledge of science. The antiscience thinkers had been ridiculed; more than that, they had been presented with competing philosophical systems. Hu Shih and Wu Chih-hui were able to take the popular success of science and build upon it a meaningful philosophy for guidance toward an unselfish life. This appealed enormously to the majority of old and young progressive thinkers during the critical years of search for a meaningful framework.

ASSESSMENT

In scanning the heavy verbiage of the Debate, one gains the impression that something important was being discussed, but that a central frame of reference was lacking in individual writings. The confusion of purpose, however, does not preclude the fact that several salient themes can be detected.

The basic contention was that of the priority of mind over matter. A corollary to this was the less philosophical contention that Eastern civilization was spiritual, while Western civilization (molded by science) was materialistic. The philosophers and metaphysicians argued strongly in favor of the existence of another world beyond the immediate world of the senses. Mind, according to them, was free and independent of the external world and was capable of forming ideals of life by itself. The scientists (including some nonscientists) repudiated this inner world of being. For them the external world of the senses determined the shape and content of mind and consciousness.

It is curious to find in these elaborate essays few attempts to analyze the nature of either mind or matter. This probably happened because both sides were facing a choice of value systems in this transition from a traditional to a modern orientation. The question of mind versus matter shed its more profound philosophical meaning and became a practical concern with the ideals and realities of life. Those who saw in China's transition a threat to traditional values were quick to point out the evils of a materialistic outlook and civilization. In order to survive, the national heritage with its highly spiritual development needed to be kept intact.

This group was opposed by those who saw the need to adopt the spirit which had strengthened and modernized the West. The former group willingly maintained a sharp division between the inner and outer life. What concerned the inner life should be discovered by intuition and inspiration; the realities of life should be studied scientifically. The scientists believed that both aspects of life, ideals and realities, must be viewed as one. Their conception of life was not individual but holistic, considering that ideals and realities interact. The task of science was to discover the realities of life and to examine the ambitions and desires of man, the social being. Science, further, was to find the means to satisfy these ambitions, desires, and needs. Science, to them, had the dual role of making clear the realities and realizing the ideals of human life.

Behind the argument about mind and matter—called ideals and realities—we see the re-enactment of the controversy between the rational and the empirical modes of thought which had characterized Chinese thought in the Sung and Ming periods and European thought in the eighteenth century. For the rationalists, true knowledge could be gained by deduction from a priori concepts and ideas; empiricists believed that truth could be obtained only from experience and perception, organized by observation and experimentation, virtues of the inductive method. For the former, true knowledge is the product of the rational intuition and does not need empirical verification. Sensory impressions were considered almost without value as compared with intuition and deduction. For the latter, no fact could be assumed to be true that has not been empirically verified. Furthermore, the scientists denied the validity of ethics, esthetics, and religion, for these are arrived at by intuition and inspiration, not by the scientific method.

The debaters had more at stake than philosophical disputation, for the role of China in the modern world was also under discussion. The question of deciding between the spiritual East and the materialistic West was a constant preoccupation. In the past, China had tried to combine the spirituality of her old civilization with those very aspects of the technology of the West which were revealing the inadequacy of China's material resources. From about 1900 until the Debate, opinion favored adoption of the scientific spirit of the West, because it was realized that guns and manufactured goods were merely the by-products of a civilization possessing a progressive spirit. Hence, the verdict of victory and defeat for either mode of civilization must be seen in light of the spiritual premises and not the material results which the two sides advocated.

Science emerged stronger than before, not so much because of the impressive names of its advocators or the general antireligious feeling in China, but because of the popularity of the scientific method itself. The scope of science was widening; it now covered aspects of natural and social life, and its possible boundaries were constantly being pushed back. The scientists seemed to have the key to the imponderables of life and the universe. The philosophers lost ground because of their unpopular way of offering solutions to the problems of human life. Their answers were, at best, speculations. The modern world demanded objectivity as the criterion for judgment of truth, honesty, reliability, and hence respectability.

To the philosophers, "philosophy of life" meant the outlook of an individual, who was not considered a component part of society and was still expected to accept the framework of transcendental values. To the believers in the scientific spirit the philosophy of life will be loftier if it is enriched by knowledge of the cosmos as well as of the immediate world. Individual life, to them, forms an inseparable part of social life. In order to be understood, society must be seen in light of the impulses and desires of its components, and individuals must be seen in light of the environment's molding forces. The scientists fought for the intellectual ascendancy of the scientific method and claimed the superiority of science in providing a conception of life, best stated as a conviction of social immortality.

In temper and in the pride shown in the "new method of science" as against the old, the Debate is reminiscent of the crisis of intellectual choice in seventeenth-century Europe between the "ancients" and the "moderns." [46] The difference, of course, is that the Debate in China

46. Fontenelle's terms to denote the superior scientist-philosophers, who were affecting the progress of knowledge, and the inferior ancient philosophers and

was complicated by the added dimension of conflicting values and cultural preferences of East and West. During these years of transformation, China was politically, economically, militarily, and technically pressed into disadvantage by the very culture whose scientific heritage she was trying to adopt. With this element—the cross-cultural movement of ideas—present, the Debate frequently seemed superficial. What it lacked in depth, it made up for in fervor. The problem of the modern transformation of China was urgent.

There was no arbiter in this Debate to pronounce the winners and losers. Thus it would seem futile to find specific evidence for maintaining that science emerged from this polemic more popular than before. If the continuation and intensification of scientism in years after the Debate are any criteria, then the side of science won. The supporters of science had received considerable help—the prestige of science itself had been accumulating for three centuries.

---

medieval scholastics. See further treatment of this "crisis" in seventeenth-century European thought in Franklin Baumer, ed., *Main Currents of Western Thought* (New York, 1952), pp. 249–57, 351–54.

Chapter 7 AFTER THE DEBATE: DOCTRINAL FINALITY

Scientism intensified rather than slackened during the decades after the Debate. Drawing upon the elements of scientism of the past thirty years, the intellectual and emotional attachment to science-as-doctrine grew in size and became the dominant theme in the thought of the day. "Science worship" describes well this expansive phenomenon of the '30s and '40s. The popularity of science progressed with the maturing of new scientific scholarship (in the physical and social sciences, but more in the idea than in the fact of the latter). The sheer force of events from the second half of the '20s on fanned the already existing sentiment into an intense mood of positivism.

Thinkers and students, caught in a restive nationalism, waited with inordinately high hopes for the outcome of the Nationalist-Communist struggle, at first veiled, but becoming an open rupture in 1926–27, to provide a solution for China. The intelligentsia contemplated a continuing revolution (now social, as well as political). Much rode on the victor, for whoever won this struggle had the responsibility of satisfying the largest notion of revolution possible. When victory came to the Nationalists, it came, as politics of the day went, from a power struggle. It left the question of social doctrines unanswered, and this disappointed a number of the intelligentsia. On the intellectual level, this dissatisfaction was strong among men (including non-Communists) who thought that their aspirations were thwarted because of the political failure of the Communists and less prevalent among those who saw in the Nationalists' victory at least a qualified success, and who hoped for a better future in some kind of unity. The combined effect of these dissatisfactions was an outbreak of new debates. The new intellectual "multilogues" turned to questions of the nature of Chinese history and society and to the nature of the century-old Western impact on China. In mood, the preference was definitely for a set of positive doctrines, whose determinism, many hoped, would push China to the correct solution. Dialectical materialism seemed a singularly appropriate doctrine to account for the so-called contradictions in events and aspirations of the times and became dominant within the general school of philosophical materialism.

Even in academic philosophical circles, the events of the times had an indirect influence on the direction of thought. Pragmatic and utilitarian ways of thinking which reached a height of popularity about 1923–24 now gradually yielded to the new idealism forming at Peita and to the new realism at Tsing Hua. The new realism was to merge into the materialism of the larger world of thought. The former fought valiantly to "make philosophy safeguard science." In the larger world of thought, as against academic philosophy, the cautious pragmatism of the '20s now lost to materialist positivism its portion of materialist scientism as well as its prestige.[1] We shall see in this chapter the growing vogue of materialist scientism; its positive conclusions were easily available and all but discredited the less rigid tenets of other intellectual systems.

POLEMIC ON THE HISTORY AND NATURE OF CHINESE SOCIETY

If the ground for this debate had been prepared by the decades of "doubting" China's past, it had also been prepared by the concomitant growth of faith in the efficacy of the scientific method in not only understanding social problems but also studying societal configurations—the nature and history of total societies. When the polemic began in 1928, its participants did not approach China's past in the cellular manner of the debate on ancient history, which began in 1926,

1. For fuller treatment of the academic world of thought, see Sun Tao-sheng, "Hsien-tai Chung-kuo che-hsüeh chih chieh-p'ei" (An Analysis of Contemporary Chinese Philosophy), *KWCP*, 12:45 (1935), 6 pp.

led by Ku Chieh-kang.[2] The 1928 polemic's method and theme can be found in Marxism. The participants expected to make Chinese history and society conform to the laws of the dialectical development of society, thus merging it with universal history and lending it cosmic meaning. The participants all considered themselves scientists of society, working out a methodological explanation of Chinese history.

The polemic was also more prolonged and involved more persons than the Debate of 1923. It lasted into the late 1930s and affected numerous books and articles,[3] reflecting the keen intellectual concerns in this time of political change. The pressing need to find accurate and reliable intellectual guidelines, with enough status in modern times the primary requirement, is clearly seen in the Preface to the large collection of essays on the nature of Chinese history and society. Wang Li-hsi, editor of the collection, summed up the feelings of all the polemicists:

> The present is no longer an age when a spontaneous peasant rebellion such as that of Ch'en Sheng and Wu Kuang [who overthrew the Han] can seize ruling power.
>
> At the same time, the present is no longer a period in which a tyrant . . . can suppress revolutions.
>
> The present is the time when blind and undirected revolutions have reached a blind alley, the time when the momentum of revolution can no longer be suppressed and therefore there is

2. A good exposition of this spirit of doubt is in the series of articles and letters concerning ancient history that appeared in the *Tu-shu tsa-chih,* a supplement of *The Effort Weekly,* involving mostly Ku Chieh-kang, Hu Shih, and Ch'ien Hsüan-t'ung. Ch'ien, especially, was noted for his disbelief in the authenticity of the past and often signed himself as I-ku Hsüan-t'ung (the doubting Hsüan-t'ung). In 1926 under the urging of the P'u-she of Peking, Ku Chieh-kang collected these writings, along with others, into the famous *Ku-shih pien* (Debates on Ancient History). He edited the next two collections in 1930 and 1931. This series, under other editorship, continued for four more collections. Ku's famous autobiographical preface to the collection is translated by A. W. Hummel, *The Autobiography of a Chinese Historian* (Leiden, 1931).

3. A count (by no means inclusive) in 1931 gives 36 books and 44 articles involving 14 journals. None of T'ao Hsi-sheng's many articles in *New Life* is included in this count. See Wang Li-hsi, "Preface" *Tu-shu tsa-chih,* 1:4-5 (1931), 18-23. This collection (abbreviated *TSTC* and not to be confused with its namesake described in n. 2) was merely the first of the writings on the debate.

> dire need of *correct* revolutionary theories to guide *correct* revolutions onto their new path. In the absence of revolutionary theory, there is no revolutionary action to speak of [following Lenin] . . .
>
> In order to search for the correct future revolution, we must first decide on the solution to a foremost problem: "Upon what stage has Chinese society already embarked?" [4]

The last sentence shows clearly the revolutionary urgency of the times. It also reveals the inextricable closeness of the nature of the "present stage" of Chinese society with a fundamental theory of societal development. From the nineteenth century on, viewing whole societies as typologically belonging to certain periods of man's history became a common practice of the new sociology; all revolutionary successes and failures were to be analyzed and accounted for by the language of this societal science. Thus, if a revolution failed to turn a society into the bourgeois stage, it is because of the continued presence of feudal elements of the previous stage.

The view of society's advancing in stages delineated by conflicts and struggles is an integral assumption of the idea of progress, which the operations of science itself have helped mold. The Marxist view of history and societal development, a part of the idea of progress, is the most dynamic theory of society to come out of the modern scientific heritage. Classical economists, with whom Marx shared the essential progressive outlook of the nineteenth century, with its epoch-making and custom-shattering industrial and technological advances, had chosen their discipline as the best method to try and understand society.

The study of economics revealed enough of the injustices and ugliness of society to earn for itself the reputation of a "dismal science." At the same time, however, it was thought to be an effective method for determining the "real" causal nexus of society. Marx, both the child and "scientist" of nineteenth-century European industrial society, could say, "In broad outline, we can designate the Asiatic, the ancient, the feudal, and the modern bourgeois modes of produc-

4. Ibid., pp. 1–2.

tion as so many epochs in the progress of the economic formation of society."[5] This passage from his "Preface" to *A Contribution to the Critique of Political Economy* became one of the most celebrated and quoted maxims of theoretical Marxism. His followers were quick to seize upon the note of scientific finality that such a statement about societal development seemed to contain. Economics was found to determine social character and societal movement; this economic determinism became synonymous with historical materialism—a group of laws explaining the entirety of human progress. Economic determinism was part of the general stream of Western thought by late nineteenth century. When Lenin revived Marxism in 1917, the Bolshevik Revolution became proof to many that the "union of theory and practice" could be achieved.

In China, Marx's law of economic determinism sparked an imagination already revolutionary in nature and temper. Nineteenth-century European industrialism, the laboratory of modern social science, did not even exist in the China of the 1920s. The dual appeal of Marx's theory and Lenin's capacity to turn it into action and success, however, gave many thinkers direction as they considered the past, present and future of China. The first laws of what we may call "social scientism" were that economic factors were at the basis of society and that revolutionary activities were signposts of basic changes in the mode of production (successful Leninist revolutions leading, moreover, to progress). Unsuccessful revolutions, such as that of the Nationalists in 1926–27 which disappointed many, gave added credence to Lenin's dictum, "without a correct revolutionary theory, there can be no revolutionary practice."[6]

The polemicists competed with each other in applying this first law of societal dynamics to Chinese history. The debate was not restricted to convinced Communists; Kuomintang theorists used the same scheme of argument. It was important to be considered the rightful heir and executor of a respectable and accurate theory of society.

5. Marx, *A Contribution to the Critique of Political Economy* (Chicago, 1904), p. 13.

6. It should be remembered that the '20s saw debates outside of China. In Russia, such "China experts" as Madyar and Radek led a petulant academic debate on Chinese society, its nature and history. Japan, too, at this time encountered the Marxian view of social history and has carried the discourse into the present.

The debaters took sides using the theories of two men, T'ao Hsi-sheng and Kuo Mo-jo. The theories of others are also worthy of note, those of Li Chi, Wang Li-hsi, Hu Ch'iu-yüan, Liang Yüan-tung, and Ch'en Pang-kuo. The two camps of combatants are usually identified with T'ao Hsi-sheng's *New Life* and the *New Thought Tide* groups. Important differences in assigning a name to the "present stage" of China's social development are evident. The former labeled it capitalism (with variants); and the latter designated it feudalism (also with variants).[7] This was, however, *not* a debate between different systems of thought. The similarity of language, theoretical assumptions, and beliefs reveals it as a debate within the same system. In it can be seen the degree to which this most dynamic social science had worked its way into Chinese intellectual premises.

T'ao Hsi-sheng (b. 1899), a well-known professor of the history of Chinese society, had been a publisher and long-time supporter and theoretician of the Kuomintang. Amidst his vast writings on Chinese society based on dialectical materialism, was the much-revised theory: Chinese society during the Western Chou was the last tribal age, with tribal relations differing from the commonly assumed feudal relations; the period from the Warring States through the Later Han was an economic stage based on slavery, an institution common in the cities as well as in the country; the time from the Three Kingdoms through the post-T'ang brief rules, was a fully developed feudal and manorial epoch; from the Sung on there was a period of the dissolution of the huge estates. Thus, an age of feudalism gave way to the urban handicraft economy of the cities, called precapitalist. Finally, after 1840, a period of semicolonialism bowing to industrial capitalism.[8]

The explanation for these changes was in economic terms. T'ao had started *The Bi-Weekly Economic Journal* (*Shih-huo pan-yüeh-k'an*), with its avowed goal to explain history by means of economics, just

7. For an excellent treatment of the debate on the "present" stage and nature of Chinese history and its Soviet involvements, see B. Schwartz, "A Marxist Controversy in China," *FEQ*, 13 (1954), 143–53. See also Ho Kan-chih, *Chung-kuo ch'i-meng yün-tung shih* (A History of China's Enlightenment Movement) (Shanghai, 1947), pp. 159–93.

8. See his "Chung-kuo she-hui hsing-shih fa-ta kuo-ch'eng ti hsin ku-ting" (A New Evaluation of the Developmental Patterns of Chinese Society), *TSTC*, 2:7–8 (1932), 2nd art.

prior to his re-evaluation of Chinese societal stages. His authority was Marx's *Das Kapital*.[9]

Such was also the scheme of another debater: to give past Chinese historical development a meaning according to the Marxian dialectic. Kuo Mo-jo is a literary figure and intellectual who weathered the mid-century political change to become spokesman of culture in contemporary China. In his study of Chinese social history, he contributed a persistent use of historical materialism to Chinese thought. From his study of oracle bones and ancient bronzes ("documents" for the study of Chinese antiquity), which he combined with the dialectical view of history, Kuo divided Chinese history as follows: pre-Chou is primitive-communal; Western Chou is slave society; Eastern Chou and on is feudal; the last hundred years have been capitalistic. He noted three major social revolutions caused by changing modes of production: The revolution establishing slavery, the revolution establishing feudalism, and the revolution erecting capitalism.[10]

The third variation along the same theme was provided by Li Chi and argued in a lengthy article in the *Reader's Miscellany* (*Tu-shu tsa-chih*). To him, pre-Shang is primitive communism, Shang is a society of the "Asiatic mode of production," Chou is feudal, Ch'in to 1840 is precapitalistic, and the period from 1840 on is capitalistic.[11]

Other variations, all attempting to locate Chinese historical divisions that would suit Marx's categories are numerous. Wang Li-hsi and Hu Ch'iu-yüan tried to incorporate Marx's "Asiatic mode of production" into their theories. Both found pre-Shang society primitive-communal, Shang a clan society, and Chou feudal. They designated the period from Ch'in to late-Ch'ing as despotism.[12]

Just about all possible meanings were given to Marx's "types" of

9. See acknowledgment in his *Chung-kuo she-hui shih* (A History of Chinese Society) (Chungking, 1944), preface. This Kuomintang theorist still believed in this mode of dividing society at this late date.

10. Kuo Mo-jo, *Chung-kuo ku-tai she-hui yen-chiu* (Studies on Ancient Chinese Society) (Peking, 1960), pp. 20–21, a reprint of a 1954 revised edition of the 1929 original. Kuo's classification of society had not changed, however.

11. "Tui-yü Chung-kuo she-hui-shih lun-chan ti kung-hsien yü p'i-p'ing" (Contributions and Criticisms Regarding the Debate on Chinese Social History), *TSTC*, 2:2–3 (1932), 3rd art.

12. See Wang, "Chung-kuo she-hui hsing-t'ai fa-chan-shih chung chih mi-ti shih-tai" (The Age of Myths in the Developmental Patterns of Chinese Social History), *TSTC*, 2:7–8 (1932), 1st art.

society manifesting changing economic formations. Arguing the interpretations of every age, the monotonous "multilogue" proceeded. New terminology appeared, such as Mei Ssu-p'ing's "Struggle of the Races" for the period preceding T'ang and Yü, "Primitive Imperialism" from Hsia through Chou, "New Feudalism" for Chou through Ch'in, and "Commercial Capitalism" from Ch'in to late-Ch'ing.[13] Tai Hsing-shao called the whole period from Ch'in to late-Ch'ing "a society in transition." [14] When this era of two thousand years is called transitory, simply because it did not fit theoretical requirements, the disregard for history is only matched by the scientistic belief in pseudo-scientific laws of societal progress. Undoubtedly, the relentless periodizing of Chinese history was to make the past meaningful to the present. But, since the "good" and "bad" of past Chinese culture were seen according to the dialectic, and not as the past culture shaped them, such attempts to link present and past China with a satisfactory "chronologic" would seem to end in meaninglessness.

This controversy, whose style has been touched upon but whose substance will have to await separate discussion, set the tone of scientism throughout the subsequent decades. At the same time it illustrates how the intellectual predilection had given way or rather, developed into the scientism of society. Social science, in general, assumes that society can be analyzed; social scientism believes that whole societies can be analyzed according to predetermined laws. The spirit of the two is the same, guided by the thought that methods explaining scientific reality could be employed to explain man and society with equal and incontestable results.

The debate reveals the inheritance of Western positivistic scientism. The works of Morgan on the American natives (*Ancient Societies*, 1877), Marx and Engels (most notably Engels' *Der Ursprung der Familie, des Privateigentums und des Staats* [*The Origin of the Family, Private Property and the State*], 1884), and Lenin, in addition to the writings of contemporary Soviet scholars, were quoted as if they were scientific maxims. Such works, of course, have meaning and value in the context of the individual society under consideration.

13. Mei Ssu-p'ing, *Chung-kuo she-hui pien-ch'ien ti kai-lüeh;* noted in Kuo Chan-po, *Chinese Intellectual History of the Past Fifty Years*, p. 337.

14. Tai, "Chung-kuo kuan-liao cheng-chih ti mo-lo" (The Demise of Chinese Bureaucracy), *TSTC*, *1:4–5* (1931), 13th art.

The industrial society of nineteenth-century Europe was revealed with clarity in its component parts and their relationship to previous stages of the European past.

The Chinese reconsideration of history carried a commitment to the idea of social science. They went beyond their Western paragons to portray Chinese traditional society according to "proven" models. They went beyond their Eastern compatriots who, by worshipping science unabashedly, had contributed a stream of scientism that did not, as social scientism does now, necessarily belong to a single mode of interpreting events, persons, and their social organizations.

With this controversy came also an intensification of materialistic, positive scientism that was to affect much of the thinking of the next twenty years. The participants believed they had found the indisputable tool with which to study human affairs. Kuo Mo-jo wrote in 1929, in the preface of his *Studies on Ancient Chinese Society,* "At this time [when traditional materials and explanations no longer correspond to reality], the Chinese people ought to wake up and fill in the words of this unwritten portion of the world's cultural history. Foreign scholars have already paved the road for us. We have a task already made easy and so ought to contribute doubly to the final product. The nature of this book can be said to be the continuation of Engels' *Der Ursprung der Familie, des Privateigentums und des Staats.* Its methodology uses him as a guide." [15]

The style of the controversy also demonstrates that the participants accepted the view of linear, unmitigated progress inherent in the outlook born of a "scientific heritage." Such a view of historical progress has a built-in criticism of the past. This impatient disregard for the past is all the more obvious, crudely handled as it was in the debate. Study of the past only lent meaning to interpretation of the present; the whole framework of Chinese civilization must be neglected in order to accommodate a linear view of societal progress. Most of China's past, in which social science was unknown, became merely "transitory." Traditional Chinese culture was explained as individual manifestations of class interest and function; the flavor of the culture was lost in the proving of theories. The scientistic critique of China's traditional past is, of course, conditioned by its own preconceptions.

15. *Ancient Chinese Society,* preface, pp. 4–5.

The new orientation in linear time was accompanied in the West, and in China somewhat later, by a new methodology. A "scientific method for the study of society" ends in vindicating the methodology itself along with its premises. The definition of scientism earlier refers to the unwavering belief in the power of the scientific method to bring knowledge of the various aspects of the natural order. Now, China's scientists of society, intent upon satisfying this new-found faith, actually reorganized history to suit their new-found method.

The demise of traditional China and the lessening of the humanistic approach to its historic culture can be explained, at least in part, as a true revolution in methodology and historical outlook. This intensifying mood of materialist scientism appeared more frequently in the coming years and eventually eliminated the more cellular and less deterministic vocabulary.

THE "INDEPENDENT" MATERIALISTS

The *Reader's Miscellany* represented Marxian dialectical thought and material scientism. Other journals carried the views of those who called themselves materialistic philosophers, and who put much stock in philosophizing on more or less the same premises as the Marxists. *Twentieth Century, Research and Criticism* (*Yen-chiu yü p'i-p'an*), and *Collections of Writings on Science* (*K'e-hsüeh lun-ts'ung*) carry this spirit most clearly. The editorial mastermind of all three publications was Yeh Ch'ing (penname for Jen Cho-hsüan) who had frequent assistance from Yang Po-k'ai, Liu Ching-pai, Shen Yin-ming, and Chang Fan-fu. In general, members of this group were not well liked in academic circles because of their penchant for interminable polemics and criticism of other schools. They may have lacked in scholarly timidity, however, but they made up for it by considering themselves full-fledged members of modern China's intelligentsia, free to speak out on a broad range of general matters.

They believed, as did so many intellectuals and scholars of the time, that contemporary Chinese thought, notably after 1927, ought to propagate their own correct scientific methodology and criticize the three decades of imported thought. Most of these men favored a division of modern Chinese history into three stages. The first goes from either the Sino-Japanese War of 1894–95 or the Reform of 1898 to either 1911 or the May Fourth years and describes the crumbling ways of old thinking accompanied by gradual importation of the new. In the second stage, from May Fourth (or 1919) to 1927, the major mode of thought was colored by the capitalist touches of imported, Western origins. The third stage, all agreed, was the stage of dialectical materialism which began after the 1926–27 "failure." [16] These independent materialists who had no party alignment illustrate the general stream of scientism. As other thinkers, discussed in the early chapters, helped to build the empirical and materialist aspects of scientism, these material monists lived the religion of scientism, quarreling and criticizing each other much in the fashion of theological disputants. Yeh Ch'ing and his group not only advocated a new kind of Marxian thought but also criticized all previous thought. They were prolific, and their writings appeared in a few specific journals.

The earliest and leading journal of this group is the *Twentieth Century*. The first issue appeared in 1931. It contained very long articles by Yeh Ch'ing and Ju-sung. Further journals appeared, such as *Research and Criticism*, a sister publication. By far the most important is the series known as the *Collections of Critiques* (*P'i-p'an ts'ung-shu*), also masterminded by the prolific Yeh Ch'ing. This ambitious publication program was centered in the Hsin-k'en Book Store of Shanghai. It came out in two series; the first, Series A, a criticism of modes of thought of Western origin, and the second, Series B, criticized individual thinkers. Series B appeared in 1933, before Series A, and dedicated its first issue to an uncomplimentary dissection of Hu Shih, who was to many the main entrepreneur of Western ideas in China. Yeh Ch'ing himself wrote the attack in two volumes, one 524 pages long (1933) and the other 1,120 pages long (1934).

This school clearly indicated its intent and premises in the "publication announcement" of the *Twentieth Century*. Its publishers called it a "theoretical publication based on science, criticism, and synthesis." On the premise that man is a creator of history, the writers of this school tried valiantly to discard the mechanistic determinism of philosophical materialism. Only by using dialectic theories of explaining history can man be seen as a creative agent. It should be noted that

16. See Hsia Cheng-nung, *Hsien chieh-tuan ti Chung-kuo ssu-hsiang yün-tung* (The Present State of China's Intellectual Movement) (Shanghai, 1937), p. 200. Kuo Chan-po, *Chinese Intellectual History*. Ho Kan-chih states that after 1928 the mode of thought of the debate was the dominant theme. (A History of China's Enlightenment Movement) (Shanghai, 1947), pp. 158–59.

Marxist thought did not resolve the question of the "father and son" of historical laws of causation. Marx himself, in stressing that man's history is the product of forces (therefore man is the object, the "son" of history), nevertheless has also said that, at the point of synthesis, man should liberate himself from the external forces which suppress him (thus man is the subject, the "father" of history).[17] Marx's conception of man as capable of creative revolution was seized upon by the *Twentieth Century* writers, who looked upon themselves as apostles of an established "religion" of science and tried throughout their writings to show up the paralysis of mechanical determinism. Their efforts at fusing the religiosity and philosophy of scientism paved much of the way to the final unification of theory and practice in China in 1949. Meanwhile, in the dynamic spirit of science, the *Twentieth Century* opened with these remarks:

> Man makes history . . .
>
> As for the process of development in history, we can see, if we are willing to be assisted by the truthful proof of various material and natural sciences, that this brilliant world, though containing much darkness, is especially suited for man's creative will and needs particularly his creative activities.
>
> The reason is that society has a structure which is systematic and obedient to laws. Its various components during the developmental process must be mutually adaptable and must be, especially, changed as a whole on a uniform basis. Such processes resemble the situation that occurs when one part of an organism changes and brings about the change of the entire organism.
>
> Therefore, only from observation of science can we obtain conclusions which complement those derived from analyzing the historical process . . . Ever since science started with Bacon, all imponderable things, such as God, soul, and so on, have been driven outside of nature, society, and the pineal gland [mind]. It

17. See, for instance, *The German Ideology,* ed. R. Pascal (New York, 1939), p. 29, and Marx and Engels, "Third Thesis on Feuerbach," *Gesamtausgabe,* abt. I, bd. 5. For a clear statement of this view of man's purposiveness within his environment, see Julian Huxley, "The Uniqueness of Man," *Man Stands Alone* (New York, 1941)

> [science] alone supports the entire realm of knowledge, and all processes. All social activities and all the spiritual workings have become the object of science and have entered the domain of science.
>
> Under such conditions, the world of nature, the world of society, and the world of knowledge are all united and form one large system. In other words, science and philosophy are not mutually exclusive; the huge gulf between natural science and social science has been filled . . . Cosmology and the philosophy of life must be united. What is this new science? It is an active view of nature, an active view of society, an active view of economics, an active view of politics, and an active view of ethics.
>
> Matter has been annihilated! [18]

After declaring the annihilation of matter, however, Yeh says that his new science is based on the new theories, laws, and spirit of the new physics. Moreover, "matter which the new physics studies is the basis of all phenomena. No living and willful beings can escape this. Even man with his biological and psychological nature and actions—indeed all social phenomena—is included totally in physical change. Its theories [of matter] are the Bible and law of all things. Therefore, the new theories of the new physics are the revolutionary signal for science, social science, and intellectual science." [19]

The seeming contradiction in declaring both the annihilation of matter and in stressing its importance in the new physics is resolved when one realizes the enormous emphasis this school puts on the power of *theory*. Yeh himself says, "Contradiction is the activator of progress; theoretical discussion can lead to further elucidation of truth." [20] The seeming contradiction is as dialectical as one can find. In his "Preface to the Critique of Political Economy," Marx postulates that man's consciousness is determined by his social existence (material conditions, including forces such as ideas and intentions), while elsewhere he exhorts men to create their own golden world. This

18. "Erh-shih shih-chi ch'uang-k'an yen" (Preface to the *Twentieth Century*), *ESSC*, *1:1* (1931), 1–3.
19. Ibid., 8.
20. Ibid., 7.

Promethean image of man is ever-present in Marx, the theoretician and the revolutionary; so it was with materialists of the '30s and '40s in China. Here, in the Marxian image of man, the creator, the Chinese theorists saw a body of new thought and a new way to think. China, too, was a world imperfect enough and plagued by enough contradictions to warrant revolutionary change. All that was needed now was the correct theory, and Yeh and company believed they possessed the way to explain and cure China's ills. With Marx, and now with the *Twentieth Century* group, we cannot identify the emphasis on man's powers to create with a belief in freedom of the will. The effectiveness of creative ideas was to mean the efficacy of theories to explain and condone social change. The creative force and reputation of these theories could not be questioned, because they were scientific and based on material facts. Science was once again summoned to serve as final arbiter. From the materialist and mechanist determinism of crude materialism, then, a new dynamism arose. Yeh Ch'ing and his school talked in terms of a science of society with lessons and conclusions gained from science proper, but they also talked as if the holder of such knowledge should be a revolutionary in the criticism of all old and unsympathetic notions. The letter and spirit of scientism are now consciously united in the '30s and '40s.

That this union was a conscious one can be seen in the second plank of the proposed platform of the *Twentieth Century,* criticism. There was criticism, as Yeh lashed out at China's working scientists as well as at proponents of the scientific outlook for being ignorant of "true" science. Liang Ch'i-ch'ao was scolded for identifying science with Western imperialism, Hu Shih for his vagueness about mechanistic determinism and individualism, V. K. Ting for knowing only the objectivity (and not the subjective, critical role) of science, Jen Hung-chün for perpetuating vague notions of science, life, nature, society, inevitability, and freedom, and Kuo Jen-yüan for his extreme, mechanistic determinism. This relentless criticism stemmed from an unswerving sense of duty "to further culture and fight for science." [21] The criterion for criticizing the scientific notions of others was the new science—theoretical, dialectical criticism.

Yeh clarifies the meaning of criticism, striving to give it cosmic significance.

21. Ibid., 4–5, 7.

> Within the universe are abrupt changes and evolutionary changes.
>
> The entire universe follows laws. The laws of all its individual parts must be made unified and contradictory [sic]. Therefore, sudden changes in nature can amply explain sudden historical changes . . . It is a law that sudden change produces progress . . . The so-called sudden change, for society, is revolution; for knowledge or culture, it is none other than criticism.
>
> Criticism of culture is the beginning, basic technique of social revolution.
>
> In all, criticism gives practical meaning to theoretical struggles and cultural struggles.[22]

What this amounts to, then, is a total theoretical and methodological revolution in China's intellectual world. The attitude of such a struggle is also commented on by Yeh:

> We recognize that revolutionary practice uses the beneficial results of revolution as the highest law, and that criticism of culture is a kind of revolutionary practice. Thus it [cultural criticism] inevitably uses the benefits of revolution as a criterion and standard. Our attitude of criticism, then, is: in the realm of thought we must attack the conservative elements in culture, reprimand the reformist groups, but sympathize with the revolutionaries; for individuals we must assume an attitude of belligerency toward those with whom we do not share the same principles, but assume an attitude of friendliness toward those with whom we share the same premises. As for those who belong to the same school of thought as ours but treat us as enemies, we shall nevertheless be friendly to them in general attitude but will not yield an inch in matters of theory.[23]

This attitude of criticism can be explained only by the confidence which the possession of what is believed to be a correct theory imparts. It reveals the emphasis placed on theory and methodology as the tools for constructing a new outlook.

The premium placed on theory is the third plank of the *Twentieth*

22. "P'i-p'an ti i-i" (The Meaning of Criticism), *ESSC*, 1:4 (1931), 1–5.
23. "P'i-p'an ti t'ai-tu" (The Attitude of Criticism), *ESSC*, 1:5 (1931), 12.

Century program. Ju-sung, close collaborator of Yeh Ch'ing, said: "During this age of scientific advance, every action must have its theory. In the past only temporary and miscellaneous thoughts would have sufficed. Nowadays, thought has to be unified, comprehensive, and systematic." Borrowing from Lenin and using the example of the October Revolution, he continues, "revolutionary theory leads to and arouses revolutionary action." [24] Placed in an intellectual context, the same "revolutionary" theory of scientism, then, corrodes the old and lays the revolutionary foundation of a new intellectual order.

Theory, or rather the necessity for theorizing, is considered the mark of science's return from its inductive phase to its deductive, synthetic, and above all, "philosophical" stage. Theory, or theorizing, these writers contend, works within an already established scientific tradition. Science only marks an early period from a later one; it cannot be used to distinguish China from the West. Thus the scientific tradition exists for all men who claim to be modern.

Such persistent attempts to extend the laws of science to all spheres of natural activity reveal clearly the religious nature of scientism—Panscientism. The independent materialists during this period were attempting to illustrate the compatibility of faith and reason, to make believing in something a reputable act once more. This attempt resembles the efforts of medieval scholastic philosophers in the syllogistic mode of reasoning and in the need to bring an entire body of thought up to date. While the Scholastics injected reason into fundamental matters of faith, the followers of scientism made articles of faith out of a body of information accumulated by reason. The results are startlingly similar—a body and mode of thought striving to achieve unity in letter and in spirit.

Synthesizing was illustrated by Ju-sung when he deliberated on the kind of theories to be studied by modern China's intelligentsia. He offered the following criteria: theories in philosophy, sociology, economics, political science, and historical science (that vague term borrowed from the nineteenth century) are preferred for their generalizing capacities; theories must have currency; they must be of a revolutionary nature (mere individualism, equated with capitalism here and therefore opposed to collective revolutionary consciousness, is not

24. Ju-sung, penname of Yang Po-k'ai. "Li-lun ti chung-yao" (The Importance of Theory), *ESSC*, 1:7 (1931), 6–9.

enough); they must be philosophical (that is, having doctrinal significance); but above all they should be scientific. "During this scientific age, only when revolutionary nature and scientific essence are joined can there be creative and accurate theory." Scientific essence, because "science is the knowledge derived from the study of the invariable laws of causation. Thus it is knowledge based on special axioms. What we mean by science, then, is founded upon materialism, because only [scientific knowledge] can stand firmly on matter and be strengthened by laws of causation."[25]

The *Twentieth Century* and its coterie of sister publications can be taken as representative of the entrenchment of the religion of science with its base in a mode of monistic, materialistic determinism and its "theology," dialectical laws. This religiosity carried with it also a multifaceted attack on thought, culture, religion, and society. This was done in the name of science with its capacity for the objectification of truth and the enrichment of practical experience. Yeh Ch'ing commented, "Only the knowledge from experience is true knowledge . . . and only science can support this view of knowledge."[26] "We feel that man cannot exist without knowledge, and the king of knowledge today is science. All other knowledge must use it as standard. All that runs counter to it will not be able to exist."[27]

The life-view of this religion of science, then, can be constructed from the criticism it heaps on knowledge, thought, and the other requisites of civilization. But right thought, right knowledge, truth, and correct belief will appear in the civilization to be reconstructed scientifically. While making some reservation that science is more exact than thought (thought being more abstract and deductive), the attitude of the *Twentieth Century* was that thought could be objectified to be commensurate with science.[28] This attitude treats science as if it were unassailable and exterior to thought and culture; thought

25. "Yen-chiu shen-mo li-lun" (What Theories Should We Study?), *ESSC*, *1:8* (1932), 8–10.

26. Yeh, "Li-lun yü shih-chien" (Theory and Practice), *ESSC*, *2:8* (1932), 6.

27. "Chüan-t'ou yü" (Prefatory Remarks), *K'e-hsüeh lun-ts'ung* (Collections of Writings on Science), 1st coll. (Shanghai, 1934), p. 3.

28. Yeh, "K'e-hsüeh yü ssu-hsiang" (Science and Thought), *ESSC*, *1:2* (1931), 14–15. The erroneous treatment of thought as an abstract commodity with metaphysical properties to be made objective by science must be seen against Yeh's impatient scientistic disregard for anything that is not yet entirely scientific. Further page citations from this article are entered in the text.

is inextricably equated with metaphysics and thus vague. Yeh Ch'ing found the proof of the objectification of thought in the history of scholarship which, to him, showed a persistent "scientification" (*k'e-hsüeh-hua*). Even though named thought, "many of the theories [treated as thought by Yeh] in the realm of society have already been revealed as invariable laws of causation by the application of scientific methods to the study of facts." Moreover, "scientific collectivism, for instance, can be said to be the law of change of modern societies, having explained clearly and with iron-like incontestability the process of rise, death, and annihilation of the capitalist system" (pp. 15–16).

Yeh then cited the triumphant marches of science over theology, religion, and metaphysics, and the rise of the social sciences in the West as indisputable proof of the possibility that science and general thought could be merged. He placed special emphasis on the rise of the social sciences, for therein lie doctrines pointing to the increasing objectification of society and the constant progression of civilization. "The development of science in the societal domain is exactly like its development in the realm of nature, inexorably increasing itself . . . Thus religion, ethics, education, and other social phenomena are all studied and reorganized by science and turned into sciences themselves . . . Economics and physics (including chemistry) are alike in being the essential sciences for modern production [production is taken as the basis for civilization]" (p. 31). Faith is placed in these sciences because they are concerned with observation, experienced facts, and practicalities. The great goal of material scientism is to make society practical and thought scientific.

In the advance of civilization, according to this group of thinkers, we must not condone any notion of freedom of will, a point the empirical scientists encountered, but avoided explaining, by alluding to it as human creativity. For Yeh Ch'ing's group, freedom of will was not tolerated. It impeded the "scientification" of thought.

> Man's possession of creative activity for elevating the value of life lies not in praising freedom of will, but in recognizing the laws of causation. No intellectual activity can surpass science. It has helped us make various tools, machines, and modes and means of communication to reduce labor, enrich life, and destroy natural obstacles. In other words, how come man, during the scientific

> age, can use nature to conquer nature? Basically it is because we can comprehend nature and understand its laws of causation . . .
>
> Therefore, only social science and intellectual science . . . can help us avoid social repression and spiritual worship so that we may be awakened in thought and conscious in action. The scientification of thought is absolutely essential (pp. 36–39).

"Scientification of thought" (making thought scientific) was easy if a new view of the universe were chosen to replace the old metaphysical approach. Yeh Ch'ing singled out Carsun Chang as the best representative of metaphysical ignorance. Yeh maintained that we should view the universe as matter and not as God's creation or the realm of the artist's imagination. As for the inevitability of the "scientification of thought," the following argument was offered:

> All phenomena are related . . . On the basis of the highest product of modern science—*dialectique* [sic], it can be said without extensive proof that in the universe there is not one independent phenomenon . . . This is the objective basis for the view that science can come from the natural realm into the realms of society and thought (pp. 44–45).

To Yeh Ch'ing, then, the deductive and inductive aspects of science served the same function of a dialectic. From the parts to the whole, and vice-versa, the message is the same—the ability of science to make scientific all ways of thinking. Yeh thought that intellectual activity contained materialistic nature (soul and mind treated as matter in motion) and the nature of logic. Coupled with accurate theories from science, then, thought, again categorically and absolutely presented by Yeh, was ably supported. The meeting of thought and science, to Yeh, exemplified the monistic nature of life and the universe which science had revealed. Hence, the inevitability that thought become increasingly scientific (p. 48).

Having defined civilization as the progressive production of and by mankind, with production seen as the reflection of man's understanding of nature's make-up and forces, the Yeh Ch'ing school went further and stated that possession of a scientific knowledge was the most accurate reflection of the understanding of nature. Progress was, thus, inevitable. In this is seen scientism's inherent optimistic outlook.

The question of who could narrow the gap between science and thought, and make the latter totally scientific, still remained. The thinkers we have discussed earlier did not fully answer this question; the Yeh school had definite ideas. The scientist could not narrow the gap because he could not see beyond his own socially determined ideas, and so could not discern theology and metaphysical attitudes. The natural scientist could not do it, for, even if he banished God from nature, he was, like Newton, Faraday, and Maxwell, unable to be thorough enough to discard religious feelings. The social scientist could not, for he was not completely familiar with natural science nor fully divorced from theology. Examples of this category are Guizot, Brewster, Macaulay. The intellectual could not do it either, for he was too much of an idealist. The right person was a revolutionary, for only he could conduct the great revolution of making thought scientific. "Scientific and intellectual revolutions cannot be separated from economic, political, and, indeed, societal revolutions" (p. 52). The successful revolutionary must first belong to the correct revolutionary class, and second, must possess all the best qualities of the intellectual, philosopher, social scientist, and natural scientist. He must be the creator of new tools, and the new Atlantis. He must emulate Bacon, creator of the new philosophy of naturalism, and Darwin and Wallace, founders of theories of evolution (p. 53). This revolutionary must be able to unite theory and practice: The scientific theories of the entire natural world and sheer revolutionary action.

New knowledge leads, through "revolutionary sociology," to new society. This new society would be based on a new philosophy, new scientific methods, new laws of society, and a new synthetic system. "The natural sciences use physics as their foundation, the human sciences use economics. Production is a fundamental key to nature and the actions and thoughts of mankind. Based on this [view], relationships among nature, society, and knowledge can be established. Their principles of movement and their laws of development can be united in one system. This system . . . is the scientific dialectic, a synthetic philosophy of the universe and life—the true 'science of science,' the cardinal law" (p. 54). This school of materialism rejects the working scientist in favor of the unifier of theory and practice—the architect of the future order. Scientism was thus fanned by these theorists, who spoke illogically but forcefully, and who anticipated by almost a decade the "final" enunciation of the unity of theory and practice (a successful revolution) by Mao Tse-tung.

SCIENTISM IN OTHER QUARTERS

The more pluralistic thinkers shared with the materialists the belief that the scientific approach should be used to study society and human affairs. They were less rigid in their conclusions about science, man, and society. Less monistic and deterministic than the materialists, empirical thinkers remained enchanted with the idea of a civilization enriched by science, not totally described by it. Their philosophical position seemed doomed from the start, however, by the stronger current of material scientism. The material scientists made it clear that they had gone beyond mere admiration of the scientific West to find a "science" of society and man befitting the modern (not just Western or Chinese) mind. Praise by unsuspecting general admirers of the West only reinforced the arguments of thinkers who had already found the "answer"—Panscientism.

Hu Shih, himself instrumental in popularizing science, spent the '30s answering charges and clarifying his thought, always reluctant to come to a conclusion of monistic determinism. The monistic disregard for other ways of thought irked and prompted him to accuse the contemporary thought of bearing a corrupt disease, namely, the use of clichés. To him, the materialists were especially guilty of parading slogans and maxims without understanding them fully and of "using an arrangement of terms to substitute for the stages of thought and to pass for a process of reasoning." [29] He considered the following clichés meaningless: "Feudalistic age," "age of commercial capitalism," "capitalist culture," "socialistic culture," "China-centered cultural reconstruction," "creative synthesis," and others.[30] This plea for intelligent commentary, instead of the vindication of one mode of thought, was the position of the *Independent Critic,* the brainchild of Hu Shih and V. K. Ting. The journal struggled to maintain a liberal (in both the political and nonpolitical senses of the word) outlook; the opinions expressed can be called empirical. V. K. Ting and Hu Shih urged

29. Hu, "Chin-jih ssu-hsiang-chieh ti i-ke ta pi-ping" (A Major Disease of Today's World of Thought), *TLPL,* 153 (1935), 3. He singled out Tao Hsi-sheng for relentless criticism.

30. Ibid., 5.

the readers to explore, experiment, and criticize ideas and institutions instead of seeking final solutions. While Hu Shih cautioned against cliché-thinking, V. K. Ting wrote on subjects ranging from militarism, to Communism, to the relativity of age and generation.[31]

Jen Hung-chün, popularizer of science, in the '30s wrote on the merits of preserving relics. He praised the League of Nations' attempt to set up an agency in Geneva for this purpose and bemoaned the passing of the old pines at T'ien-tai in Peking.[32] His professional writings could still be found in scientific journals, but his "extra-curricular" writings covered a wide range of subjects from poetry to politics. His silence on the cultural aspects of science does not mean that he had given up the scientific attitude. Jen now took for granted the pervasiveness and persuasiveness of culture enriched by science. T'ang Yüeh spent the '30s and '40s in little or no popularization of science. He became more and more concerned with administrative aspects of academic life; there is no indication of a basic change in his attitude toward science.

Even though they were materialists, Wu Chih-hui and Ch'en Tu-hsiu stood with the empirical scientists during the 1923 Debate. They did not join the material monists of the '30s and '40s for political and personal reasons, but this did not seriously weaken the monists. The latter took the voluminous writing on the subject of these once prolific men and would often acknowledge, rather weakly, Wu and Ch'en as early contributors to material monism. Wu Chih-hui did continue in the same vein but was no longer as prolific as before on the benefits of "motors." [33] Ch'en Tu-hsiu's political disappointment in the '30s resulted in a personal and literary detachment from the cultural debate. He turned his attention to such writings as "A Study of Lao-tzu," "Confucius and China," and "A Chronological Chart of Ancient Chinese History." [34] The effort at scholarly pursuits by this one-time

31. Ting, "Hsien-tsai Chung-kuo ti chung-nien yü ch'ing-nien" (Contemporary China's Middle Aged and Youth), *TLPL, 144* (1935), 8–11. See his "credo," Chapter 5.

32. Jen Hung-chün, "Pao-ts'un ku-wu tsuo ti shen-mo" (Why Preserve Relics?), *TLPL, 126* (1934), 4–6.

33. See pp. 40–41.

34. In this order: "Lao-tzu k'ao-lüeh" (A Study of Lao-tzu), *TFTC, 34:11* (1937), 7–15, "K'ung-tzu yü Chung-kuo" (Confucius and China), *TFTC, 34:18–19* (1937), 9–15, "Chung-kuo ku-shih piao" (A Chronological Chart of Ancient Chinese History), *TFTC,* 37:22 (1940), 35–38.

firebrand popularizer of modern ideas was in a sense a victory for the humanistic approach to culture, ideas, and scholarship; on the other hand, he approached these matters as a loner, and his basic philosophical assumptions about life had not changed. The indecisive and incohesive language of the so-called empiricists and the sprawling activities of a few well-known materialists caused the eventual triumph of monistic determinism.

The strength of empirical attitudes in being generous to other schools of thought actually made for its own weakness in the '30s and '40s. This is clearly seen when Carsun Chang, archenemy of the supporters of science in the 1923 Debate, once again took up his position on science and life, in 1934.[35] Chang was never as strongly opposed to science, and in favor of humanistic investigation alone, as his opponents have charged. The heat of the Debate had passed, and he reflected on the whole problem, again revealing himself as taking a reasonable position on the question of whether science should be set above culture, as if the latter could be educated by science, or should be considered part of cultural activities. Carsun Chang felt called upon to keep philosophical dialogue open. He and Chang Tung-sun were responsible, with such writers as Lin Tsai-p'ing, Chang Chen-ju, Ch'ü Chü-nung, Ho Lin, Chou Fu-ch'eng, Hsü Hsü-sheng, and others, for the popularity of the new school of idealism represented by the Peita philosophy department.

Reflecting the general outlook of this school, Chang now approached science and culture in three ways. First, he believed that science, since its birth in sixteenth-century Europe, had been responsible for unprecedented progress in various aspects of human life, and that China should hurry to correct its past lack of the sense of objective truth and natural knowledge by promoting not the outward trappings but the "mind" of science. Second, all arguments based on philosophical naturalism and materialism (referring to Wu Chih-hui, Hu Shih, and Ch'en Tu-hsiu) were really not conclusive about the ultimate reality, for science (around 1930) had already pointed to the indeterminacy of knowledge. The materialistic arguments really aimed at the destruction of prevailing religious, artistic, and scholarly thought. Third, future thinkers, of China especially, should emphasize

35. See his "Jen-sheng-kuan lun-chan chih hui-ku" (Reflections on the Debate on the Philosophy of Life), *TFTC,* 31:13 (1934), 5–13.

intellectual development, updating and disseminating scientific advances, and giving continued attention to philosophy; philosophy should be used as a check and balance. To this school, science by itself is only an operation based on theories and mathematical symbols which members of the larger cultural world could not possibly understand. Therefore, the philosophers must render intelligible the emerging concepts of the workings of the natural order. It was up to philosophy to put science into the larger stream of thought. The world, to these thinkers, could not be divided simply into the material and the spiritual; it was above all a world of consciousness and experience, both public and private, of which science was a part.

In academic circles of thought the school of empirical scientism saw its various intellectual endeavors rising to more sophisticated heights. The new idealist philosophy replaced the pragmatism which Hu Shih had made famous. Serious and academically philosophical activities during the '30s and '40s in China were, on the whole, led by this school. A rash of philosophies of life, under the impetus of a pluralistic approach to life's problems (called for by Chang Tung-sun), came forth again in the '30s; various collections recorded a bewildering variety of life-views of noted men.[36] These declarations of faith reveal that the debate between science and metaphysics no longer existed and that science had become a part of the general outlook on life. This does not mean that all who liked science understood its meaning and workings; more often than not, the psychological and emotional impact of science had evoked a sympathetic response.

One did not have to be a scientist or a philosopher to speak glowingly of the role of science in modern culture. As seen before, this participation in the popular province of science weakened the empirical style of thought. The aroused spirit for science looked, during the impatient and chaotic '30s and '40s, not to the gradual and pluralistic ways of empirical thought but to the dogmatic conclusions of materialist scientism. The new school of philosophy at Peita helped to make respectable a general philosophical tendency and had no control over its outcome. While popular on the academic level, this new school, which dealt even with the philosophy of science, could not win in

36. For example, the collection by Huang Ching-wan and Hsü Wan-ch'eng, *Ko-chung jen-sheng-kuan* (Varieties of Philosophies of Life) (Shanghai, n.d.).

the public forum, where language is less refined, patience for intellectual discernment limited, and the emotional reaction to the appeal of science was rapidly harnessed by a style of thought, modern in premise, simple in reasoning, and resolute in conclusion. The material monist possessed these qualities and used them to good advantage.

The open-mindedness inherent in empirical, non-monistic schools also invited strange philosophical fellow-travellers. Borrowing the popularity of science for its modernity, respectability, and timely open-mindedness, fellow-travellers did not have to be philosophically based in science at all. An example which in the end diminished the influence of empiricism in the '30s is the philosophy of the Nationalists.[37] Born of the Nationalists' primarily political desire to regiment thought and action after the 1927–28 political revolution, this philosophy was called vitalism or vita-ism (*wei-sheng lun*). It went hand in hand with Chiang Kai-shek's New Life Movement, initiated in 1934. Vitalism articulated chiefly by Ch'en Li-fu, revolved around a activitist concept of life's vital force (*sheng*). It turned back to the classics, borrowed a few concepts from Hans Driesch and Henri Bergson, and proclaimed its suitability for modern times by announcing that it was compatible with science. The result is a metaphysics that does not face the problem of knowledge which concerned even the empirical and materialistic scientistic schools. Skirting the problem of knowledge, vitalism sought its own unity of thought and action, spirit and matter, by taking for itself the key concepts of those two Confucian canons, the *Great Learning* (*Ta-hsüeh*) and the *Doctrine of the Mean* (*Chung-yung*), "attainment of knowledge lies in the investigation of things (*chih-chih ke-wu*)." Chiang Kai-shek, in a lecture to the Party at Lu Shan on September 15, 1934, declared:

> I believe that the book, *Great Learning*, is not only China's orthodox philosophy but also the forebear of scientific thought, undoubtedly the source of Chinese science. If we bind together the *Great Learning* and the *Doctrine of the Mean*, we will have the most complete text on the harmony of philosophy and science

37. For Kuomintang philosophy, see Mary C. Wright, "From Revolution to Restoration: The Transformation of Kuomintang Ideology," *FEQ*, 14 (1955), 515–32; H. H. Dubs, "Recent Chinese Philosophy," *Journal of Philosophy*, 35 (1938), 345–55.

> and the unity of spirit and matter. Thus I call it the "Scientific Nature of the Great Learning and the Doctrine of the Mean." [38]

A year later, he commented again on science:

> Actually what we nowadays call science is none other than what we Chinese in the past have called the learning of *ke-chih* [investigation of things leads to knowledge]. [As this approach is found in the *Great Learning*] we can see that China had science two thousand years ago. Since there was science, there must have been the scientific method. Thus the scientific method is not discovered in modern times, much less is it a sole possession of foreign countries. During the age of Confucius this fact is already clear. What Confucius meant by "everything has its source, and everything has its beginning and end; when one knows the order of things, he is indeed close to the Tao" is the best scientific method for any scholarship and every way of handling affairs.[39]

Science was anachronistically appropriated by the Nationalist theorizers to lend their philosophical efforts a measure of dignity. "The pursuit of knowledge lies in the investigation of things," may sound scientific, but it refers to the pursuit of truth among ancient books for moral perfection and not to the search for exact knowledge or to the creation of a vocabulary to explain the new data.

The incorporation of science into Kuomintang philosophy, on a higher level, was left to Ch'en Li-fu, long the guardian of theory for the Party, but first and foremost a politician. He gave a series of Lectures to the Central Political Institute in 1934, which he published under the title of vitalism, *Wei-sheng-lun*. Ten years later he revised it and added another title, *Principles of Life* (*Sheng chih yüan-li*). An English edition appeared in 1948 entitled *Philosophy of Life*. This work gave metaphysical justification to the political activities of the Kuomintang in arousing what Chiang called a "spiritless" people. It contains questionable metaphysics and efforts to seek historical, psy-

38. Reprinted in *K'e-hsüeh ti Hsüeh-Yung* (The Scientific Nature of the Great Learning and the Doctrine of the Mean) (Taipei, 1959), p. 52.

39. From a lecture of January 28, 1935, originally entitled "K'e-hsüeh ching-shen yü k'e-hsüeh fang-fa" (Scientific Spirit and Scientific Method). This lecture reappeared as a pamphlet, *K'e-hsüeh ti tao-li* (Principles of Science) (Taipei, 1958), pp. 3–4.

chological, and figurative justification for the task of the Kuomintang. This major work, exposing Ch'en's philosophy, sees the universe as change, a cornerstone of his thought based on the *Book of Divination* (*I Ching*). But since "there cannot be any changing phenomena without an ontological body," he postulates the ontological body, "life-substance," which includes material force and spiritual power. Life-substance is more basic than change because the "possibility of change in all the phenomena arises from the regenerating ability of the life-substance."[40] Ch'en admitted that his own view suggested a monism, but felt that he had avoided the real problem—materialism (for Ch'en the same as Communism)—by fusing the spiritual and physical into life-substance. He then compared his ontological body to the Absolute (*t'ai-chi*) of the *I Ching*, with its positive and negative tendencies. The negative aspect became the static state of material force; the positive assumed the dynamic qualities of spiritual power. At this point Ch'en jumped from Confucian analogies to comparisons with modern science.

> Material force is . . . that which is capable of receiving the power of other things. According to physics, the primary nature of material things is inertia. Inertia means the tendency not to move. This inertia is precisely the evidence that such material things do have the power of receiving and storing up power, whereby they are enabled to maintain their own state of existence.[41]

Apparently Ch'en was referring to mechanical motion and to the power of matter to stay in motion.

Ch'en tries to use Einstein's theory of relativity to explain how his life-substance could act as both a function and a body.

> Matter means the conservation as well as the latent state of power, which is energy . . . Thus matter becomes the function of energy; that which is not carried out or hidden is the state, whereas that which is expressed or emerges forth is function.[42]

To Ch'en, since change is the most fundamental fact of the universe, energy has a slight edge over matter.

40. Ch'en, *Philosophy of Life* (New York, 1948), p. 22.
41. Ibid., p. 24.
42. Ibid., p. 25.

It is obvious that Ch'en's use of science is, at best, eclectic, an effort to bolster his own scheme. He avoids, for instance, concepts of modern science which might have some negative implications for his belief that energy is the master of matter. His loose use of "energy" and "matter" to mean "the soul" and "the will," and his inaccurate use of "inertia" to mean "a state of unreleased power" show that these terms serve nonscientific ends.

Ch'en was only superficially attracted to Hans Driesch and Henri Bergson. He borrowed their concepts and labels to suit his own philosophy. Ch'en equated *ch'eng* (*ch'eng*, usually translated as sincerity, a concept in the *Doctrine of the Mean*) with Driesch's entelechy and Bergson's *élan vital* with no effort at showing relationships beyond the labels.[43] He was then faced with an almost impossible task of analyzing the Western origins of this school of vitalism in China. It is obvious that Ch'en's philosophy was primarily intended to justify Kuomintang actions. His choice of imported and modern labels permits him to deny both the materialistic philosophy of the Communists and the materialistic values of Western culture; both are the result of highly developed technology deprived of a corresponding "spiritual" philosophy. His allusions to the materialistic temptations of "jazz, goods, and profits" are repeated with comic frequency. By his philosophy, Ch'en wanted to provide a will (spiritual power) for the people (matter which in his philosophy goes from individual existence to collective existence). This will would make them behave first as individuals, then—more importantly—as effective citizens, all culminating in sincerity. Ch'en's philosophy turns out to be a manipulation of systems of thought, psychology, and tradition. It was meant for the public at large and, because of this, its language was a serious impediment to the public's understanding of the Kuomintang intent. For our purposes, Ch'en's indiscreet use of science demonstrates a coarser variety of scientism and the strange company the popularity of science invites. The fumbling ways of vitalism in the larger world of thought actually reinforced monistic materialism, the very school it was meant to destroy.

43. See Ch'en's *Wei-sheng lun* (Vitalism) (Shanghai, 1947), I, 109–33. Hans Driesch, *The History and Theory of Vitalism,* Eng. trans. C. K. Ogden (London, 1914), p. 202. Henri Bergson, *Creative Evolution,* Eng. trans. Arthur Mitchell (London, 1954).

The popularity of science affected yet other quarters in the '30s. In 1929 Hu Shih had advocated wholesale Westernization of China. The empirical spirit of argument produced a series of debates in the '30s on the question of wholesale modernization versus China-centered mode of modernization. In the early '30s, professors and other intellectuals often lectured on "wholesale modernization." Their lectures were published in 1934, as *Collections of Speeches and Essays on the Question of Total Westernization* (*Ch'üan-p'an hsi-hua yen-lun chi*). Two additional collections appeared in 1935 and 1936. The majority of the writers, led by Ch'en Hsü-ching, favored wholesale Westernization. The counterattack appeared in 1935 in a work by ten professors[44] entitled *Manifesto of a China-Centered Cultural Reconstruction* (*Chung-kuo pen-wei ti wen-hua chien-she hsüan-yen*).

In general, three views were expressed: the empirical creed; veneration of traditional civilization; and selectivism. Of these, the first and the last were the most widespread. On the surface, the debate of the '30s seems to have drawn the battle line between the pro-West and the protradition factions. A closer look reveals that this was not entirely the case. The ten professors' *Manifesto* shows weariness at their countrymen's attempts at following various Western models. It argues for a sense of pride that would arise from the self-reconstruction of Chinese civilization and culture on the basis of Chinese needs. The *Manifesto* was not anti-West, as were the "metaphysicians" in the '20s. It pressed for a review of China's past, a grasping of China's present, and a building of China's future. The professors proposed to do this in a critical spirit with the help of the scientific method. Their opponents made them out to be defenders and restorers of the old order. Even clear-minded Hu Shih succumbed to this unreasonable accusation.[45] What the ten professors were asking for was modernization in China, but they misunderstood the term "Westernization" as used by their opponents. The proponents of Westernization reciprocated this misunderstanding; they actually wanted modernization also.

44. They are Wang Hsin-ming, Ho Ping-sung, Wu Yü-kan, Sun Han-ping, Huang Wen-shan, T'ao Hsi-sheng, Chang I, Ch'en Kao-yung, Fan Chung-yün, and Sa Meng-wu.

45. Hu, "Shih p'ing so-wei 'Chung-kuo pen-wei ti wen-hua chien-she'" (A Trial Criticism of the so-called 'China-centered Cultural Reconstruction'), *HSWT*, 4th coll., bk. 4, 535–40. This was written in March 1935.

There was never any question about the benefits of science, its spirit and method, for a new China. The debate lasted into the Sino-Japanese Incident in 1937. The next ten years saw few intellectual debates conducted in the empirical spirit. The war ended with a strong surge of scientism once again. This time it was the scientism of materialist monism.

In face of the resolute, materialist school, a clear understanding of the operations of science and an appreciation of its scope and power were hampered by a number of factors. First, empirical scientism could not help but follow the natural development of scientific research and theory. It could not seek closed systems of the union of scientific premises with scientific conclusions. Awareness of the quickly developing post-Heisenberg science was registered also in China. Chang Tsung-ping writes in "The Limitations of Science" in *Far Eastern Miscellany:*

> Among . . . the discoveries in science for the past fifty years, the most important is the change wrought in the scientist's intellectual faith. For some time now the materialism of Newton has governed the belief of the scientist, the direction of his work, and the spirit of his research. The reason for materialism's enormous popularity with the people is its simplicity and unified nature . . . The wavering of [the claims of] materialism has its greatest impact in the world of thought. The fact that the scientist has now lost his one and only faith is as important as the loss to science itself of a unifying and central idea.[46]

The indeterminacy of physical phenomena meant the scattering of the Newtonian view of matter and motion and of the Newtonian universe itself. But this awareness in China was restricted to a small number of scientists and nonscientists during these two decades. The language of real science was not the language of the general public which, during these years, still favored the simple and emotional language of the inexorable laws and the "reality" which they described.

46. Chang, "K'e-hsüeh chih hsien-chih," *TFTC,* 40:6 (1944), 35. See also his "I-ke k'e-hsüeh-chia ti tsung-chiao-kuan" (The Religious Outlook of a Scientist), *TFTC,* 40:9 (1944), 27–29 for a "cellular" view of life based on concepts of "truth" (*chen*), "ethics" (*shan*), and "esthetics" (*mei*).

Second, the repute of empirical thought was often lessened by parasitic intellectual systems which borrowed the respectable stature of science in attempts to make their philosophies, not always refined, exportable. Materialists, like Ch'en Tu-hsiu and Wu Chih-hui, continued to talk about the blessings of science without true understanding of the theories of science or appreciation for the popular implication of their scientism. Thinkers of the Nationalist camp also tried to borrow from science without contributing to the empirical style any real efforts of their own.

Third, while scientism in general received enormous impetus during the '30s and '40s through the popularity of science in the numerous schools of thought, all this popularity in the end supported the style of thought which disregarded most the scientific spirit, and this materialism possessed rigidity of conclusion. It boasted that all "scientific" testing would be conclusive, with science looked on as the final arbiter. It is no accident that scientism in China triumphed in its highest form—a materialist monism which claims cosmic significance and scientific quality by finding the key to all causal relations.

THE UNION OF THEORY AND PRACTICE

While the Nationalists were remaking ideology to suit their purposes for ruling China, the Communists were busy making the intellectual world safe for their philosophy. A major difference between them is that the Nationalists' revolution "succeeded" without a real workable set of beliefs, despite (or because of the looseness of) Sun Yat-sen's "People's Principles"; the Communists still had a revolution to achieve. One is ad hoc ideological reconstruction and rationalization; the other sees "successful" revolution as the inevitable outcome of the correct view of the theory of history, man, and the cosmos. Of the thirty years before the triumph of the Communists, twenty were spent in intense intellectual and theoretical stockpiling. The result was that the successful revolution vindicated the theory. This triumph of theory is also the victory of scientism in its most developed and comprehensive form.

The intellectual world had been prepared to appreciate science. All modern-minded Chinese had contributed to this task. The empiricists publicized the objective premises of a scientific outlook; independent materialists, such as Wu Chih-hui, had joined with those who believed in a general scientific outlook to make science the indispensable helpmate of progress; still other positivists, whether Communists or not, had transferred the theories of science itself into "scientific" theories of society. Communist theorizers shared the wellsprings and assumption of this heritage. They appropriated its broadest conclusions, developed its most resolute language, and predicted the eventual triumph of their own outlook which they identified with the scientific heritage itself (a circular argument). While participating in the general trend of China's Westernization (that is, becoming ever more conscious of the idea of science, even if just for cultural and emotional reasons), the Communist theorizers, such as Ch'ü Ch'iu-pai, Ai Ssu-ch'i, Ch'en Po-ta, Li Ta, Ho Kan-chih, Yang Chien-hsiu, Hu Sheng, Kuo Mo-jo, and Mao Tse-tung, lent a tradition of their own to the ideological struggle for power in the years before their triumph. Marxian dialectic, which had been one of many dialogues in the ceaseless discussions in modern China, in the end became the "intellectual science." The world to be objectified and the method with which to do it were both validated.

It is generally agreed that Ai Ssu-ch'i has been the Communist Party's chief thinker. He spearheaded the movement of the '30s in 1934 to capture the intelligentsia with his *Philosophy of the Masses* (*Ta-chung che-hsüeh*). Intended as a popularization, it went through thirty-two editions in twelve years.[47] In contrast to the heavily theoretical writings of Ch'en Po-ta and Li Chi and others,[48] this work is marked by its effectiveness as propaganda. It is a skillful piece of writing to instill in the people a sense (not necessarily a complete understanding) of dialectical materialism, giving the people the terms and directions of thought. Using concrete examples and immediate situations, Ai classifies all ideas "up to the present" as preconditioned by superstition and inexact habits. He shows that it is necessary to

47. Noted by Brière, p. 78.

48. Li Ta was the first systematic interpreter of Marx. His principal work is *Elements of Sociology* (*She-hui-hsüeh ta-kang*), 1939, a continuation of which appeared in 1947 called *Modern Sociology* (Hsien-tai she-hui-hsüeh). Ch'en Po-ta is reputed to have provided a good part of the philosophy to Mao Tse-tung's "New Democracy" of 1940. Li Chi, expelled along with Ch'en Tu-hsiu from the Party, was also a theoretical Marxist noted for his three-volume biography of Marx, *Ma-k'e-ssu chuan,* and for his participation in the Debate of Chinese Society and History.

liberate oneself from these vague notions. Proficiency in philosophizing is not enough, according to this manual, although philosophy (theory) is essential in dispelling untruths. The right philosophy must be found. Marxian philosophy, of course, is the right one because of its progressiveness, exactness, and its scientific theory and method. It is scientific because dialectical materialism is the law that governs all nature.

Ai Ssu-ch'i continued to write thin, but effective, tracts throughout the '30s. *How to Study Philosophy* (*Ju-ho yen-chiu che-hsüeh*) and *On How to Think* (*Ssu-hsiang fang-fa lun*) appeared in 1935. Some were collections of essays, such as *Philosophy and Life* (*Che-hsüeh yü sheng-huo*) which appeared in 1937. In 1939 he came out with many works, the more important of which were *Practice and Theory* (*Shih-chien yü li-lun*), appearing soon after Mao's classics, "On Practice" (*Shih-chien lun*) and "On Contradiction" (*Mao-tun lun*), *Philosophical Selections* (*Che-hsüeh hsüan-chi*), and, with Wu Li-p'ing, *Textbook on the Scientific View of History* (*K'e-hsüeh li-shih-kuan chiao-ch'eng*). Innumerable writers followed Ai's example and wrote short tracts. Of these, Hu Sheng is noted for his indefatigable labors as writer and editor from the time of the Sino-Japanese Incident on. He produced numerous pamphlets which were reprinted many times. Among them were *New Philosophy's Conception of Life* (*Hsin-che-hsüeh ti jen-sheng-kuan*), 1937; *Introducing Dialectical Materialism* (*Pien-cheng-fa wei-wu lun ju-men*), 1938; *How to Think and How to Study* (*Ssu-hsiang fang-fa yü tu-shu fang-fa*), 1947. Shen Chih-yuan edited, with Hu Sheng, *Theory and Reality* (*Li-lun yü hsien-shih*), a journal on ideas of culture. It was in print from 1939 to 1946, in Chungking, and was a treasure house of Marxian views.

One of the best statements of the scientistic assumptions behind these bold popular proclamations is given by Ch'ü Ch'iu-pai. A one-time Party stalwart, becoming its Secretary-General in 1927–28, he was much beleaguered by the "left" and "right" of the shifting party line, intermittently called a "leftist deviationist" and a "rightist opportunist," until his death in 1935. Party vicissitudes did not shake his conviction in the correctness of the materialistic historical outlook. The scientistic premises of Communism's view of history, man, society, and destiny were stated by Ch'ü in the early '30s.

> Science arose fully during the age of capitalism. But the capitalist class could not fully develop science, for science must be based entirely on pure materialism. The capitalists vacillated between idealism and materialism; thus science could never become secure. The proletariat, however, grew up under capitalism, and its strength lies in its being a productive force of its own . . . Inevitably it will oppose existing systems as well as change society in order to liberate itself. Therefore, its revolutionary activities and reformist deeds must require the most accurate social science and natural science for an intimate understanding of society and nature . . . With the socialist society, in which every man is a scientist, true equality appears.[49]

In the same publication, Ch'ü explains the compatibility of science and social science, of nature and society. Forces and means of production, being the arrangement of matter, provide the meeting point between man (producer) and nature (matter), and therefore are the bases of historical (social) materialism. Society is the product of the complicated relationships of matter (productive force). The causes and effects of these relationships are accounted for by economics and can be understood if scientific laws are used. Dialectical materialism explains the base (economics) and the superstructure (the entire spectrum of culture) of society. Understood in this way, society can be changed if the right view of history is upheld and the right method applied to matter in its natural course of change. No difference is seen between the laws of science proper and the maxims supposedly describing society.[50] Ai Ssu-ch'i enlarged this inseparability of the natural and social worlds by saying that human life and activity, the objective world, and the views regarding them, subjective recognition, cannot be separated. Thus party strife and natural struggle are the same.

> A realization of the nature of party difference and an accurate and progressive understanding of things must first be predicated upon a knowledge which uses scientific theory as the fundament. True science is the knowledge which holds firm the develop-

49. Ch'ü, *She-hui k'e-hsüeh kai-lun* (Elements of Social Science) (Shanghai, 1949), pp. 55–56.
50. Ibid., pp. 61–68.

> mental laws of various things. Why is it that science can accurately hold firm the axiomatic nature of all things? The reason is that science itself is the product of the grand total of mankind's practical experience. The precision of its theories and principles has already been validated by mankind's long enduring practical experience.[51]

While the doctrine of materialist determinism is the kernel of Communist thought, the role of ideas is equally stressed, with the proviso that the right ideas lead to the right existence. Lenin's belief in the indispensability of theory to revolution reflects Marx's own view of man as both the object, matter to be studied scientifically, and the subject, the creator of a better world through revolutions, of history. Chinese materialists continued and refined this flexible concept of the union of theory and practice. Mao Tse-tung, in the early Yenan period, began to prepare, as a part of a general effort at Party reform, the theoretical basis for present and future action. In July and August of 1937 he came out with two classic documents, "On Practice" and "On Contradiction." Both were originally lectures delivered to the Anti-Japanese Military and Political College in Yenan.

Mao, interpreting practice as the reality of social existence, the composite of "forces of production, struggle of the classes, and the processes of scientific experimentation," repeated what all the materialists of the '30s and '40s were saying: "If man wants to succeed in his work, in other words, to achieve what is anticipated, he must train his thought to be compatible with the laws governing the objective external world; if they are not compatible, he will fail in practice."[52] Once again, then, the importance of theory and practice to each other was stated. These repeated assertions illustrate further the belief of the Marxist-Leninists that they had found the system of laws revealing a world of facts which could prescribe remedies for all ills. Mao said:

> Dialectical materialism's epistemology is rational knowledge that depends upon a perceptive knowledge which is in the process of developing into rational knowledge. Both "rationalism" and "empiricism" in philosophy do not understand the historical or dia-

51. Ai Ssu-ch'i and Wu Li-p'ing, *K'e-hsüeh li-shih-kuan chiao-ch'eng* (Textbook on the Scientific View of History) (Shanghai, 1939), pp. 4–5.

52. Mao, "Shih-chien lun," *MTTHC*, 1 (Peking, 1961; 1951), 273.

> lectical nature of knowledge, and although each of the two contains some truth (that is, regarding materialist rationalism and empiricism, and not rationalism and empiricism), both of them are incorrect for the whole of knowledge . . .
>
> But the process of knowing does not end here . . . What is regarded as the most important problem in Marxist thought does not lie in merely the understanding of the laws governing the objective world in order to explain it, but in *using this knowledge of the objective laws to actively change the world.*[53]

Mao wanted to give his movement dynamism during the late '30s. He achieved this dynamism by making theory (knowledge) commensurate with and substantiated by the growth of historical and practical experiences. He declared it the intellectual science (now meaning only reliable views of the entire cosmos) which could make a better world (this was and still is the intent of science proper itself). To further justify his reasoning, he wrote "On Contradiction" a month after he finished "On Practice."

"On Contradiction" is a philosophical justification of Mao's thought and a primer on the art of argumentation, a lesson on applying the dialectical world outlook. To Mao, traditional Marxist dialectic is based on the universality and the particularity of contradiction. The first is to solve "large" problems in history, such as the bourgeois-proletariat struggle, which is solved by the socialist revolution, and the contradiction between colonies and colonizers, resolved by national revolutionary wars. The second is to deal with the qualitatively important small problems, such as "the contradiction between the proletariat and the the peasantry in socialist society [which] is solved by the collectivization and mechanization of agriculture; the contradiction within the Communist Party [which] is solved by the method of criticism and self-criticism."[54] Opposition within each contradiction is nurtured by antagonism and results in struggle. Thus the duty of the Party "scientist-revolutionary" is to be constantly alert to the fundamental laws of the historically developed Marxism-Leninism and to see to the proper application of the maxims according to the particulars of time and space.

53. Ibid., 280–81. Italics added.
54. Mao, "Mao-tun lun" (On Contradiction), *MTTHC, 1*, 292–98.

Mao attached this reasoning to his theory of knowledge and action. The flexibility and intent of this "scientific" approach is seen in an official note that accompanies these two major theoretical documents in Mao's *Selected Works.*

> Within our Party there used to be a section of formalistic comrades who, discarding long ago the experience of the Chinese revolution and shunning the truth that "Marxism is not a dogma but a guide to action," have been deceiving people with undigested words and sentences lifted from Marxian works. There also used to be a group of empiricist comrades who, long clinging to their individually partial experiences, could neither understand the importance of revolutionary practice nor see the whole of the revolutionary situation; thus, [they] toil diligently but blindly; . . . Comrade Mao Tse-tung's "On Practice" is intended to expose, using the Marxian theory of knowledge, such subjective errors within the Party as formalism and empiricism, especially formalism.[55]

Mao's two pronouncements clearly reveal his determination to become both the theoretical and the practical scientist of society and its revolution. What started as a tendency, shared by materialists and empiricists of all political shades, to perfect a knowledge of society had turned into a science of sociology with the ability to predict, even in the human realm. The dynamic language of this sociology sometimes helped to hide the contrived theorizing and assisted the science of Marxian analysis and forecasting to give the Party a unity of outlook and approach. It also attracted many converts.

Li Shih-ts'en, one of the converts, was known during the New Culture period as an accomplished student of Nietzsche, Bergson, and other "idealistic" philosophers. He startled the intellectual world in the late '20s (after a trip to Europe) by reversing his position and declaring that the direction of the New Thought would be scientific materialism.[56] Chang Tung-sun was another convert who reflected

55. Ibid., 272.

56. Li Shih-ts'en, "San-shih-nien lai shih-chieh che-hsüeh chih chin-chan" (The Progress of World Philosophy of the Past Thirty Years), *TFTC, 31:1* (1933), 137–44, in which he uses 1917 (Bolshevik Revolution) as the dividing line between the old and the new thought. See also his *Che-hsüeh ta-kang* (Outline of Philosophy) and *Chung-kuo che-hsüeh shih-chiang* (Ten Lectures on Chinese Philosophy), both Shanghai, 1933.

the scientistic tenor of the times and helped to popularize it. Chang was reputed to reflect all the best in Western idealistic philosophies. He, along with Carsun Chang and Li Shih-ts'en, gave philosophy an exalted position in China's leading universities. He had wrestled with the Kantian problem of knowledge, emerging with his own "pluralism of knowledge," only to go through the Second World War to appear as a partial convert to dialectical materialism. His early works were abandoned in favor of sociology, or rather, the philosophy of sociology, which he called "epistemological sociology." His writings, which were increasingly political as he joined the Democratic League after the war, now showed a craving for sociological content as well as a propensity for "settling" postwar China's social and political ills.[57] By 1948, when he wrote *Democracy and Socialism* (*Min-chu chu-i yü she-hui chu-i*), he had committed himself quite readily to the Marxist view of society and culture, a view he had abhorred before the war.

The dissemination of scientism went on. A barrage of editions of *Elements of Social Science* (She-hui k'e-hsüeh kai-lun) appeared from the late '30s on. All seem to be modeled on Yang Chien-hsiu's edition of 1929, with the "definitive" edition by Ch'en Po-ta in 1938. In 1949, three of these *Elements* appeared with various editors (Ch'en Po-ta et al., Wu Li-p'ing and Yang Sung, Hsü Mou-yung and Ho Kan-chih) and no difference in subject matter. All such publications assumed the equation of natural and social science and aimed at providing an intellectual science (historical materialism) for making this union meaningful. All begin with this prefatory declaration:

> The purpose of this book is to help young readers first in understanding the laws of the development of man and society and the direction of the international situation of the last twenty years . . . This way they can proceed to study the classic writings of Marx, Engels, Lenin, and Stalin; they can also be enabled to observe and study independently the reality of the world and the historical laws of its development.

Equipped with "absolute" knowledge of society and a method to interpret society's intended direction, Mao Tse-tung could say that

57. For fuller treatment of Chang Tung-sun, see Brière, *Chinese Philosophy*, pp. 66–72.

the New Democracy (the topic of another of his major theoretical works) has a scientific culture.[58] This was in January 1940, in Yenan. By June 1949, Mao had occasion to "prove" that his unity of theory and practice was feasible. Who was to judge the objective viability of any thought or action? The answer lay in the Bolshevized role that Mao gave to the Party elite during the Party reforms at Yenan.[59] Not just anyone would hold the correct view, but the Leninist "vanguard" of Party members would be the final arbiters. Only by declaration could there be objective assessment of any given revolutionary tradition. Only by faith in having the "method," scientific and tested, could such views be upheld.

By June 1949, the Communists were close to achieving the world that would negate all past, obscurantist, and unscientific worlds. At this time Mao passed judgment on another dreamer of better worlds, K'ang Yu-wei, author of *A Book on Universal Harmony* (*Ta-t'ung shu*). Mao commented that K'ang's "best of possible worlds," written a half-century earlier, was merely descriptive. He continued, "K'ang Yu-wei has written the *Ta-t'ung shu,* but he has not found a way [method] to achieve this universal harmony." [60] The occasion for Mao's boast of having found a method himself was the twenty-eighth anniversary of the Chinese Communist Party, when Mao exhorted his comrades to bring about the true unity of theory and practice. With full confidence in the means of validation, Mao boasted of the method and the promise of a world united in theory and practice in a speech entitled "The Dictatorship of the People's Democracy."

For fifty years, China's intellectuals presented, introduced, argued, proclaimed, and debated a variety of ideas and intellectual systems. These fifty years may be seen as the era of China's truly conscious response to the impact of the idea of world civilization; conscious because, in the unceasing intellectual multilogues, often impatiently and coarsely stated, is seen the fundamental stirring of the Chinese mind in search of an integrated, modern identity. Whether the mid-

58. See Chapter 1, p. 19 n.

59. See *Cheng-feng wen-hsien* (Peking, 1949), the Party reform documents during this period. An English treatment and translation is by Boyd Compton, *Mao's China: Party Reform Documents 1942–44* (Seattle, 1952).

60. "Lun jen-min min-chu chuan-cheng" (On the Dictatorship of the People's Democracy), *MTTHC, 4,* 1476

century "union of theory and practice" represents unqualified success in the search for this integrated identity, is, of course, open to various interpretations.

Scientism affects various areas of human endeavor without really helping science itself to advance. Reality, for the scientists, is represented by equations, its language in the purest form is mathematical; reality for the nonscientist, the man of letters, is represented by ordinary language, with its noble imperfections. It is one thing to say that the discoveries and achievements of science should be admired, and quite another to say that all of human life and behavior can be represented by the pure languages of science. The latter attitude, born of an admiration for science that has come to equate scientific verification with precise verifiability of all phenomena, and scientific objectivity with objectifiability of human endeavors, assumes for science a doctrinal finality improbable for any essentially human situations. Through worship of the methods of science came the metaphysics of methodology, without which intellectual undertakings would be called "unscientific"—a derisive term. Many leading thinkers of modern China failed to distinguish between the critical attitude and methodological authority, between scientific objectivity and absolute rationality, and between scientific laws and irrefutable dogmas. This failure left behind an era of open contests of ideas. It helped initiate the next era, a monolithic intellectual supersystem.

GLOSSARY OF PROPER NAMES AND TERMS

Ai-kuo hsüeh-shih she 愛國學士社
Ai Ssu-ch'i 艾思奇
Chang Chen-ju 張真如
Chang Chih-tung 張之洞
Chang Ching-chiang 張靜江
Chang Chun 張羣
Chang Chün-mai (Carsun) 張君勱(嘉森)
Chang Fan-fu 張凡夫
Chang I 章益
Chang, Neander C. S. 張欽士
Chang Tsung-ping 張宗炳
Chang Tung-sun 張東蓀
Chang Wen-po 張文伯
Chang Yüeh-jui 張越瑞
chen 真
Ch'en Heng-che 陳衡哲
Ch'en Hsü-ching 陳序經
Ch'en Kao-yung 陳高傭
Ch'en Li-fu 陳立夫
Ch'en Pang-kuo 陳邦國
Ch'en Ping-k'un 陳炳堃
Ch'en Po-ta 陳伯達
Ch'en Sheng 陳勝
Ch'en Tu-hsiu (Chung-fu, Shih-an) 陳獨秀(仲甫,實庵)
Ch'en Tuan-chih 陳端志
ch'eng 誠
Chiang Kai-shek 蔣介石
chih-chih ke-wu 致知格物
Ch'ien Hsüan-t'ung ("I-ku") 錢玄同("疑古")
Ch'iu-shih shu-yüan 求實學院
Chou Chen-fu 周振甫
Chou Fu-ch'eng 周輔成
Chou Yün-ch'ing 周雲青
Chow Tse-tsung 周策縱
Chu Ching-nung 朱經農
Chu Hsi 朱熹
chuan 篆
Chung-yung 中庸
chü-jen 舉人
Ch'ü Chü-nung 瞿菊農
Ch'ü Ch'iu-pai 瞿秋白

Ch'üan-kuo tu-yin t'ung-i hui 全國讀音統一會
Fan Chen 范縝
Fan Chung-yün 樊仲雲
Fan Shou-k'ang 范壽康
Feng En-jung 馮恩榮
Fu Ssu-nien 傅斯年
han-hsüeh 漢學
Ho Kan-chih 何幹之
Ho Lin 賀麟
Ho Ping-sung 何炳松
hsi-hsüeh 西學
Hsia Cheng-nung 夏征農
Hsia, C. T. 夏志清
Hsia K'ang-nung 夏康農
Hsin-k'en shu-tien 辛墾書店
hsin ssu-ch'ao 新思潮
hsiu-ts'ai 秀才
Hsü Ch'ung-ch'ing 許崇清
Hsü Hsü-sheng 徐旭生
Hsü Kuang-ch'i 徐光啟
Hsü Mou-yung 徐懋庸
Hsü Wan-ch'eng 許晚成
Hsü Yen-chih 徐彥之
hsüan-hsüeh kuei 玄學鬼
Hu Ch'iu-yüan 胡秋原
Hu Sheng 胡繩
Hu Shih 胡適
Huang Ching-wan 黃警頑
Huang Wen-shan 黃文山
jen-hua 人化
Jen Hung-chün (Shu-yung) 任鴻雋(叔永)
jen-sheng-kuan 人生觀
Ju-sung 如松
Kao I-han 高一涵
K'ang Yu-wei 康有為
ke-chih 格知
k'e-hsüeh-hua 科學化
k'e-hsüeh ti hsi-li 科學的洗禮
Kiang Wen-han 江文漢
Ku Chieh-kang 顧頡剛
kung 公
kung 功
Kuo Chan-po 郭湛波
Kuo Jen-yüan 郭任遠
Kuo Mo-jo 郭沫若
kuo-ts'ui 國粹
Lao-tzu 老子
Li Chi 李季
li-chih-hua 理智化
Li Shih-tseng 李石曾
Li Shih-ts'en 李石岑
Li Ta 李達
Li Ta-chao 李大釗
Liang Ch'i-ch'ao 梁啟超

Liang Sou-ming 梁漱溟
Liang Yüan-tung 梁園東
Lin Tsai-p'ing 林宰平
Liu Ching-pai 劉静白
Liu Shao-ch'i 劉少奇
Liu Shu-ya 劉叔雅
Lu Hsiang-shan 陸象山
Lü Hsüeh-hai 呂學海
Mao Tse-tung 毛澤東
mei 美
Mei Kuang-ti 梅光迪
Mei Ssu-p'ing 梅思平
Mo Fa-ying 麦發穎
mo-t'o chiu-kuo 摩托救國
Mo-tzu 墨子
pa-ku 八股
pai-hua 白話
Peita 北大
P'u-she 樸社
Sa Meng-wu 薩孟武
shan 善
she-hui-hua 社會化
Shen Chih-yüan 沈志遠
Shen Yin-ming 沈因明
sheng 生
shih 適
Ssu-ma Kuang 司馬光
Sun Han-ping 孫寒冰
Sun Hsing-che 孫行者
Sun Tao-sheng 孫道昇
Sun Yat-sen 孫逸先
Ta-hsüeh 大學
Tai Hsing-shao 戴行軺
t'ai-chi 太極
T'ang Yüeh (Pi-huang)
唐鉞（擘黄）
T'ao Hsi-sheng 陶希聖
T'ao Meng-ho 陶孟和
te 德
Ting Wen-chiang (V. K., Tsai-chün)
丁文江（在君）
Tsien Tsuen-hsuin 錢存訓
Ts'ai Yüan-p'ei 蔡元培
T'ung-meng hui 同盟會
Wang Hsin-ming 王新命
Wang Hsing-kung 王星拱
Wang Li-hsi 王禮錫
Wang Tsi C. 王苣章
Wang Yang-ming 王陽明
Wang Yü-ch'üan 王毓銓
wei-sheng lun 唯生論
wei-wu lun 唯物論
Wei Yün-kung 魏允恭
wen-yen 文言
Wu Chih-hui (Ching-heng)
吴稚暉（敬恆）
Wu Ch'i-yüan 伍啟元

Wu Kuang 吳廣
Wu Li-p'ing 吳黎平
Wu Yü-kan 武堉幹
Yang Chien-hsiu 楊劍秀
Yang Chu 楊朱
yang-pa-ku 洋八股
Yang Po-k'ai 楊伯愷
Yang Sung 楊松
Yeh Ch'ing (Jen Cho-hsuan) 葉青(任卓宣)
yen 言
Yen Fu 嚴復
Yüan Shih-k'ai 袁世凱

BIBLIOGRAPHY

Frontispiece of *New China*, written in ancient seal script, praising mechanization.

Ai Ssu-ch'i, *Che-hsüeh hsüan-chi* 哲學選輯 (*Philosophical Selections*), Shanghai, Ch'en-kuang, 1939.

——, *Che-hsüeh yü sheng-huo* 哲學與生活 (Philosophy and Life), Shanghai, Tu-shu sheng-huo, 1937.

——, *Ju-ho yen-chiu che-hsüeh* 如何研究哲學 (How to Study Philosophy), Shanghai, Ch'en-kuang, 1935.

——, and Wu Li-p'ing, *K'e-hsüeh li-shih-kuan chiao-ch'eng* 科學歷史觀教程 (Textbook on the Scientific View of History), Shanghai, Ch'en-kuang, 1939.

——, *Shih-chien yü li-lun* 實踐與理論 (Practice and Theory), Shanghai, Tu-shu sheng-huo, 1939.

——, *Ssu-hsiang fang-fa lun* 思想方法論 (On How to Think), Shanghai, Tu-shu sheng-huo, 1935.

——, *Ta-chung che-hsüeh* 大衆哲學 (Philosophy of the Masses), Shanghai, Tu-shu sheng-huo, 1934.

Baumer, Franklin L., ed. *Main Currents of Western Thought*, New York, Knopf, 1952.

Bergson, Henri, *Creative Evolution*, Eng. trans. Arthur Mitchell, London, Macmillan, 1954.

Bernard, Henri, "Notes on the Introduction of the Natural Sciences into the Chinese Empire," *Yenching Journal of Social Studies*, 3 (1941), 220–41.

Brière, O. J., *Fifty Years of Chinese Philosophy 1898–1950*, Eng. trans. Laurence G. Thompson, London, G. Allen & Unwin, 1956.

Chang, Neander C. S., ed., *Kuo-nei chin shih-nien-lai chih tsung-chiao ssu-ch'ao* 國內近十年來之宗教思潮 (Religious Thought Movements in China 1917–1927), Peking, Yen-ching Hua-wen hsüeh-hsiao, 1927.

Chang Chun, "Wu-shih-nien-lai Chung-kuo chih k'e-hsüeh" 五十年來中國之科學 (Chinese Science of the Past Fifty Years), *Tsui-chin chih wu-shih-nien* (The Past Fifty Years) (Shanghai, Shen Pao, 1923), 2, 4th art.

Chang Chün-mai (Carsun Chang), "Jen-sheng-kuan" 人生觀 (The Philosophy of Life) *KHYJSK*, *1*, 1st art.

———, "Jen-sheng-kuan lun-chan chih hui-ku" 人生觀論戰之回顧 (Reflections on the Debate on the Philosophy of Life), *TFTC*, *31:13* (1934), 5–13.

———, "Ou-chou wen-hua wei-chi chi Chung-kuo hsin wen-hua chih ch'ü-hsiang" 歐洲文化危機及中國新文化之趨向 (The European Crisis in Culture and the Direction of China's New Culture), *TFTC*, *19:3* (1922), 117–23.

———, "Tsai lun jen-sheng-kuan yü k'e-hsüeh ping ta Ting Wen-chiang" 再論人生觀與科學並答丁文江 (Again on Philosophy of Life and Science, and also In Answer to V. K. Ting), *KHYJSK*, *1*, 3rd art.

Chang Tsung-ping, "I-ke k'e-hsüeh-chia ti tsung-chiao-kuan" 一個科學家的宗教觀 (The Religious Outlook of a Scientist), *TFTC*, *40:9* (1944), 27–29.

———, "K'e-hsüeh chih hsien-chih" 科學之限制 (The Limitations of Science), *TFTC*, *40:6* (1944), 34–37.

Chang Tung-sun, *K'e-hsüeh yü che-hsüeh* 科學與哲學 (Science and Philosophy), Shanghai, Commercial Press, 1924.

Chang Wen-po, *Chih-lao hsien-hua* 稚老閒話 (Random Notes on Wu Chih-hui), Taipei, Chung-yang wen-wu, 1952.

Chang Yüeh-jui, *Chin-jen chuan-chi wen-hsüan* 近人傳記文選 (Biographical Essays on Recent Men), Changsha, Commercial Press, 1938.

Ch'en Li-fu, *The Philosophy of Life*, New York, Philosophical Library, 1948.

———, *Wei-sheng lun* 唯生論 (Vitalism), Shanghai, Cheng-chung, 1947.

Ch'en Ping-k'un, *Tsui-chin san-shih-nien Chung-kuo wen-hsüeh shih*

最近三十年中國文學史 (A History of Chinese Literature of the Past Thirty Years), Shanghai, The Pacific Ocean Book Co., 1930.

Ch'en Po-ta, et al., *She-hui k'e-hsüeh kai-lun* 社會科學概論 (Elements of Social Science), Dairen, Hsin-hua, 1949.

Ch'en Tu-hsiu, "Chi-tu-chiao yü Chung-kuo-jen" 基督教與中國人 (Christianity and the Chinese), *THWT*, *1*, 425–29.

——, "Chin-jih chih chiao-yü fang-chen" 今日之教育方針 (Policy and Direction for Modern Education), *HCN*, *1:2* (1915), 1st art.

——, "Ching-kao ch'ing-nien" 敬告青年 (My Solemn Plea to Youth), *HCN*, *1:1* (1915), 1st art.

——, "Chung-kuo ku-shih piao" 中國古史表 (A Chronological Chart of Ancient Chinese History), *TFTC*, 37:22 (1940), 35–38.

——, "Fa-lan-hsi-jen yü chin-tai wen-ming" 法蘭西人與近代文明 (The French People and Modern Civilization), *HCN*, *1:1* (1915), 2nd art.

——, "Hsüeh-shu yü kuo-ts'ui" 學術與國粹 (Scholarship and the National Heritage), *THWT*, 2, 52–54.

——, "Jen-sheng chen-i" 人生真義 (The True Meaning of Life), *HCN*, 4:2 (1918), 90–93.

——, "K'e-hsüeh yü jen-sheng-kuan hsü" 科學與人生觀序 (Preface to Science and the Philosophy of Life), *KHYJSK*, *1*, 1st preface.

——, "K'e-hsüeh yü shen-sheng" 科學與神聖 (Science and the Divine), *THWT*, 2, 5–7.

——, "K'e-lin-te pei" 克林德碑 (The Von Ketteler Monument), *HCN*, *5:5* (1918), 449–58.

——, "K'ung-chiao yen-chiu" 孔教研究 (The Study of Confucianism), *THWT*, *1*, 625–27.

——, "K'ung-tzu chih tao yü hsien-tai sheng-huo" 孔子之道與

現代生活 (The Confucian Way and Modern Life), *HCN*, 2:4 (1916), 1st art.

———, "K'ung-tzu yü Chung-kuo" 孔子與中國 (Confucius and China), *TFTC*, 34:18–19 (1937), 9–15.

———, "Lao-tzu k'ao-lüeh" 老子考略 (A Study of Lao-tzu), *TFTC*, 34:11 (1937), 7–15.

———, "Ou-hsiang p'o-huai lun" 偶像破壞論 (On the Destruction of Idols), *HCN*, 5:2 (1918), 89–91.

———, "Pen-chih tsui-an chih ta-pien shu" 本誌罪案之答辯書 (A Reply to the Charges Against Our Journal), *HCN*, 6:1 (1919), 10–11.

———, *Shih-an tzu-chuan* 實庵自傳 (Autobiography), Shanghai, Ya-tung, 1938.

———, "Shih-chü tsa-kan" 時局雜感 (Random Thoughts on the Current Situation), *HCN*, 3:4 (1917), 1st art.

———, "Ta Chieh-p'ing" 答皆平 (Answering Chieh-p'ing) *THWT*, 3, 273.

———, "Ta Shih-chih" 答適之 (Answering Hu Shih), *KHYJSK*, 1, pp. 33–42 of 2nd preface.

———, "Tang-tai liang ta k'e-hsüeh-chia chih ssu-hsiang" 當代兩大科學家之思想 (The Thought of Two Great Scientists of the Modern Era), *HCN*, 2:1,3 (1916), 10th and 7th art. respectively.

———, "Tsai lun K'ung-chiao wen-t'i" 再論孔教問題 (Again on the Problem of Confucianism), *HCN*, 2:5 (1917), 1st art.

———, "Tung-hsi min-tsu ken-pen ssu-hsiang chih ch'a-i" 東西民族根本思想之差異 (Basic Intellectual Differences between Peoples of East and West), *HCN*, 1:4 (1915), 1st art.

Ch'en Tuan-chih, *Wu-ssu yün-tung chih shih-ti p'ing-chia* 五四運動之史的評價 (An Historical Evaluation of the May Fourth Movement), Shanghai, Sheng-huo, 1935.

Cheng-feng wen-hsien 整風文獻 (Documents on Reform), Peking, Hsin-hua, 1949.

Chiang Kai-shek, *Chung-kuo chih ming-yün* 中國之命運 (China's Destiny), Chungking, Cheng-chung, 1943.

——, *K'e-hsüeh ti Hsüeh-Yung* 科學的學庸 (The Scientific Nature of the Great Learning and the Doctrine of the Mean), Taipei, Chung-yang wen-wu, 1959.

——, *K'e-hsüeh ti tao-li* 科學的道理 (Principles of Science), Taipei, Chung-yang wen-wu, 1958.

China's Own Critics, Peiping, China University Press, 1931.

Chou Chen-fu, ed., *Yen Fu ssu-hsiang shu-p'ing* 嚴復思想述評 (A Critical Study of the Thought of Yen Fu), Shanghai, Chung-hua, 1940.

Chow Tse-tsung, "The Anti-Confucian Movement in Early Republican China," *The Confucian Persuasion*, ed. A. F. Wright (Stanford, Stanford University Press, 1960), pp. 288–312.

——, *The May Fourth Movement: Intellectual Revolution in China 1915–1924*, Cambridge, Mass., Harvard University Press, 1960.

Ch'ü Ch'iu-pai, *She-hui k'e-hsüeh kai-lun* 社會科學概論 (Elements of Social Science), Shanghai, Ch'ün-i, 1949.

Ch'üan-p'an hsi-hua yen-lun chi 全盤西化言論集 (Collections of Speeches and Essays on the Question of Total Westernization), 1st coll., 1934, ed. Lü Hsüeh-hai; 2nd coll., 1935, ed. Feng En-jung; 3rd coll., 1936, ed. Mo Fa-ying; Canton, Lingnan University Press.

Compton, Boyd, *Mao's China: Party Reform Documents 1942–44*, Seattle, University of Washington Press, 1952.

Dampier, Sir William C., *A History of Science*, 4th rev. ed. New York, Macmillan, 1949.

Driesch, Hans A. E., *The History and Theory of Vitalism*, Eng. trans. C. K. Ogden, London, Macmillan, 1914.

Dubs, H. H., "Recent Chinese Philosophy," *Journal of Philosophy*, 35 (1938), 345–55.

Elegant, Robert S., *China's Red Masters*, New York, Twayne, 1951.

Fan Shou-k'ang, "P'ing so-wei 'K'e-hsüeh yü hsüan-hsüeh chih-cheng'" 評所謂'科學與玄學之爭' (A Critique of the so-called "Debate on Science and Metaphysics"), *KHYJSK*, 2, 16th art.

Forke, Alfred, *Geschichte der neuren Chinesischen Philosophie*, Hamburg, Friedrichsen, De Gruyter & Co., 1938.

Fu Ssu-nien, "Wo so jen-shih ti Ting Wen-chiang hsien-sheng" 我所

認識的丁文江先生 (The Ting Wen-chiang that I Knew), *Fu Meng-chen hsien-sheng chi* 傅孟真先生集 (Collected Works of Fu Meng-chen), 2, section B, bk. 6 (3 vols. Taipei, Kuo-li Taiwan ta-hsüeh ch'u-pan pu, 1952).

Ho Kan-chih, *Chung-kuo ch'i-meng yün-tung shih* 中國啓蒙運動史 (A History of China's Enlightenment Movement), Shanghai, Sheng-huo, 1947.

Hodgkin, Henry Theodore, ed., *China Christian Yearbook*, Shanghai, Christian Literature Society, 1929.

Hsia, C. T., *A History of Modern Chinese Fiction 1917–1957*, New Haven, Yale University Press, 1961.

Hsia Cheng-nung, *Hsien chieh-tuan ti Chung-kuo ssu-hsiang yün-tung* 現階段的中國思想運動 (The Present State of China's Intellectual Movement), Shanghai, I-pan, 1937.

Hsia K'ang-nung, *Lun Hu Shih yü Chang Chün-mai* 論胡適與張君勱 (On Hu Shih and Chang Chün-mai), Shanghai, Hsin-chih, 1948.

Hsü Mou-yung and Ho Kan-chih, *She-hui k'e-hsüeh kai-lung* 社會科學概論 (Elements of Social Science), Liaotung, Chien-kuo, 1949.

Hu Sheng, *Hsin che-hsüeh ti jen-sheng-kuan* 新哲學的人生觀 (The New Philosophy's Conception of Life), Shanghai, Sheng-huo, 1937.

———, *Pien-cheng-fa wei-wu-lun ju-men* 辯證法唯物論入門 (Introducing Dialectical Materialism), Shanghai, Hsin-chih, 1938.

———, *Ssu-hsiang fang-fa yü tu-shu fang-fa* 思想方法與讀書方法 (How to Think and How to Study), Shanghai, Keng-yün, 1947.

Hu Shih, "An Oriental Looks at the Modern Western Civilization," *Modern Education and Human Values*, 5 (1954), 47–60.

———, "Chang Chün-mai yü Sun Hsing-che" 張君勱與孫行者 (Carsun Chang and the Monkey King), *KHYJSK*, 1, 5th art.

——, *Ch'ang-shih chi* 嘗試集 (A Collection of Experiments), Shanghai, Ya-tung, 1925.

——, "Cheng-li kuo-ku yü ta-kuei" 整理國故與打鬼 (Tidying the National Heritage and Catching Ghosts), *HSWT*, 3rd coll., bk. 2, 207–12.

——, "Chi-ke fan-li-hsüeh ti ssu-hsiang-chia" 幾個反理學的思想家 (Several Anti-Li-hsüeh Thinkers), *HSWT*, 3rd coll., bk. 2, 112–85.

——, "Chieh-shao wo tzu-chi ti ssu-hsiang" 介紹我自己的思想 (Introducing My Own Thought), *HSWT*, 4th coll., bk. 4, 607–24.

——, "Chih-hsüeh ti fang-fa yü ts'ai-liao" 治學的方法與材料 (Method and Materials of Study), *HSWT*, 3rd coll., bk. 2, 187–205.

——, "Chin-jih ssu-hsiang-chieh ti i-ke ta pi-ping" 今日思想界的一個大弊病 (A Major Disease of Today's World of Thought), *TLPL*, 153 (1935), 2–5.

——, "Ch'ing ta-chia lai chao-chao ching-tzu" 請大家來照照鏡子 (Let Us All Look at Ourselves in the Mirror), *HSWT*, 3rd coll., bk. 1, 39–50.

——, "Ch'ing-tai hsüeh-che ti chih-hsüeh fang-fa" 清代學者的治學方法 (The Research Method of the Scholars of the Ch'ing Period), *HSWT*, 1st coll., bk. 2, 205–45.

——, *Chung-kuo che-hsüeh shih ta-kang* 中國哲學史大綱 (An Outline of Chinese Philosophy), Shanghai, Commercial Press, 1917.

——, "Fei·ko-jen chu-i ti hsin sheng-huo" 非個人主義的新生活 (A Nonindividualistic New Life), *HSWT*, 1st coll., bk. 4, 173–89.

——, "Hsin ssu-ch'ao ti i-i" 新思潮的意義 (The Significance of the New Thought), *HSWT*, 1st coll., bk. 4, 151–64.

——, *Hu Shih liu-hsüeh jih-chi* 胡適留學日記 (Hu Shih's

Diary of Student Days Abroad), 4 vols. Shanghai, Commercial Press, 1947.

——, *Hu Shih wen-hsüan* 胡適文選 (Selected Essays of Hu Shih), Hongkong, Hsien-tai, 1958.

——, "I-po-sheng chu-i" 易卜生主義 (Ibsenism), *HSWT*, 1st coll., bk. 4, 13–38.

——, "K'e-hsüeh ti jen-sheng-kuan" 科學的人生觀 (The Scientific Philosophy of Life), *Hu Shih wen-hsüan* (Hongkong, 1958), pp. 74–78.

——, "K'e-hsüeh yü jen-sheng-kuan hsü" 科學與人生觀序 (Preface to the Debate on Science and the Philosophy of Life), *KHYJSK*, 1, 2nd preface.

——, *Living Philosophies, A Series of Intimate Credos* (New York, Simon & Schuster, 1931), pp. 235–63.

——, "Man-yu ti kan-hsiang" 漫遊的感想 (Impressions of My Journey), *HSWT*, 3rd coll., bk. 1, 51–72.

——, "Pi shang Liang-shan—wen-hsüeh ke-ming ti k'ai-shih" 逼上梁山—文學革命的開始 (Compelled into Rebellion—the Beginnings of the Literary Revolution), *TFTC*, 31:1 (1934), 15–31.

——, "Pu-hsiu, wo ti tsung-chiao" 不朽，我的宗教 (Immortality, My Religion), *HSWT*, 1st coll., bk. 4, 105–18.

——, "Shih p'ing so-wei 'Chung-kuo pen-wei ti wen-hua chien-she'" 試評所謂'中國本位的文化建設' (A Trial Criticism of the so-called "China-centered Cultural Construction"), *HSWT*, 4th coll., bk. 4, 535–40.

——, "Shih-yen chu-i" 實驗主義 (On Pragmatism), *HSWT*, 1st coll., bk. 2, 75–145.

——, *Ssu-shih tzu-shu* 四十自述 (Autobiography at Forty), Shanghai, Ya-tung, 1933.

——, *The Chinese Renaissance*, Chicago, University of Chicago Press, 1934.

——, "The Civilizations of the East and of the West," in Charles A. Beard, ed., *Whither Mankind* (New York, Longmans Green, 1928), pp. 25–41.

———, *The Development of the Logical Method in Ancient China,* Shanghai, The Oriental Book Co., 1922.

———, "Ting Tsai-chün che-ke-jen" 丁在君這個人 (This Man Ting Tsai-chün), *Chin-jen chuan-chi wen-hsüan* 近人傳記文選 (Biographical Essays on Recent Men), ed. Chang Yüeh-jui (Changsha, Commercial Press, 1938), pp. 92–102.

———, "Ting Wen-chiang ti chuan-chi" 丁文江的傳記 (Biography of Ting Wen-chiang), *Annals of Academia Sinica,* no. 3 (Taipei, 1956), pp. 1–123.

———, *Ts'ang-hui-shih ta-chi* 藏暉室劄記 (Notebook of the Hidden Brillance Study), 4 vols. Shanghai, Ya-tung, 1939.

———, "Wen-t'i yü chu-i" 問題與主義 (On Problems and Isms), *HSWT,* 1st coll., bk. 2, 147–98.

———, "Wo-men tui-yü Hsi-yang chin-tai wen-ming ti t'ai-tu" 我們對於西洋近代文明的態度 (Our Attitude Toward the Modern Civilization of the West), *HSWT,* 3rd coll., bk. 1, 3–23.

———, "Wu-shih-nien lai chih shih-chieh che-hsüeh" 五十年來之世界哲學 (World Philosophy of the Past Fifty Years), *HSWT,* 2nd coll., bk. 2, 217–303.

Huang Ching-wan, and Hsü Wan-ch'eng, *Ko-chung jen-sheng-kuan* 各種人生觀 (Varieties of Philosophies of Life), Shanghai, Ching-wei, n. d.

Hughes, E. R., *The Invasion of China by the Western World,* New York, Macmillan, 1938.

Hummel, Arthur W., trans., *The Autobiography of a Chinese Historian,* Leiden, E. J. Brill, 1931.

Huxley, Julian, "The Uniqueness of Man," in *Man Stands Alone,* New York and London, Harper, 1941.

Jen Hung-chün, "Ho wei k'e-hsüeh-chia" 何謂科學家 (What is a Scientist), *HCN,* 6:3 (1919), 247–53.

———, "Jen-sheng-kuan ti k'e-hsüeh huo k'e-hsüeh ti jen-sheng-kuan" 人生觀的科學或科學的人生觀 (A Science of the Philosophy of Life or A Scientific Philosophy of Life), *KHYJSK,* 1, 6th art.

——, "K'e-hsüeh ching-shen lun" 科學精神論 (On Scientific Spirit), *K'e-hsüeh t'ung-lun* (Essays on Science) (Shanghai, Science Society of China, 1919), pp. 1–9.

——, "K'e-hsüeh yü chiao-yü" 科學與教育 (Science and Education), *K'e-hsüeh* (The Science Journal), *1:12* (1915), 1343–1352.

——, "Pao-ts'un ku-wu tso ti shen-mo" 保存古物做的什麼 (Why Preserve Relics?), *TLPL*, *126* (1934), 4–6.

——, "Science: Its Introduction and Development in China," in Sophia H. Zen, ed., *Symposium on Chinese Culture*, Shanghai, Institute of Pacific Relations, 1931, pp. 165–75.

——, "Shuo Chung-kuo wu k'e-hsüeh chih yüan-yin" 說中國無科學之原因 (On the Reasons for China's Lack of Science), *K'e-hsüeh t'ung-lun* (Essays on Science) (Shanghai, Science Society of China, 1919), pp. 183–89.

——, "Wo-kuo hsüeh-shu ssu-hsiang chih chiang-lai" 我國學術思想之將來 (The Future of Thought in Our Country), *K'e-hsüeh t'ung-lun* (Essays on Science) (Shanghai, Science Society of China, 1919), pp. 190–99.

——, "Wu-shih-nien-lai chih shih-chieh k'e-hsüeh" 五十年來之世界科學 (World Science of the Past Fifty Years), *Tsui-chin chih wu-shih nien* 最近之五十年 (The Past Fifty Years), *1*, 1923, 6th art.

Ju-sung, "Li-lung ti chung-yao" 理論的重要 (The Importance of Theory), *ESSC*, *1:7* (1931), 5–17.

——, "Yen-chiu shen-mo li-lun" 研究什麼理論 (What Theories Shall We Study?), *ESSC*, *1:8* (1932), 5–15.

K'e-hsüeh lun-ts'ung 科學論叢 (Collections of Writings on Science), eds. Yeh Ch'ing et al., 4 colls. Shanghai, Hsin-k'en, 1935.

K'e-hsüeh t'ung-lun 科學通論 (Essays on Science), Shanghai, Science Society of China, 1919.

Kiang Wen-han, *The Chinese Student Movement*, New York, King's Crown, 1948.

Ku Chieh-kang, ed., *Ku-shih pien* 古史辨 (Debates on Ancient History), 3 vols. Peiping, P'u-she, 1927–31.

Kuo Chan-po, *Chin wu-shih-nien Chung-kuo ssu-hsiang shih* 近五十年中國思想史 (Chinese Intellectual History of the Past Fifty Years), Peiping, Jen-wen, 1935.

Kuo Mo-jo, *Chung-kuo ku-tai she-hui yen-chiu* 中國古代社會研究 (Studies on Ancient Chinese Society), Peking, Jen-min, 1960.

Levenson, Joseph R., "The Abortiveness of Empiricism in Early Ch'ing Thought," *FEQ*, 13 (1954), 155–65.

Li Chi, "Tui-yü Chung-kuo she-hui-shih lun-chan ti kung-hsien yü p'i-p'ing" 對於中國社會史論戰的貢獻與批評 (Contributions and Criticisms Regarding the Debate on Chinese Social History), *TSTC*, 2:2–3 (1932), 3rd art.

Li Shih-ts'en, *Che-hsüeh ta-kang* 哲學大綱 (Outline of Philosophy), Shanghai, Commercial Press, 1933.

———, *Chung-kuo che-hsüeh shih-chiang* 中國哲學十講 (Ten Lectures on Chinese Philosophy), Shanghai, Commercial Press, 1933.

———, "San-shih-nien lai shih-chieh che-hsüeh chih chin-chan" 三十年來世界哲學之進展 (The Progress of World Philosophy of the Past Thirty Years), *TFTC*, 31:1 (1933), 137–44.

Li Ta, *Hsien-tai she-hui-hsüeh* 現代社會學 (Modern Sociology), Shanghai, K'un-lun, 1947.

———, *She-hui-hsüeh ta-kang* 社會學大綱 (Elements of Sociology), Shanghai, K'un-lun, 1939.

Liang Ch'i-ch'ao, *Chung-kuo chin san-pai-nien hsüeh-shu shih* 中國近三百年學術史 (An Intellectual History of China in the Past Three Hundred Years), Taiwan, Chung-hua, 1956.

———, "Jen-sheng-kuan yü k'e-hsüeh" 人生觀與科學 (The Philosophy of Life and Science), *KHYJSK*, 1, 8th art.

———, "K'e-hsüeh ching-shen yü Tung-Hsi wen-hua" 科學精

神與東西文化 (The Scientific Spirit and the Cultures of the East and West), *Liang Jen-kung hsüeh-shu chiang-yen chi* 梁任公學術講演集 (Collections of Liang Ch'i-ch'ao's Academic Writings) (2nd ser. Shanghai, Commercial Press, 1922), pp. 144–52.

——, "Kuan-yü hsüan-hsüeh k'e-hsüeh lun-chan chih chan-shih kuo-chi kung-fa" 關於玄學科學論戰之戰時國際公法 (Concerning the International Law of the Battle of Metaphysics and Science), *KHYJSK*, *1*, 4th art.

——, *Liang Jen-kung chin-chu* 梁任公近著 (Recent Writings of Liang Ch'i-ch'ao), 3 vols. Shanghai, Commercial Press, 1922–23.

Liang Sou-ming, *Tung-Hsi wen-hua chi ch'i che-hsüeh* 東西文化及其哲學 (East-West Cultures and Their Philosophies), Shanghai, Commercial Press, 1922.

Lin Mou-sheng, "Symposium on Science and the Philosophy of Life—Abstracts and Reviews," *China Institute Bulletin*, 3:2 (November 1938), 35–50.

Lin Tsai-p'ing, "Tu Ting Tsai-chün ti hsüan-hsüeh yü k'e-hsüeh" 讀丁在君的玄學與科學 (Having Read V. K. Ting's "Metaphysics and Science"), *KHYJSK*, *1*, 11th art.

Liou Ho, "Notice biographique sur C. H. Wood," *Annales Franco-Chinoises de Lyon*, ler trimestre (1931), 2–4.

Liu, C. H., "Introduction of Modern Science into China," *China Journal*, 34:3 (1941), 120–25; 34:5 (1941), 210–19.

Mao Tse-tung, "Hsin min-chu chu-i lun" 新民主主義論 (On New Democracy), *MTTHC*, 2 (1952), 655–704.

——, "Lun jen-min min-chu chuan-cheng" 論人民民主專政 (On the Dictatorship of the People's Democracy), *MTTHC*, *4* (1960), 1473–1486.

——, "Mao-tun lun" 矛盾論 (On Contradiction), *MTTHC*, *1* (1951), 287–326.

——, "Shih-chien lun" 實踐論 (On Practice), *MTTHC*, *1* (1951), 271–86.

Marx, Karl, *A Contribution to the Critique of Political Economy*, Eng. trans. N. I. Stone, Chicago, C. H. Kerr, 1904.

———, *The German Ideology,* ed. R. Pascal, New York, International Publications, 1939.

Marx, Karl and Friedrich Engels, *Historisch-kritische Gesamtausgabe,* issued by the Marx-Engels Institute in Moscow, Frankfurt-Berlin, 1927–33.

Needham, Joseph, *Science and Civilization* (Cambridge, England, the University Press, 1954), 2.

Nef, John U., "The Genesis of Industrialism and of Modern Science (1560–1640)," *Essays in Honor of Conyers Read,* ed. Norton Downs (Chicago, University of Chicago Press, 1953), pp. 200–69.

Owen, R. G., *Scientism, Man, and Religion,* Philadelphia, The Westminster Press, 1952.

Peake, Cyrus H., "Some Aspects of the Introduction of Modern Science into China," *Isis,* 22 (1934), 173–219.

Russell, Bertrand, *The Problem of China,* New York, Century, 1922.

Schwartz, Benjamin, "A Marxist Controversy in China," *FEQ,* 13 (1954), 143–53.

———, "Biographical Sketch, Ch'en Tu-hsiu, Pre-Communist Phase," *Papers on China,* Harvard Regional Studies, 2, Cambridge, Mass., Harvard University Press, 1948.

———, "Ch'en Tu-hsiu and the Acceptance of the Modern West," in "Chinese Reactions to Imported Ideas, A Symposium," *Journal of the History of Ideas,* 12 (1951), 61–72.

———, *Chinese Communism and the Rise of Mao,* Cambridge, Mass., Harvard University Press, 1951.

Shryock, John K., *The Origin and Development of the State Cult of Confucius,* New York, The Century Co., 1932.

Sun Tao-sheng, "Hsien-tai Chung-kuo che-hsüeh chih chieh-p'ei" 現代中國哲學之解剖 (An Analysis of Contemporary Chinese Philosophy), *KWCP,* 12:45 (1935), 6 pp.

Tai Hsing-shao, "Chung-kuo kuan-liao cheng-chih ti mo-lo" 中國官僚政治之歿落 (The Demise of Chinese Bureaucracy), *TSTC,* 1:4–5 (1931), 39 pp.

T'ang Yüeh, "Che-hsüeh-che chih yen-chung-ting—hsin-li-hsüeh" 哲學者之眼中釘—心理學 (Psychology—The Nail in the Philosopher's Eye), *TYWT,* 1st coll., 205–20.

———, "Chi-hsieh yü jen-sheng" 機械與人生 (Machines and Human Life), *TYWT,* 1st coll., 221–40.

———, "Chung-kuo hsüeh-shu ti tsui-ta ping-ken" 中國學術的最大病根 (The Root of the Disease in Chinese Scholarship), *TYWT*, 2nd coll., 293–302.

———, "Chung-kuo shih ti hsin-yeh" 中國史的新頁 (A New Leaf in Chinese History), *TYWT*, 2nd coll., 321–32.

———, "Han-hsüeh shih k'e-hsüeh ma?" 漢學是科學嗎？ (Is the Han Learning Science?), *TYWT*, 1st coll., 249–74.

———, "Hsin-li hsien-hsiang yü yin-kuo-lü" 心理現象與因果律 (Psychological Phenomena and the Laws of Causation), *KHYJSK*, 2, 2nd art.

———, "I-ke i-jen ti shuo-meng" 一個癡人的說夢 (The Dream-talks of a Derelict), *KHYJSK*, 2, 9th art.

———, "K'e-hsüeh yü te-hsing" 科學與德行 (Science and Morality), *TYWT*, 1st coll., 115–26.

———, "Kuo-jen pu-k'o-pu hsing ti ta mi-meng" 國人不可不醒的大迷夢 (The Great Illusion from which the Chinese Must Awaken Themselves), *TYWT*, 2nd coll., 303–09.

———, "Ping-kuo lun" 病國論 (On a Sick Country), *TYWT*, 2nd coll., 277–88.

———, "Wu kuo-jen ssu-hsiang hsi-kuan ti chi-ke jo-tien" 吾國人思想習慣的幾個弱點 (Several Weak Points in the Habit of Thought of Our Countrymen), *TYWT*, 1st coll., 127–38.

T'ao Hsi-sheng, "Chung-kuo she-hui hsing-shih fa-ta kuo-ch'eng ti hsin ku-ting" 中國社會形式發達過程的新估定 (A New Evaluation of the Developmental Patterns of Chinese Society), *TSTC*, 2:7–8 (1932), 2nd art.

———, *Chung-kuo she-hui shih* 中國社會史 (A History of Chinese Society), Chungking, Wen-feng, 1944.

Thomson, John A., *An Outline of Science*, 4 vols. New York, London, Putnam, 1922.

Ting, V. K., "Che-ssu hsüeh yü p'u-tieh" 哲嗣學與譜牒 (Eugenics and Heredity), *KT*, 3:4,5,6 (1920, 1921), 37–44, 31–36, 7–15.

———, "How China Acquired Her Civilization," *Symposium on Chinese Culture,* ed. Sophia Zen (Shanghai, Institute of Pacific Relations, 1931), pp. 1–24.

———, "Hsien-tsai Chung-kuo ti chung-nien yü ch'ing-nien" 現在中國的中年與青年 (Contemporary China's Middle Aged and Youth), *TLPL,* 144 (1935), 8–11.

———, "Hsüan-hsüeh yü k'e-hsüeh" 玄學與科學 (Metaphysics and Science), *KHYJSK,* 1, 2nd art.

———, "Hsüan-hsüeh yü k'e-hsüeh, ta Chang Chün-mai" 玄學與科學，答張君勱 (Metaphysics and Science, and the Answer to Carsun Chang), *KHYJSK,* 2, 1st art.

———, "K'e-hsüeh-hua ti chien-she" 科學化的建設 (Scientific Reconstruction), *TLPL,* 151 (1935), 9–13.

———, "Wo ti hsin-yang" 我的信仰 (My Belief), *TLPL,* 100 (1934), 9–12.

Tsien Tsuen-hsuin, "Western Impact on China Through Translation," *FEQ,* 13 (1954), 305–27.

Tsui-chin chih wu-shih-nien, Shen-pao kuan wu-shih chou-nien chi-nien 最近之五十年，申報館五十年週年紀念 (The Past Fifty Years, in Commemoration of the Fiftieth Anniversary of the Shen Pao, 1872–1922), 2 vols. Shanghai, Shen Pao, 1923.

Wang Hsing-kung, "K'e-hsüeh yü jen-sheng-kuan" 科學與人生觀 (Science and the Philosophy of Life), *KHYJSK,* 2, 10th art.

Wang Li-hsi, "Chung-kuo she-hui hsing-t'ai fa-chan-shih chung chih mi-ti shih-tai" 中國社會形態發展史中之謎的時代 (The Age of Myths in the Developmental Patterns of Chinese Social History), *TSTC,* 2:7–8 (1932), 1st art.

———, ed., *Chung-kuo she-hui-shih lun-chan* 中國社會史論戰 (Debates on Chinese Social History), 4 vols. Shanghai, Tu-shu, 1932.

———, *Chung-kuo she-hui-shih lun-chan hsü-mo* 中國社會史論戰序幕 (Prologue to the Debate on Chinese Social History), *TSTC,* 1:4–5 (1931), 23 pp.

———, "Ti-san pan chüan-t'ou yü 第三版卷頭語 (Preface to the Third Printing), *TSTC*, 1:4–5 (1931), 4 pp.

Wang Tsi C., *The Youth Movement in China*, New York, New Republic, 1927.

Wang Yü-ch'üan, "The Development of Modern Social Science in China," *Pacific Affairs*, 11 (1938), 345–62.

Wei Yün-kung, *Chiang-nan chih-chao-chü chi* 江南製造局記 (A Record of the Kiangnan Arsenal), Shanghai, 1905.

Wellmuth, John, *The Nature and Origins of Scientism*, Milwaukee, Marquette University Press, 1944.

Wightman, W. P. D., *Science and Monism*, London, Allen & Unwin, 1934.

Woodhead, H. G., and H. T. Montague Bell, eds., *China Year Book, 1914*, London, Routledge, 1915.

Wright, Mary C., "From Revolution to Restoration: The Transformation of Kuomintang Ideology," *FEQ*, 14 (1955), 515–32.

Wu Chih-hui, "Chen yang-pa-ku-hua chih Li-hsüeh" 箴洋八股化之理學 (A Critique of the Thought of Foreign Eight-Leggedism), *WWT*, 1, 151–59.

———, "Chi-ch'i ts'u-chin ta-t'ung shuo" 機器促進大同說 (On the Promotion of Universal Harmony by Machines), *HCN*, 5:2 (1918), 158–60.

———, "Ch'ing-nien yü kung-chü" 青年與工具 (Youth and Tools), *HCN*, 2:2 (1916), 2nd art.

———, "Chung-kuo-jen chih fu-pai-ping" 中國人之腐敗病 (The Disease of Corruption of the Chinese), *WCC*, bk. 6, 135–40.

———, "Erh-pai-chao p'ing-min ta wen-t'i tsui ch'ing-pien ti chieh-chüeh-fa" 二百兆平民大問題最輕便的解決法 (The Easiest Way to Solve the Problem of Two Hundred Million People), *TFTC*, 21:2 (1924), L-1–L-30.

———, "Fu Ts'ai Chieh-min shu" 復蔡孑民書 (A Return Letter to Ts'ai Yuan-p'ei), *WWT*, 1, 146–51.

———, "I cheng-hsüeh chih fei-cheng-hsüeh" 以政學治非政學 (Use Political Science to Study the Science of Nongovernment), *T'ai-p'ing yang* (The Pacific Ocean), 1:2 (1917), 1–2.

———, "I-ke hsin hsin-yang ti yü-chou-kuan chi jen-sheng-kuan" 一個新信仰的宇宙觀及人生觀 (A New Belief's Conception of the Universe and the Philosophy of Life), *WWT*, 1, 168–308.

———, "K'e-hsüeh chou-pao fa-k'an-yü" 科學週報發刊語 (Preface to the Publication of the Science Weekly), *WWT*, 1, 73–76.

———, "Mo-t'o chiu-kuo chih i-chien" 摩托救國之肌見 (My Sincere View on Saving the Country with Motors), *HCH*, 1:13 (1933), 1–4.

———, *Shang-hsia ku-chin t'an* 上下古今談 (Sayings About the World and Times of Old and New), 2 vols. Taipei, Chung-yang wen-wu, 1955.

———, "Ta jen-shu—chiao-yü . . . ke-ming" 答人書 — 教育....革命 (An Answer to a Letter—Education . . . Revolution), *Wu Chih-hui hsüeh-shu lun-chu* 吳稚暉學術論著 (Selections of Wu Chih-hui's Academic Writings), Shanghai, Ch'u-pan ho-tso she, 1925.

———, "T'an wu-cheng-fu chih hsien-t'ien" 談無政府之閒天 (The Carefree Realm of Anarchy), *WCC*, bk. 8, 49–55.

———, "Tsai lun kung-chü" 再論工具 (Again on Tools), *HCN*, 2:3 (1916), 9th art.

———, "Tsung-chiao tao-te yü she-hui-chu-i" 宗教道德與社會主義 (Religion, Morality, and Socialism), *WCC*, bk. 6, 1–6.

———, "Tsung-chiao wen-t'i" 宗教問題 (The Problem of Religion), *WCC*, bk. 6, 12–16.

———, "Wan-kao T'ai-ko-erh" 婉告太戈爾 (My Sincere Advice to Tagore), *WWT*, 1, 30–34.

———, *Wu Chih-hui hsüeh-shu lun-chu* 吳稚暉學術論著 (Selections of Wu Chih-hui's Academic Writings), Shanghai, Ch'u-pan ho-tso she, 1925.

———, *Wu Chih-hui wen-hsüan* 吳稚暉文選 (Selected Essays of Wu Chih-hui), ed. Hsü Yeh-ju, Shanghai, Wen-lin, 1936.

———, "Yü yu-jen lun wu-li shih-chieh chi pu-k'o-ssu-i shu" 與友人

論物理世界及不可思議書 (A Letter to a Friend on the Physical World and Imponderables), *WCC*, bk. 4, 1–7.

Wu Ch'i-yüan, *Chung-kuo hsin-wen-hua yün-tung kai-kuan* 中國新文化運動概觀 (China's New Culture Movement), Shanghai, Hsien-tai, 1934.

Wu Li-p'ing and Yang Sung, ed., *She-hui k'e-hsüeh kai-lun* 社會科學概論 (Elements of Social Science), Shanghai, Hsin Chung-hua, 1949.

Yamamoto, T. and S., "The Anti-Christian Movement in China, 1922–27," *FEQ*, 12 (1953), 133–48.

Yang Chien-hsiu, ed., *She-hui k'e-hsüeh kai-lun* 社會科學概論 (Elements of Social Science), Shanghai, Hsien-tai, 1929, 1932.

Yeh Ch'ing, "Chüan-t'ou yü" 卷頭語 (Prefatory Remarks), in Yeh Ching et al., eds., *K'e-hsüeh lun-ts'ung* (Collections of Writings on Science), 1st coll. (Shanghai, Hsin-k'en, 1935), 3–8.

———, "Erh-shih shih-chi ch'uang-k'an yen" 二十世紀創刊言 (Preface to the Twentieth Century), *ESSC*, *1:1* (1931), 1–9.

———, "K'e-hsüeh yü ssu-hsiang" 科學與思想 (Science and Thought), *ESSC*, *1:2* (1931), 13–61.

———, "Li-lun yü shih-chien" 理論與實踐 (Theory and Practice), *ESSC*, *2:8* (1935), 5–38.

———, "P'i-p'an ti i-i" 批判的意義 (The Meaning of Criticism), *ESSC*, *1:4* (1931), 3–12.

———, "P'i-p'an ti t'ai-tu" 批判的態度 (The Attitude of Criticism), *ESSC*, *1:5* (1931), 3–12.

———, ed. *P'i-p'an ts'ung-shu* (Collections of Critiques), Series B, 2 vols. Shanghai, Hsin-k'en, 1933, 1934, respectively.

Yen Fu, "Lun shih-pien chih chi" 論世變之極 (On the Extremes of World Change), *Yen Fu shih-wen hsüan* (Selected Poems and Essays of Yen Fu), ed. Chou Chen-fu, Peking, Jen-min wen-hsüeh, 1959.

Zen, Sophia H., ed. *Symposium on Chinese Culture,* Shanghai, Institute of Pacific Relations, 1931.

Zilsel, Edgar, "The Genesis of the Concept of Scientific Progress," *Journal of the History of Ideas*, 6 (1945), 325–49.

OTHER PERIODICAL MATERIALS IN CHINESE

Ching-yeh hsün-pao 競業旬報 (*Struggle Tri-monthly*)
Chung-hua hsin-pao 中華新報 (*China's New Journal*)
Hsin Chung-kuo 新中國 (*New China*)
Hsin-ch'ao 新潮 (*New Tide*)
Hsin sheng-ming 新生命 (*New Life*)
Hsin ssu-ch'ao 新思潮 (*New Thought Tide*)
Hsüeh-i 學藝 (*Wissen und Wissenschaft*)
K'e-hsüeh 科學 (*The Science Journal*)
K'e-hsüeh chou-pao 科學週報 (*Science Weekly*), Supplement of *Min-kuo jih-pao* 民國日報 (*Republican Daily*)
K'e-hsüeh ti Chung-kuo 科學的中國 (*Scientific China*)
Li-lun yü hsien-shih 理論與現實 (*Theory and Reality*)
Nu-li chou-pao 努力週報 (*The Effort Weekly*)
Shao-nien Chung-kuo 少年中國 (*Young China*)
Shih-chieh hua-pao 世界畫報 (*The Illustrated World*)
Shih-huo pan-yüeh k'an 食貨半月刊 (*The Bi-weekly Economic Journal*)
Su-pao 蘇報 (*The Kiangsu Journal*)
T'ai-p'ing yang 太平洋 (*The Pacific Ocean*)
Tu-shu tsa-chih 讀書雜誌 (*Readers' Journal*), Supplement of *Nu-li chou-pao*
Yen-chiu yü p'i-p'an 研究與批判 (*Research and Criticism*)

INDEX